IS RESCUING RIGHT?

BREAKING THE LAW
TO SAVE THE UNBORN

RANDY C. ALCORN

INTERVARSITY PRESS
DOWNERS GROVE, ILLINOIS 60515

InterVarsity Press is the book-publishing division of InterVarsity Christian Fellowship, a student movement active on campus at hundreds of universities, colleges and schools of nursing in the United States of America, and a member movement of the International Fellowship of Evangelical Students. For information about local and regional activities, write Public Relations Dept., InterVarsity Christian Fellowship, 6400 Schroeder Rd., P.O. Box 7895, Madison, WI 53707-7895.

All Scripture quotations, unless otherwise indicated, are from the Holy Bible, New International Version. Copyright © 1973, 1978, International Bible Society. Used by permission of Zondervan Bible Publishers.

Cover illustration: Photo Assignments Unlimited

ISBN 0-8308-1301-2

Printed in the United States of America ∞

Library of Congress Cataloging-in-Publication Data

Alcorn, Randy C.
   Is rescuing right?/Randy Alcorn.
     p.   cm.
   ISBN 0-8308-1301-2
   1. Abortion—Religious aspects—Christianity. 2. Pro-life
movement—United States. 3. Civil disobedience—United States.
4. Abortion services—United States. I. Title.
HQ767.25.A43   1990
363.4'6—dc20   90-38819
                                  CIP

13	12	11	10	9	8	7	6	5	4	3	2	1
99	98	97	96	95	94	93	92	91	90			

To my precious family,
Nanci, Karina and Angela Alcorn,
and our dear friends
Ron, Kathy, Amy, Jenny and Skeets Norquist,
who know the costs and rewards
of loving Christ
and his little ones

1
Purpose & Foundation

*The church is the
conscience of the state.*
John Calvin

A s I write, more than forty thousand rescuers have been arrested in the United States, far more than all those arrested in the civil rights demonstrations of the fifties and sixties.[1] The rescue movement has spread to Canada, England, France, Australia and other countries as well. No matter where we stand on the issue, we must recognize that rescuing has become a major force in both church and society today.

On the one hand, rescuing has graphically drawn attention to the plight of unborn children. People inside and outside the church are being forced to deal with the fact that a number of citizens really believe the unborn are human beings. These citizens are also willing to make considerable sacrifices to stand up for unborn children's right to live. The lives of babies are being saved. And, despite strong opposition from pro-choice forces, a tired and sagging pro-life movement has been revitalized by the growing involvement of Christians in rescuing.

On the other hand, rescuing has been a confusing, frustrating and sometimes explosive issue in the Christian community. Respected voices are crying out conflicting messages. "Rescuing is right" or "rescuing is wrong." "Everyone should do it" or "no one should do it." Sermons are being preached, articles written, church position papers drafted, and press releases issued. The Bible is quoted to support contradictory positions on this issue. The lines are being drawn, brothers and sisters in Christ are being polarized, and motives are being questioned by those on all sides.

People who actively oppose rescuing will not enjoy this book. Neither will those who defend rescuing without taking stock of the questionable attitudes and counterproductive actions that sometimes accompany it. In short, this is not a party-line book. It will not receive an unqualified endorsement from anyone.

Some in the rescue movement will feel I have not gone far enough. But I am convinced there is need for better perspective and balance both outside *and* inside the rescue movement. I believe civil disobedience is a biblical means of rescuing the unborn. I also believe it is not the only means, nor is it the only important or effective means.

Furthermore, while intervention for the unborn children is vital and close to the heart of God, it is *not* the only responsibility of the church. It can and should be done by some, but it need not and should not overshadow the other central callings of the church. These include prayer, evangelism and intervention for other desperately needy people. It is no more or less spiritual to rescue the unborn than to reach out to the lost, feed the hungry or care for the sick.

God has called all of us to obey him and minister to the needy. But he has not called all of us to intervene at abortion clinics any more than he has called all of us to inner-city street ministry, prison ministry or the foreign mission field. Just because a ministry is right, important and even vital doesn't mean we should all do it all of the time. If we did, other vital ministries would be neglected, and other needy people wouldn't be rescued from spiritual and physical death, abuse, injustice and poverty.

Though this book is designed to tackle the rescue issue, its implications go far beyond it. Our answer to the question of civil disobedience in this area will have great influence on how we answer it in other areas. This is why we must take pains to scrutinize our position in the light of Scripture. Important as the issue of rescuing is, it is not an isolated issue. More and more, Christians in the Western world are facing painful ethical dilemmas from which we have previously been preserved.

Must Rescuing Divide the Church?

So far, the debate over rescuing has generated much more heat than light. I do not want to turn up the heat. Rather, I want to try to shed some light. I am committed to dialog on this matter and pray regularly that God will point out flaws in my own thinking. Criticisms of this book are sure to come. I invite and welcome them and will take each of them seriously. I will examine them not in the posture of defensiveness, but with openness and prayer.

Perhaps it is partially because of my own slow and reluctant pilgrimage that I do not condemn others for their reservations or criticisms about rescuing. I do not judge a person's spirituality by his position on this issue. One's personal integrity and walk with God does not stand or fall with the question of rescuing. Many who will disagree with my conclusions are very godly people. Some who will agree with my conclusions may not be godly at all.

Rescuing has great potential to divide the church. This fact has no bearing on whether or not it is right, of course, for the church has been divided by right things as well as wrong ones. I have seen rescuers create unnecessary division, and I have seen those who oppose rescuing create unnecessary division. The key word is *unnecessary,* for I am convinced this issue will divide us only if we choose to let it divide us. Our differences in perspective need not, should not, *must not* turn us against each other.

I do not say this theoretically—I know it firsthand. Some of my fellow elders at our church do not believe in civil disobedience to rescue unborn children. Our significantly different positions have made it difficult for us all.

This has not, however, kept us from fellowship, dialog, praying together, or moving forward in our ministry. Our positions sometimes differ, but our loyalty to each other goes deeper than those differences. Our unity is all the more significant because it is not that artificial unity based on mindless uniformity. It is a true and tested unity that has been forged in the crucible of diversity. (In the interests of unity and clarity I need to emphasize that this book is an expression of my own convictions. It should *not* be construed as the position either of my church or my co-elders.)

Rescuing, then, is not only a challenge to the unity of the church. It is a great opportunity to develop and demonstrate a unity that both incorporates and transcends our differences.

The Foundational Issue: Who Are the Unborn?

The most critical premise behind rescuing is that the unborn are human children. They are created in the image of God, and are as valuable in the sight of God as born persons. The unborn should not be less than this in our minds. If they are, then beneath the surface will be the unspoken thought, "It might be right to violate civil law to save a real human life, but unborn life is different." I have found that when the point is actually pressed, some who think of themselves as pro-life often make a distinction between the nature and value of born people and unborn people. This distinction is silent and subtle. It may color one's opinion of any pro-life ministry, and will definitely and dramatically affect one's view of rescuing.

It is therefore crucial, before entering into the main body of this book, that attention be given to this fundamental conviction. Due to limitations of space, I can only present briefly the scientific and biblical arguments for the humanity of the unborn child. Far more thorough presentations have been made by others.[2] I highly recommend a careful study of this issue by any reader with even a trace of doubt as to who the unborn really are.

The Scientific Evidence

One of the most common public misconceptions of our day is that there is a medical and scientific uncertainty as to whether an unborn child is a human being. On the contrary, there is a *strong* scientific consensus that human life begins at conception.[3] Therefore every abortion results in the death of a human being.

A panel of prominent scientists and medical researchers gave their testimonies to the Senate Judiciary Subcommittee in 1981. All but one affirmed with certainty that human life does indeed begin at conception. Though invited to do so, pro-choice advocates failed to produce even a single expert witness who would testify that life begins at any point other than conception.

The most they could come up with was one witness, and only one, who said no one can tell when life begins.[4]

In the early 1960s Dr. Alan Guttmacher of Planned Parenthood was still affirming that a human baby is present from the point of conception. Planned Parenthood literature warned women about the dangers of abortion, explicitly stating that abortion "kills the life of a baby."[5]

Dr. Landrum Shettles was a pioneer in sperm biology, fertility and sterility, and is famous for being the discoverer of male- and female-producing sperm. His intrauterine photographs of preborn[6] children appear in over fifty medical textbooks. In his book, *Rites of Life: The Scientific Evidence of Life Before Birth,* Dr. Shettles states, "No knowledge has emerged since the sixties that would cause Planned Parenthood to alter its view on scientific grounds. Though alter its view it has. Indeed, all the new knowledge we have about the unborn only *further* supports the idea that it is meaningful human life. The biological facts have not changed direction. But society has."[7]

Dr. Bernard Nathanson, internationally known obstetrician and gynecologist, was a co-founder of the National Abortion Rights Action League (NARAL). He owned and operated a New York abortion clinic that was the largest in the Western hemisphere, and personally presided over tens of thousands of abortions. But in studying the science of fetology, and using ultrasound to actually observe the unborn inside his mother, Nathanson came to the conclusion that he had made a horrible mistake.

In his documentary, *The Silent Scream,* Nathanson affirmed, "Modern technologies have convinced us that beyond question the unborn child is simply another human being, another member of the human community, indistinguishable in every way from any of us." *The Silent Scream* and its sequel, *The Eclipse of Reason,* graphically portray this reality by showing the actual abortions of unborn—and visibly human—children.

Examine any medical textbook or popular picture book that deals with the development of the unborn child. You will find an amazing portrait that is conspicuously absent from pro-choice literature. By eighteen days the unborn's heart is forming and his eyes are starting to develop. By twenty-four days his heart is fully developed and beating. By twenty-eight days the child has budding arms and legs. By thirty days he has multiplied in size by 10,000 times. He has a brain and blood flows through his veins.[8]

By this stage of development, the unborn child responds to stimulus. At eight weeks, if the nose is tickled the child will move his head backward.[9] An abortion at this point will certainly be felt by the child, who is already obviously human in appearance.[10] Yet many women aren't even sure they're pregnant at this point, and almost none get an abortion before then. In our area, the largest clinic refuses even to attempt an abortion until at least eight weeks, fifty-six days, of development. Yet two weeks earlier than this, at only forty days, the unborn child's brain waves can be recorded.[11] The absence of heartbeat and brain waves indicate a person has died. Don't the presence of heartbeat and brain waves indicate a person is living?

Where does human life begin? It begins at the beginning. Life is a continuum from conception to death. The biological evidence confirms what common sense has always led people to believe. That is that an unborn baby is a baby, and an abortion is the killing of that baby. This is not pro-life rhetoric. It is simply the truth. This actively suppressed truth[12] is resurfacing in legislatures and the judicial system, despite the fact that *Roe* v. *Wade* silenced it so effectively for years. A man who beat up a pregnant woman, resulting in the death of her unborn, is being prosecuted for murder. The state of Illinois forbids pregnant women from taking drugs because of the harmful effects on their preborn babies. Women can actually be prosecuted for "delivering a controlled substance to a minor." Washington, D.C., and Portland, Oregon, are two of the most pro-choice cities in the nation. Yet judges in these cities have sent women to jail to keep them from taking drugs because of adverse effects on their unborn children. The health of the unborn is being protected under the law, even when it requires sending people to jail.

This means that it is illegal for doctors and women to make choices that risk indirect *harm* to unborn children. Yet it is perfectly legal to make the choice to directly *kill* the same children by abortion. Mothers who risk harm to unborn children are being sent to jail. At the same time people who peacefully try to save the same unborn children from a brutal death are also being sent to jail. This glaring contradiction points out that the laws that grant the right to abortion are not founded in reality. Any honest recognition of the medical and scientific facts must lead to the conclusion that abortion is the killing of a human being.

The Biblical Evidence

We are made in the image of God (Gen 1:27). This means we are human from our beginning. Birth is not that beginning. It is simply the point at which the child who is already there joins others in the outside world. That child is a person before birth just as an adult is a person when alone and also when he joins a room full of other people.

The Old Testament word used for the unborn (Ex 21:22-25) is not an equivalent to our words *zygote, embryo* or *fetus.* It is simply the normal word for child.[13] The Hebrews did not need a separate word for the unborn. The Bible refers to born children and unborn children, but recognizes no such thing as potential, possible, or "almost" children.

Job graphically described the way God created him before he was born (Job 10:8-12). The person in the womb was not simply something that might become Job, but was actually Job himself. The unborn child was a younger version of exactly the same man.

Psalm 139:13-16 paints the most graphic picture in all Scripture of the intimate involvement of God with each preborn person. God created David's "inmost being," not at birth but before birth. David says to his Creator, "You knit me together in my mother's womb." Every person, regardless of his parentage or handicap, has been knitted together by God in the womb. All the days of the life ahead of him have been planned out by God before any have come to be (Ps 139:16).

David also affirms that his sin nature was present from the time of his conception (Ps 51:5). Who but an actual person can have a moral nature?

Jacob was given a place over Esau "though not yet born" (Rom 9:11). Jacob was Jacob before he was born. When Rebekah was pregnant with Jacob and Esau, Scripture says, "The *babies* jostled each other within her" (Gen 25:22). "The Lord who made you and formed you in your womb, he will help you" (Is 44:2, 24). What you are—not merely what you might become—was present in your mother's womb.

God tells Jeremiah, "I knew you in the womb" (Jer 1:5). The Hebrew word translated "knew" in this verse is *yadah.* It refers to the intimate acquaintance of persons with one another, and is even used of a married couple's sexual intimacy (e.g., Gen 4:1). God knows his people, and his people know him (Dan 11:32). God could not know Jeremiah in his mother's womb, unless Jeremiah, the person, was present in his mother's womb. God is involved in a knowing relationship not only with born people, but with preborn people.

When their pregnant mothers were together, the unborn John the Baptist was near the unborn Jesus. The "baby" John moved dramatically in response to the presence of his Lord (Lk 1:41). What were inside these women were not lumps of tissue, but distinct individual human beings. In fact, the word translated "baby" in this passage is the Greek word *brephos*. This word is used to refer to the already-born baby Jesus (Lk 2:12, 16), and for already-born babies whose parents were bringing them to Jesus to receive his blessing (Lk 18:15-17). It is also the same word used for the newborn babies killed by Pharaoh (Acts 7:19).

Scripture says Mary was "with child" (Lk 1:31). In the first century, and in every century, to be pregnant is to be with child. Women were not merely pregnant with that which might become a child. The incarnation did not begin in Bethlehem, but Nazareth. Any unborn child, whether nine months or six or three or one month after conception, is a child. This is not only the clear teaching of Scripture, but has been the consistent view of Christians throughout church history.[14]

Conclusion

This, then, is the foundational assumption upon which my examination of rescuing will be based. Even if some readers have the least uncertainty as to the nature and value of the unborn, can't we agree that we should err on the side of life created by God?

There are the further semantic issues of what to call the unborn, and whether abortion should be referred to as "murder."[15] Those interested may check the endnotes for an explanation of why I have chosen to use certain terms rather than others.

I do hope our vocabulary of unborn children and abortion can increasingly become consistent with reality. If we succumb to the world's euphemistic terminology that makes child-killing sound acceptable, we become unwitting partners in the depersonalization of the unborn children. We must learn to use words that give windows to the womb. Such words remind us and our society that someone is in there who must not be forgotten.

The peril of the unborn can be illustrated by a science-fiction story. A spaceship crew member picks up a radio transmission of a little girl's voice. The girl is stranded on a dying planet. But the "Prime Directive," which binds the crew to a policy of noninterference, persuades them they cannot rescue the little girl. Only one crew member feels differently. That is the one who has actually heard her voice.

Just as they are about to leave her to die, the ship's officers receive another transmission. This time they *all* hear the girl's voice. Suddenly they change their minds. They realize that no matter what the cost, they must save this girl's life. What has happened? The policy has not changed. The girl has not changed. Their knowledge of her dilemma has not changed. What has happened is that in that moment their perspective changed. Now, in their hearts they know that *this is indeed a little child who is about to die.* This is no longer a theory, but a fact. The understanding is now not only in their heads but also in their hearts.

Our willingness to come to grips with the fact that the unborn are real and precious little girls and boys—not just in theory, but in fact, not just in our heads but in our hearts—will largely determine what we will do for the children who are about to die.

2
A Slow & Reluctant Pilgrimage

Let this be written for a
future generation, that a people
not yet created may praise the LORD.
David (Psalm 102:18)

*I*n this chapter I will tell my own story. In so doing I am not assuming that God calls everyone to the same conclusions or actions. I am simply sharing the process he took me through in relation to rescuing.

Deeply Disturbed
In the fall of 1985 I sat in my office, deeply disturbed. I had been thinking about a message I was preparing on abortion. In a few months I would be preaching this message on Sanctity of Human Life Sunday. For some years our church had observed this special day on the Sunday in January closest to the anniversary of the infamous *Roe* v. *Wade* decision.

In past years I and other pastors at our church had preached against abortion. But year after year abortions were continuing, one and a half million annually. Very little had changed. Abortion was now part of the warp and woof of American culture.

In the previous ten years I had thought through the issues, studied the

Scriptures, and read countless books and articles on the subject. I had prayed, written letters to congressmen and the president, supported pro-life candidates, and given money to pro-life groups. I'd served on the board of Portland's first Crisis Pregnancy Center. My wife and I opened our home to a pregnant girl, saw her through the birth and adoption, and had the joy of seeing her come to Christ while with us. I counseled women not to get abortions, ordered and distributed pro-life materials for our church, wrote against abortion, preached against abortion, and attended anti-abortion rallies. But, on this day as I sat with open Bible and considered the children who were suffering and dying day after day, all I had done just didn't seem to be enough.

Recently a few abortion clinics had been bombed. This was disturbing (and still is) to everyone, including me. I also knew there were some peaceful protesters at the clinics. Some were even getting arrested, though I wasn't exactly sure why. Like most evangelical Christians I thought of these nonviolent "protesters" as sincere, but misguided. In fact, I thought they were more than a little kooky.

Still, I was struck with the fact that abortion was taking innocent lives, and at least these people were treating it that way. After all, what if these were three- or six- or nine-year-old children who were being cut to pieces in our city every day? If the police would do nothing, wouldn't we go right to the killing places and try to save some lives?

So I determined that my message on Sanctity of Human Life Sunday was not going to be like one more sermon against Jew-killing preached to people in a German church forty years earlier. This time it would be different.

In the sermon I pointed out that the combined American casualties of the Revolutionary War, Civil War, Spanish-American War, World War 1, World War 2, Korean War, and the Vietnam War were one and a half million people. This was roughly the same number of children being killed by abortion in America every year.

Then I put on the overhead projector a map of the United States. I crossed out the states of Montana, Wyoming, Colorado, North Dakota, South Dakota, Nebraska, Kansas, Minnesota and Iowa. The combined populations of these states at the time (counting men, women and children) was just over sixteen million. This is about the number of children that had been killed by abortion since 1973. Forty-five hundred children were being killed each day. One-third of all pregnancies were ending in abortion. In some cities, including our nation's capital, abortions were outnumbering live births. Then I compared all this to the holocaust. I pointed out that already the number of children killed by abortion had far exceeded those murdered by the Nazis.

Citing numerous biblical examples, I drew what was at the time a surprising conclusion. If abortion was not stopped by legal means, then we as Christians would need to seriously consider nonviolent civil disobedience to attempt to save lives. This was a new thought both to me and to my church. Still, the general reaction to the message was positive. At least, few negative opinions were expressed directly to me. I realized later that as long as arguments are theoretical, they pose few problems. The concept of civil disobedience to save human lives is one thing. It is another thing when you actually go out there and start doing it! At the time I was either unready or unwilling to actually do it. So my message served the purpose of planting seeds that might later bear fruit. But for now it was safe enough that no one had to grapple with it past midweek, when sermons are normally forgotten.

Another Year, Another Message

Three years later it was another fall, and I was anticipating another Sanctity of Human Life Sunday. I pulled out the overhead transparency I had made three years earlier, on which I'd crossed out those nine states. I now did some figuring and found that since my last message on the subject, I would need to cross out four more states—Oregon, Nevada, New Mexico and Utah. The proportions of this holocaust of the unborn were staggering. They defied belief.

As I crossed out those states with my red felt pen, I could not escape the implications. I really believed these were human beings, mercilessly slaughtered in my own city every day. So why wasn't I doing what I told myself I would be doing if they were older and bigger people as in Nazi Germany? Abortion was killing innocent people. Why wasn't I doing for them what I would do for other innocent people killed in other ways?

I asked myself, what if my next-door neighbor decided to kill his children and it was perfectly legal for him to do so? What would I do? Write a letter to my congressman? Send money to a child-care center? Picket my neighbor's driveway? Prepare a sermon or write an article against child-killing? I might do some of these things and others as well. But my immediate action would be to do something *now* to save the lives about to be taken. If the police were unavailable or unwilling to help, I would physically intervene to try to prevent the murders. I imagined myself prayerfully and fearfully talking to my neighbor to help him realize he must not do this terrible thing. I would tell him that his children are precious and deserve to live. I would tell him that I would help him in any way I could to deal with the problems that led to his desperation. If he felt he could not handle the burden of raising his children, I would volunteer to have them live with me or to find them a home.

Why wasn't I doing this for the desperate or misguided mothers and the innocent babies about to be killed at the abortion clinics?

I was saying "the unborn are human beings," yet day after day I was not acting as if that were true. As a father and pastor the conviction was doubly weighty. How could I expect my children or my congregation to take my words seriously when my own life demonstrated I didn't really believe the words I was saying? I might as well stand up and preach a sermon against materialism while living in opulence, or a sermon on feeding the poor while I let my next-door neighbor starve, or a sermon on evangelism while quietly watching as those around me go to hell.

My mind went to Rev. Mari, one of the trustees of ECWA, the largest evangelical denomination in Nigeria. Mari had visited our church on a Sunday a year after my last message on abortion. I had asked him to bring a greeting to our church. This was to be translated by a friend who was a Nigerian attending a nearby seminary. Mari first said some nice things about our country and our churches. Then he said something very disturbing. Mari said, "But with all the good things I see in your country and in your churches, there is something here that troubles me deep in my soul." Mari kept saying how troubled he was, and how awful this thing was, before telling us what he was actually talking about. While he was building up to it, I guessed a half dozen things, including unbelief, materialism, immorality, superficiality, prayerlessness, and lack of zeal for the unsaved. What he said took me by surprise. "This horrible thing I speak of," he said, "is that you kill your children before they are born." What was particularly troublesome was that Mari made no distinction between what our country was doing and what the church was doing. He seemed to think that the church was responsible for the moral choices of the country.

There I was in 1988, three years and five million slaughtered children since my last message, trying to figure out how in the world I could preach one more sermon against abortion. I was haunted by my own convictions, Mari's words, and the unending statistics of murdered children. Fortunately this particular message wasn't scheduled to be preached for another three months. Though one child in America was being killed every twenty seconds, I still had some time to think and pray before having to preach the message.

"Never Again"

As God would have it, during this time I was speaking for a week at a Christian liberal arts college on the East Coast. The subject was not abortion, but that was where my mind was dwelling. On November 9, I was about to stand up to speak in chapel. The school president, who was sitting next to me, whispered, "Do you mind if I take some of your time to say something before you speak?" One does not say, "Yes, I mind" to the president, so I said, "No, not at all." He stood up behind the podium.

He began to speak in his distinctive German accent. I immediately realized something unusual was happening. His eyes were full of tears. This was a man who commanded respect. So his uncharacteristic display of emotion was causing the whole student body to be riveted to his words.

"To most of you," he began, "today is like any other day. But it is an extremely important day to me. For today is the fiftieth anniversary of Crystal Night. This was the night the Nazis broke the glass in the Jewish synagogues, and homes and shops, and beat and ridiculed the Jews. It happened throughout Germany."

By now the president was choking back a sob. "I was there, as a young boy. I can still hear the sound of the shattering glass."

The haunting memories filling his head, this soft-spoken and godly intellectual said, "There were many of us who were Christians, but we did nothing to stop it. That was the beginning of the holocaust, because then the Jew-haters knew that the people of Germany would not stand up for the Jews."

To conclude these powerful moments he quoted the words now posted at the concentration camp in Auschwitz, Poland. There, where unspeakable crimes against God and man were committed by the Nazis, a sign says, "Never again." "Christian young people," he said, "at all costs *we must never let it happen again.*"

To most of the students, I suppose, the warning was inspirational, but fairly irrelevant. "Of course we would never let it happen again. What kind of people do you think we are anyway?" To me, though, it was the proverbial last straw. All I could think of was, "It *is* happening again. Just like the Christians of Germany we are letting it happen. *I* am letting it happen." In fact, it had been happening in America for longer than it happened in Germany, and with many more casualties. What's more, the victims in America had much less chance to defend themselves or escape than those in Germany. We say, "Never again." We gather in our churches and talk about holiness and justice and morality and compassion. Yet the holocaust goes on incessantly, day after day, bathed in the blood of millions of innocent children.

I knew as I sat there what I must do. That day I spoke to the students about something that, for the moment, I cared nothing about. As I shook the president's hand afterward, I knew the time had come. This was not a knee-jerk reaction to inspiring words. It was the culmination of years of conviction. I would no longer be a spectator to the holocaust. I would begin to treat the unborn children as human beings. I would physically intervene for them in the name of Christ, regardless of the cost. I would do it even if it meant breaking man's law.

The Reluctant Convert

C. S. Lewis called himself "the most reluctant convert in England." He said he had been "dragged, kicking and screaming, into the kingdom of God." This is precisely how I felt about my decision to rescue. I believed it was right, and still do. But it was also terribly difficult, for I had powerful vested interests in not doing it. Much of the built-in resistance was due to my own background and makeup. I was raised to respect and obey the law, and I taught others to do the same. My theological training was at a conservative Bible college and seminary. They were conservative not just in theology but in action. I had since served on the part-time faculty of both schools. Civil disobedience may be acceptable in some Christian circles. It was definitely not acceptable in mine!

The decision brought simultaneous peace and turmoil. Peace because I had finally succumbed to the Hound of Heaven. I was finding rest in him and in the sense of rightness about the commitment to which I had so reluctantly come. Turmoil because now I would have to take the actual steps. I would have to try to explain my convictions and actions to my family, friends, fellow elders, my church, and the greater Christian community to whom I ministered.

My wife understood and came to total agreement. But it was terribly hard on her at first. She understood this would mean her husband must endure physical pain, arrest, standing before courts, and spending time in jail. Since I am an insulin-dependent diabetic, the physical and emotional stress could jeopardize my health. This troubled her. Among other things, my rescuing might eventually mean being sued by an abortion clinic and losing our house and everything else we owned. Being a faithful servant of God and loyal wife, she was soon 100 per cent supportive. In fact, she has spent more time at abortion clinics than I have. Every week she goes to share her faith in Christ and talk women into letting their babies live.

My daughters, then nine and seven, were among the very few who understood instantly. They didn't know any better than to actually believe what we had told them about unborn children being real people. My decision made perfect sense to them. But I was afraid it would make little sense at all to most of the adults I knew.

The word that best describes what I felt the next two months is *lonely*. Thankfully, there was no abortion clinic in my own town. However, there were several in Portland, fifteen miles from my church and home. I found out there was an upcoming meeting about rescuing. I planned to go, but my biggest fear was that I would be associating with "off the wall," militant people, unbalanced rebels, shouters or malcontents. These are the very type of people who can make life miserable for a pastor. I would not want to share a one-hour appointment with them, much less a police car, a jail cell or a lawsuit.

I went to the meeting by myself. It was probably the most lonely evening I have ever spent. Though I was surrounded by people, I didn't know any of them. Many of them, unlike me, had rescued before. It turned out to be a very friendly group, consisting of surprisingly normal people, clothed and in their right minds. The worship and prayer was strong and Christ-centered, but I still felt alone. It was as if God was saying, "You must first draw your strength from me in this, not from others."

At one point the leader asked, "Do we have any pastors here tonight?" Three of us raised our hands, the others noticeably higher than mine. The leader then asked if any of us wanted to say something. The others did. I didn't. I didn't even want to be there, and I certainly wasn't going to encourage others in what I had not yet done myself. But as the evening went on I discovered that God had graciously led me to the like-minded. These were people who had come down different paths. But each had arrived at the same place I had. This confirmed to me that the work of the Spirit was here.

At the close of the evening they asked that each of us write out his name and address. I wrote, "Please pray for me. I can't rescue tomorrow because I haven't worked it through with my fellow church leaders." The drive home was even more lonely. But this time it was a different loneliness. I wanted to be with those people the next morning intervening for the unborn. But I knew I owed it to my co-elders to share my heart and convictions with them first. It was also important to listen to their response, in case they had Scriptural input that could change my thinking. The way I felt, I would have welcomed it!

The next day I sat down to write out a letter to the other elders of the church. I had served there for twelve years, since its very conception. Christmas was coming and we wouldn't meet for a few weeks, so I wanted them to have time to think and pray it through. I explained how I had arrived at my position and asked for their counsel. Pointing to relevant Scripture, I asked their permission to share my perspective with the church family in the upcoming message on abortion. I said I would not impose these convictions on anyone. I simply wanted them to hear why I had made this decision before they saw me on the news being dragged away by the police.

In the next three weeks I had occasion to see all the elders. Only one of the twelve mentioned the letter to me. The idea was so shocking, I think, that they just didn't know how to respond. When it came time, we discussed my decision for two meetings. A variety of perspectives were raised. It was a very disturbing issue to them, just as it was for me. But they are godly men. So they gave me the green light to preach the message as I believed God would have it preached.

The next rescue was two weeks away, and I was planning on participating. Meanwhile I had shared my conviction with a friend and mentioned what a lonely process it had been. Later she told her husband what I was planning to do. He called me and said, "I want you to know that I share your conviction, and I'd like to go to the rescue with you." I was overcome with emotion and could barely say "thanks for calling" before I hung up and wept. It is impossible to describe how much it meant that someone I knew and respected, a member of my church family, believed like I did, and wanted to join me. Just eight days before my message on abortion and civil disobedience, we went to our first rescue together. It was not easy, but as we drove home we said to each other that we were certain it was right.

Another Message, a Different Response

Sunday morning came and I preached on abortion. I shared the biological and biblical evidences for the humanity of the unborn. I made the parallels to the holocaust and the American slavery issue. I told the story of the college president who said, "Never again." I talked about the logical connection between killing preborn and killing already born babies, as well as the euthanasia of the elderly, ill, and mentally and physically handicapped. I spoke of God's judgment on the nation Israel for the slaughter of innocent blood.

Finally I asked, where was the church in Germany during the holocaust, and where is the church today? Quoting Proverbs 24:11-12 and similar passages, I said, "These verses command us to rescue innocent people who are being led to slaughter. Does this include unborn children?" I invited them to return in the evening to hear thirty-five means they could use to intervene for the unborn, thirty-four of which were perfectly legal. I told them the thirty-fifth means would be blocking access to abortion clinics.

Many people returned that night. After listing all the other ways to fight abortion, and encouraging people to pursue them, I explained in brief the basic themes of this book. My friend who had rescued with me shared his perspective. A few weeks later at the next rescue there were twenty-five of us from the church. As I write, about fifty of our church people have rescued, not a large number for a church our size. Some have gone only one time and probably won't again. Others are regulars. Still others, like my wife, go down to the clinics weekly to talk with women as they come in for pregnancy tests and abortions.

Many of our people have for the first time become involved in legal pro-life activities, including helping in pregnancy centers and all forms of political action. The week after the message two hundred people from our church traveled to our state's capital to march on behalf of the unborn children. Our people were suddenly standing up for the innocent as never before, despite the fact that we had encouraged them to be involved in these ways for many years.

In the year and a half since that message our church has, among other things, placed a series of large pro-life newspaper advertisements offering to help pregnant women, taken a very large pro-life offering, increased our pro-life budget, distributed thousands of pieces of literature, staged a major pro-life youth rally, and become widely known as a strong pro-life force in our community. Recently one hundred sixty of our people committed themselves to legal picketing against abortion and the unjust treatment of rescuers. These have not been my personal efforts, but the efforts of many people in our church.

All the years of preaching on this subject had generated relatively little involvement on behalf of the unborn. What made the difference this time? Without a doubt, it was the decision of a small number to rescue. We were willing to do for the unborn what we would do for the born. We would intervene to save lives even if it required trespassing. This gave authenticity to a cry that had years earlier begun to ring hollow: "the unborn are human beings, and abortion is child-killing." It was as if we were now saying, "We really mean business." The majority have chosen not to engage in civil disobedience. But they are much more serious in their efforts for the unborn than ever before. Many have said, "I don't feel I can rescue at the clinics, but I will commit myself to faithfully stand for the unborn in these other ways."

The bottom line is that rescuing has had its own direct effect, *and* has become a major catalyst to other forms of intervention. Those of us from our church who choose to rescue do not regard it as superior to any other ministry. To us it is another important and legitimate way to intervene in the name of Christ for innocent, vulnerable and needy people created in God's image.

The year and a half that I've been involved in rescuing has brought many difficulties into our lives. However, in the midst of these difficulties my family and I have deeply sensed the presence and approval of our Lord Jesus. He has faithfully walked ahead of and beside us. We have experienced peace and joy. These have transcended every difficult circumstance that has come out of our choice to rescue the unborn.

3
Test Cases of Civil Disobedience

*If there is no final place for civil disobedience, then
the government has been made autonomous, and as such,
it has been put in the place of the Living God.*
Francis Schaeffer

For many sincere Christians the issue of civil disobedience hangs like a storm cloud over the practice of rescuing. This cloud casts ominous shadows on the wisdom, motivations and ultimate rightness of those who choose to rescue. Is civil disobedience for the Christian ever right? If so, is it right in the specific case of trying to save the lives of preborn children?

The following fifteen cases raise the question of whether it is sometimes right for Christians to break civil laws. Most are situations that have actually occurred. A few are true-to-life situations that have likely occurred or will occur in the future. For maximum benefit from reading this book, approach this chapter as a group of exercises. Please read each case carefully. Put yourself in the situation described. In the margin of the book, or on a separate sheet of paper, write a yes or no answer.

Case #1
You are a first-century Christian. The Roman government doesn't care whether you worship Christ, but it does insist that you also recognize the ultimate authority of Caesar. To show your total allegiance to him, you must offer a

sacrifice to Caesar. If you do, you are free, but if you refuse, you will be imprisoned, tortured and executed. Would it be right for you to disobey the law that says you must offer a sacrifice to Caesar?

Case #2

You are a Christian living in the second century. Roman law grants fathers absolute right over their children. It is common practice for newborn babies to be discarded, and left outside the city gates to die. It is also common practice for Christians, believing in the sanctity of human life, to rescue these children from death and raise them as their own. Roman authorities regard this as an infringement on the father's rights over his children. It is therefore illegal for anyone to care for a discarded infant.[1] Would it be right for you to disobey the law and try to save the child's life and provide him a home?

Case #3

You live in a Middle Eastern country where the law specifically prohibits you from proselytizing or sharing the gospel with Muslims. In private conversation with a Muslim neighbor you see an opportunity to share with him the good news of salvation in Christ. Would it be right to disobey the law to share Christ with him?

Case #4

The year is 1855 and you are a Black slave living in the southern United States. Though you have served him well, your master beats you, rapes your wife, and now has his eye on your ten-year-old daughter. He allows you no private family life, nor an education for your children. According to the law of the land, upheld by the Supreme Court, it is illegal for you either to resist your master or to run from him. You have appealed to him to have mercy on your family, but to no avail. Would it be right for you to attempt to run away to gain safety and freedom for your family?

Case #5

The year is, again, 1855 but this time you are a White American, living in the

North. The Black slave and his family described in the previous case, fleeing from their master, come to your house and ask for a meal and to spend the night in your barn. According to the Fugitive Slave Law of 1850 it is absolutely illegal for you to feed or house this family. In fact, your legal duty is to turn them in to the authorities. Would it be right for you to break the law by feeding and housing them?

Case #6

You are a Christian living in India some years ago. It is a legally sanctioned social custom that when the head of a household dies, his widow is burned to death. A woman nearby has lost her husband. Tomorrow she is scheduled to be killed. Though you would be violating the law, would it be right for you to try to rescue this innocent woman from the legalized killing that is imminent unless you intervene?

Case #7

It is World War 2, shortly after the bombing of Pearl Harbor by the Japanese. The U.S. Supreme Court has declared it legal for the government to move 70,000 Japanese Americans, including children and elderly, into concentration camps for the duration of the war. This is done with no due process of law, and they are guilty of no crime, other than being of the wrong race.

You have developed a close relationship with the Japanese family next door. You have shared the gospel with them. You know them to be fine people and loyal Americans. You have made an official appeal for them, but to no avail. They will soon be taken to the camps. Would it be right for you to break the law by inviting them to live secretly in your basement for the duration of the war, or until other arrangements could be made?

Case #8

It is 1955 and you are a Black living in Montgomery, Alabama. You are not permitted to sit on a bus in a seat parallel to Whites. A White person is seated near you, so the bus driver orders you to move to the back of the bus. You paid your fare, and though you and your fellow Blacks have acquiesced to such treatment for years, you know it is wrong. Would it be right for you to refuse to move and be arrested in order to draw attention to racial injustice, hopefully thereby becoming a catalyst for social change?

Case #9

You are a Christian currently living in Sweden. You believe the Bible's instructions to discipline your children by using appropriate corporal punishment (Prov 13:24; 22:15; 23:13-14; 29:15). But for some years now Swedish law has specifically prohibited spanking or any other corporal punishment. You would of course never abuse your children, but you love them enough to raise them the way God says to. Would it be right for you to violate the law by spanking your children?

Case #10

You are a doctor living in the Netherlands. The law allows for euthanasia, and doctors are given considerable latitude in determining who will be permitted to die. One of your fellow doctors orders the withholding of care from an elderly patient with no family, whose chances for recovery are slim. It is the doctor's legal right to do so. Would it be right for you to violate the law by secretly giving medical care to the woman?

Case #11

You are a nurse living in the United States a few years from now. You are working the night shift and you discover a baby with Down's Syndrome. You see a note above the baby which states "No food or care." The hospital policy, supported by previous court decisions, is to allow parents and doctors the freedom to deny care to deformed or extremely retarded children. You have appealed to hospital administration and staff in the past, and they have not changed their policy.

It will take several days, perhaps a week, for the child to slowly die of neglect. Would it be right for you to violate the law by feeding the child? Or, knowing he will otherwise die, would you be right to go a step further and smuggle the child out of the hospital to give him to a friend who has been wanting to adopt a Down's Syndrome child?

Case #12

You are a Christian living in Nazi Germany in 1942. By law, Jews are now considered nonpersons, devoid of rights. As the government rounds them up for extermination in the camps, it is your legal responsibility to give them no aid whatsoever. Even your church leaders have said it is important that the law be obeyed. You hear of a Jewish family hiding in an abandoned building six blocks away. You know that unless they are well hidden the SS is sure to find them and send them to the camps. Would it be right for you to go to them and bring them into your own home, even if it meant putting yourself and your family at great risk?

Case #13

It is some time in the future, and you are alive during a period of great social and economic turmoil. A gifted leader rises up who promises to deliver your country from economic disaster. Part of his plan, approved by the legislature and judicial system, is that everyone will have a mark put on his right hand or forehead. Without this mark no one can buy or sell food, or anything else. Those who do not comply with this law are not only considered unpatriotic and anarchists, but are prosecuted as criminals. Not only your responsibility to obey the law, but your personal and family welfare is at stake. Should you obey the law and receive the mark? Or would it be right for you to disobey the law and refuse it?

Case #14

You live in a country where the laws state any or all of the following: only those licensed by the state can preach in churches; churches can only be open on Sundays; churches can only address religious issues, not "political" ones; home Bible studies cannot be held in many neighborhoods due to zoning restrictions; churches must not discriminate by refusing to hire homosexual staff members; churches cannot dismiss a staff member for his private sexual activities; churches are not permitted to make public statements to the assembly in accord with Matthew 18:15-20.

In any of these situations, would you or your church leaders be right in breaking the law? If so, which situations, and why?

Case #15

After eighteen years of legal attempts by yourselves and others to protect the lives of unborn children, babies are still being killed every day in your country. In your own city there are four abortion clinics where a steady stream of children are daily killed by appointment.

You have picketed the clinics, and while you may be influencing public opinion, the vast majority of the women still enter the clinics and get their abortions. Only a few appear to take your signs seriously. You try to talk to the women, but clinic personnel have warned them in advance not to listen to you. In fact, you have watched clinic workers take away and tear up the literature you give to the expectant mothers. You know that most of these women have never been told the truth about the living person inside them. You know that in their ignorance they are about to have their babies killed.

A small number of local Christians have been "rescuing," peacefully placing their bodies in front of abortion-clinic doors. They do this to buy time for the babies and give opportunity for sidewalk counselors to talk with the mothers coming for abortions. Even those who won't talk don't get in for their abortions. You have heard that Planned Parenthood has stated that 20 per cent of the women who miss their appointments, for whatever reason, do not reschedule their abortions. You know that some babies have definitely been saved through these rescues. In fact, a family in your church recently adopted one of them, and you have held him in your arms.

You want to try to save these precious lives. But you wonder whether a Christian should break a no-trespassing law, subject himself to the possibility of arrest, go to jail, or be sued by the abortion clinic.

Would you be right in joining this group of Christians to try peacefully to save the lives of unborn children, even if it means violating a trespass law to do so?

Where Do You Stand?

Did you answer yes in any of these cases? If so, you have affirmed your belief in civil disobedience.[2] You believe that it is sometimes, in certain situations, God's will for Christians to disobey civil law.

Or perhaps there were none of the fifteen cases you said yes to, but you can imagine a situation in which it would be right to disobey the law. In that case you too believe that civil disobedience is sometimes right, even if rarely. The only question that remains is "When is it right and when is it wrong, and how can we decide?"

Obviously, even those of us who said yes a number of times would draw the line somewhere. You might not believe it is right, for instance, for someone to burn a slave-owner's crop, bomb a Nazi-operated Jewish extermination camp, or fire-bomb an abortion clinic, even if you knew no one would be hurt. Violent or physically destructive action "ups the ante" in issues of civil disobedience. If the cases had asked about the rightness of violent or destructive actions some of your answers would almost certainly have been different.

Nonetheless, in answering the above questions, most readers will have taken the position that civil disobedience is sometimes permissible for the conscientious Christian. In fact, in some of these cases you may personally believe it is not only permissible but mandatory. You may feel that it would be wrong not to disobey the law. However, that is not the primary issue of this book.

The question I wish to address is not "Is civil disobedience to save unborn babies always right for everyone?" The question is "Is civil disobedience to save unborn babies ever right for anyone?" I am not asking if biblically and morally all Christians must rescue. I am asking if biblically and morally any Christians may rescue. If the reader concludes that such civil disobedience is indeed right, or may be right for some people in some situations, that reader will need to decide before God what his own actions will be.

Civil Disobedience around the Globe

Several of the fifteen cases relate to the early church or to Christians alive today in other countries. These may seem like theoretical cases to us, but they were and are painfully real to our brothers and sisters in Christ.

The Christian church was born and raised in frequent conflict with civil government. The governments of England, France, Spain, Portugal, Japan, Burma, India, Madagascar, Grenada, Cambodia, China, the Soviet Union, Romania, Nepal, Saudi Arabia and a host of other countries have at one time persecuted Christians. Many still do so today. The commitment of such governments to opposing Christianity requires daily civil disobedience on the part of Christians. Our brothers and sisters are often not legally allowed to assemble, share their faith, possess or distribute Christian literature, or exercise many of their basic biblical convictions.

In China, where pastors over fifty have spent an average of fifteen years in prison, unauthorized meetings of three or more persons are illegal. Every Christian parent must decide whether to obey the law of the state which says children under eighteen are not to be taught a religious faith. The Chinese abortion policy has resulted in horrifying experiences. For instance, in 1981 abortion "posses" rounded up expectant mothers in animal trucks and took them to abortion clinics. In a single town 19,000 abortions were performed in fifty days.[3] In China alone, fifty-three million unborn infants were slaughtered between 1979 and 1984. Christian families must decide whether it is right to obey the law that says you must have an abortion after the first or second child. They must also decide whether or not they should break the law by helping other parents avoid abortions.

I once met with Christian leaders in a Muslim country. One of them shared that a Christian friend had recently found a microphone under his dining room table. The police were monitoring his conversations. Many of the Christian activities of the men I met with are illegal. One of them stated to those of us from the West, "If one of you is found, they kick you out. But if one of us is found, they kick us in."

Today Eastern Europe is experiencing a resurgence of freedom. But we must not forget the challenges faced by believers there in the last four decades. Many Hungarian Christians refused to comply with the government's laws that churches be registered. The church in Poland stood up against the state's attempts to infringe on their religious and moral convictions. In Bulgaria and Romania illegal prayer meetings and Bible classes have been the norm. In Albania it is against the law not only to assemble as Christians, or to share the faith, but even to be a Christian. To love Christ is to live each moment in civil disobedience.

Most evangelicals hailed the December 1989 toppling of Romania's dictator Ceausescu and the subsequent civil and religious freedoms it brought. Many, however, still do not understand that it was the courageous civil disobedience of Christians that sparked the move to freedom. Laszlo Tokes, pastor of a small church in Timisoara, publicly opposed the evil policies and practices of the government, which was denying human rights. Fearing government disapproval, his own church officials disowned him.[4]

After months of harassing Tokes and his family, government troops came to forcibly remove him. They were met by hundreds of Christian families forming a human chain around the pastor. Troops opened fire on a line of children, then mowed down the adults as well. Many people were killed in the massacre. When word spread, the country was outraged. Within days Ceausescu was dead and Romania free.[5]

Prior to 1990, in the Soviet Union many Christians were fired from their jobs just because of their faith. Many of them were in work camps, others in prison. Some have had their children taken away. Others have been imprisoned because they would not give up their Scriptures to the authorities. Alexander Solzhenitsyn, who was not permitted to write in prison, tricked the authorities by scratching out lines in his cell, then memorizing them. When he was released, he had 12,000 lines committed to memory, and he promptly wrote them out for the benefit of the world and his suffering brethren.

When I personally attended an illegal gathering of pastors behind the iron curtain, I was moved and humbled by their godliness, humility and courage. I was only risking expulsion from a country I wouldn't want to stay in anyway. But they were risking their families, their jobs, and what limited freedoms they had. They gathered to fellowship with brothers from the West and to study God's Word with us. They desired to deepen their reservoirs so they might have more to share with their congregations. It was one of the most meaningful meetings of my life. It was also in violation of civil law.

At the time I was not involved in rescuing. I remember thinking about previous discussions with Christians who were categorically against civil disobedience. They argued that Bible smuggling, illegal radio broadcasts, unlawful meetings and other such activities were displeasing to God.

A large portion of the body of Christ in many parts of the globe today must daily disobey civil law in order to obey the law of God. So I believe we must be careful not to sit in comfort and freedom and make sweeping condemnations of civil disobedience.

We are a unique generation of Christians, both historically and globally. We have lived so long without having to break laws that we have forgotten it has been normal for God's people to have to choose between obeying God and men. We have the luxury of debating an issue which is already settled for Christians in sixty per cent of the world's population areas, where to be a Christian and to obey the Lord requires regular civil disobedience.

In fact, we who are so accustomed to not living in conflict with civil laws may find in years ahead that we are unprepared when it comes to counting the cost and making hard decisions that put us at odds with our government and society. For that reason the subject of this book is relevant not only to abortion and rescuing, but to many other issues we may eventually face.

Current Ethical Issues in the United States

In recent years more and more situations have arisen that have forced Christians in America to choose between violating biblical convictions and violating the laws of the state. An Oklahoma church lost a lawsuit over a case of church discipline in which they had tried to follow the guidelines of Matthew 18. I know church leaders who now question whether they should follow the pattern of this passage in light of threatened lawsuits. Churches in our country may soon be routinely forced to choose between what is legal and what is biblical.

The Faith Baptist Church of Louisville, Nebraska, refused to comply with the the state requirements that the church's school have teachers from state-approved institutions. The church and its families felt the state was intruding into their God-given responsibility of educating their children. Even when the court ordered compliance or closure, the church did not budge. Police arrested the pastor in the middle of a church service and padlocked the church doors. Fathers were jailed for refusing to testify about school operations. Whether or not the church and pastor handled this situation well, what happened there could become more common in the future.

A national leader in the home-school movement told me that there are thousands, probably tens of thousands of Christians across America who are currently in violation of civil law by teaching their children at home in a way other than what their states allow. However, major legal progress has been made in certain states as a direct result of noncompliance with unjust laws.

In 1987 thirteen doctors and psychiatrists examined a six-year-old girl who claimed her father had raped her. Eleven of them testified in a D.C. court that she had in fact been sexually abused. But the judge ruled the evidence was inconclusive and ordered that the girl spend a two-week unsupervised visit with her father.

The girl's mother sent her daughter into hiding and was subsequently put in jail for contempt of court. She was told she would not be released until she fulfilled the court order to give her daughter over to the man who, she is convinced, was sexually abusive. In September 1989 this woman was released after spending twenty-five months in jail. She had stated that she would stay there another eleven years until her daughter turned eighteen, if that's what it took to keep her safe. Given the same situation, what would you do?

At least two families in our church have had to choose between violating kidnapping laws and letting an innocent child die from abuse or neglect. They had previously pursued legal recourses to no avail. In such cases does one obey the law and allow the child to suffer and die, or does he disobey the law and save the life?

The issue of trespassing at abortion clinics to save the lives of unborn children is not theoretical. Of course we should pursue every legal means to save the lives of babies. But it eventually comes down to the fact that an innocent child will be killed on this day and at this place. Is it right or wrong to nonviolently break a trespassing law to try to prevent the killing and save the life? Is it right even if the consequences include arrest, imprisonment, and being sued by the abortion clinic?

I have tried to take civil disobedience from the theoretical to the real. I find that when Christians are asked if they believe in civil disobedience they often say "no." But when you give them specific examples their true position comes out. The idea of civil disobedience is repugnant to the decent law-abiding Christian citizen. In most cases, it should be. But the reality is that the very fact that he is a Christian and a decent person would compel him to civil disobedience in a significant number of actual cases.

However, the fact that we have said we would think it right to disobey the law in one or more of these cases does not thereby make it right. Neither does the fact that Christians around the world have and are making choices to break civil laws. To determine when if ever civil disobedience is right, we must go directly to the Scriptures.

4
Civil Disobedience in the Bible

*What belongs to God
is outside the Emperor's power.*
Ambrose, A.D. 385

M oses was born in Egypt at the time when Pharaoh commanded
that all boys born to Hebrews be killed at birth. Pharaoh's command *was* civil law. With the lives of innocent children at stake,
the Hebrew midwives disobeyed that law. "The midwives, however, feared God and did not do what the king of Egypt had told them to do"
(Ex 1:17). How did God respond to their choice to place the sanctity of human
life over obedience to government? "So God was kind to the midwives and
the people increased and became even more numerous. And because the
midwives feared God, he gave them families of their own" (Ex 1:20-21). God
gave his approval and blessing upon those who refused to obey civil law when
it came to the taking of innocent lives.

Likewise, Moses' parents and sister disobeyed the government to protect
the life of their child, hiding him for three months (Ex 2:1-4). His parents are
used as examples of people with faith in Hebrews 11 because "they hid him"
and "were not afraid of the king's edict" (Heb 11:23).

A Christian leader has argued against rescuing and other forms of civil
disobedience. Concerning the account in Exodus 2 he has said, "Consider the
faith that Moses' parents had in God's ability to work through human author-

ities. They complied with an evil law as far as they could by placing their baby in a basket on the river."[1] In contrast, Scripture itself demonstrates that Moses' parents did everything they could *not* to comply with the evil law in order to save their child. Any Christian recognizes God can indeed work through human authorities. However, the faith for which Moses' parents are commended in Hebrews 11 was not a faith in "God's ability to work through human authorities." Theirs was a faith in God's edict rather than the king's command. This demonstrated a fear of God that was greater than their fear of the king (Heb 11:23).

God, Moses and the Exodus

Moses modeled a correct approach to human government by first appealing to Pharaoh to allow the people of Israel to go into the desert for three days to worship God (Ex 5:1-5). At first Pharaoh refused. But, after a great deal of divine persuasion in the form of the ten plagues, he finally gave permission. Each plague is related to a specific god of Egypt. The plagues culminated in the striking down of Pharaoh's firstborn, the "divine" heir to the throne. This is a vivid reminder that there is only one true authority over all.

Acting on their legal right, "Pharaoh and his officials changed their minds about them and said, 'What have we done? We have let the Israelites go and have lost their services' " (Ex 14:5). They then pursued the Israelites, "who were marching out boldly" (Ex 14:8). But instead of submitting and going back to slavery to Pharaoh, as was their legal duty, the children of Israel followed God and Moses and crossed the Red Sea into freedom. Even the Egyptians had to admit, "The LORD is fighting for them against Egypt" (Ex 14:25). God and his people actively opposed the authority of Egypt's government.

The exodus was an act of disobedience to the civil laws of Egypt. These laws recognized the Israelites as property of the Egyptians, and gave Pharaoh the right to let them go or call them back at his whim. The exodus was justified to attain the higher good of greater freedom to worship, as well as deliverance from the physical abuse and economic and social oppression of Egypt. The greatest act of redemption in the entire Old Testament was a divinely orchestrated act of civil disobedience in which God rescued millions of his people from bondage.

Rahab Saving the Spies

In Joshua 2 we find the account of Rahab. She saved innocent lives by hiding the two Hebrew spies from the soldiers who searched for them. The spies had no legal right to be in Jericho, while the soldiers had every legal right to apprehend them. In doing this, Rahab certainly violated civil law. All nations have laws against aiding and abetting the enemy. She assisted an enemy of the state to which she was subject. Thus she became a traitor to her own government.

In my ethics classes in Bible college and seminary, students argued against Bible smuggling. Concerning Rahab some said, "God didn't approve of Rahab's actions, just her attitude." Scripture specifically contradicts this position. It says, "Was not even Rahab the prostitute considered righteous for what she *did* when she gave lodging to the spies and sent them off in a different direction?" (Jas 2:25). Rahab is considered righteous for what she did—her actions, not her attitude.

Rahab graduated from her role as a heathen prostitute to take a vital place in the messianic line. She became the great-great grandmother of King David, and Christ himself was her direct descendent (Mt 1:5). Rahab is also listed as a hero of faith in Hebrews 11:31. There the Bible says, "By faith the prostitute Rahab, because she welcomed the spies, was not killed with those who were disobedient."

It is interesting that Rahab, who violated weighty civil laws, is set in contrast to those who were "disobedient" and subsequently killed. According to Scripture, it is those who were the law-abiding citizens of Jericho who were disobedient to God, whereas Rahab, the breaker of civil law, was considered obedient to God. Had she obeyed civil law and given over the spies, she would have been disobedient to God and we would not know her name today. Rahab is a clear example of being judged ultimately righteous or unrighteous based on conformity to divine law, not civil law.

The Rescue of Jonathan

In Israel, as in virtually all of the ancient world, the King's word was law. In 1 Samuel 14:24 a proud and unreasonable King Saul issued a law. In the heat of battle he said, "Cursed be any man who eats food before evening comes, before I have avenged myself on my enemies!" The law put the men of Israel "in distress" (v. 24) and made them faint (v. 28). Jonathan unwittingly violated the law. But ignorance of the law is no excuse. When told about the law he said, "My father has made trouble for the country. . . . How much better it would have been if the men had eaten today" (vv. 29-30).

Saul called together the leaders of the army to find out who had violated his law. The men refused to incriminate Jonathan. When Saul found that Jonathan broke the law, he was determined to enforce it and to punish Jonathan with death (v. 44). But the men of Israel, flying in the face of both the law and the consequences of breaking it, responded this way:

> But the men said to Saul, "Should Jonathan die—he who has brought about this great deliverance in Israel? Never! As surely as the LORD lives, not a hair of his head will fall to the ground, for he did this today with God's help." *So the men rescued Jonathan,* and he was not put to death. (1 Sam 14:45)

The men of Israel illegally rescued this innocent person from the unrighteous penalty for an unrighteous law. Jonathan was rescued from the unrighteous lawmaker and the unrighteous law-enforcer. The men made clear that if their appeal to the lawmaker was denied they would intervene as necessary. They said, "As surely as the LORD lives, not a hair of his head will fall to the ground" (1 Sam 14:45).

In this passage it is not an individual acting on his own, but a group action. The soldiers reflected determined solidarity to stand together to keep the innocent person from being legally but wrongly killed. For Jonathan to be killed for eating honey was almost as senseless as an unborn child being killed for being too small, too young or too inconvenient.

If Saul would have moved forward at that point to kill Jonathan, the soldiers would have not continued to talk. They would have physically intervened on his behalf. How would they have done this? They would not attack Saul. They still respected him as their leader. They would likely stand side by side in front of his innocent victim, Jonathan. This action would send the message, "We stand in the gap for this innocent person. You cannot harm him unless you move past us first." This is the intent and the method by which many people are choosing to rescue unborn children today.

Remember, the decree of the king was recognized as law. Therefore civil law was clearly on Saul's side. But those who intervened for innocent Jonathan appealed to a higher law, the moral law of God. This law transcended the law of the king.

Obadiah Saves the Prophets

In 1 Kings 18, Queen Jezebel and King Ahab were seeking to execute the prophets of God. In an act of treason, the king's officer, Obadiah, hid a hundred prophets in caves and supplied them with food and water. This was his attempt to keep them from being killed. Obadiah realized his duty was not to passively "not kill" the prophets but to actively, and illegally, intervene to keep them from being killed. The fact that their murder would have been legal made it no less deplorable either to God or to Obadiah.

Obadiah's rescue of the prophets was a model for the mid-nineteenth-century Underground Railroad in America and the mid-twentieth-century resistance in occupied Europe. These movements provided food, shelter and protection for slaves and Jews, saving them from the abuse permitted by the laws of the state.

Some might argue that the text does not specifically state that what Obadiah did was right. However, it does describe Obadiah as "a devout believer in the LORD" (1 Kings 18:3). The following verse tells the story of how he hid the prophets from the queen. This was a demonstration of just how devout he was. In other words, Obadiah was regarded as devout *because* he disobeyed the law at his own risk to save lives that were precious to God.

The Rescue of Joash

The queen mother Athaliah wanted to insure none of her family would take her throne, so she ordered the rest of the royal family killed. But her stepdaughter Jehosheba took the infant Joash and "put him and his nurse in a bedroom to hide him from Athaliah; so he was not killed. He remained hidden with his nurse at the temple of the LORD for six years while Athaliah ruled the land" (2 Kings 11:1-3).

The temple priests participated in the six year cover-up from the head of state, Queen Athaliah. So they were also "guilty" of this treasonable rescue of a young innocent life. This action culminated in the godly priest Jehoida crowning Joash king while the ruling civil authority Athaliah cried "Treason" (2 Kings 11:12-16). The text indicates that all this civil disobedience brought both spiritual and social good to God's people (2 Kings 11:17-20).

Jeremiah the "Traitor"

Jeremiah violated the will of the government officials of Judah by advising the people to surrender to the Babylonians (Jer 38:1-6). Jeremiah was concerned for the lives of innocent people. He said that only by surrender would their lives be saved. They stayed "loyal to their government" by continuing in a battle that was already lost. This only insured they would "die by the sword, famine or plague." "Whoever goes over to the Babylonians," Jeremiah declared, "will live. He will escape with his life; he will live" (v. 2).

For this Jeremiah was labeled a traitor by those in authority. Their charges were easily proven, and they wanted to put him to death. With King Zedekiah's approval, they lowered him into a cistern and sank him down into the mud. Jeremiah knew he was violating laws of allegiance to king and state. But he continued to speak God's words. His purpose was to be obedient to the Lord and save as many lives as possible.

Daniel's Friends and the Fire

Shadrach, Meshach and Abednego violated the laws of Babylon by refusing to fall down before the king's image of gold. The king was furious, and promised he would throw them immediately into a blazing furnace. Having pulled his trump card he then asked, "Then what god will be able to rescue you from my hand?" (Dan 3:15). Their answer left no question about their position on civil disobedience. They said,

O Nebuchadnezzar, we do not need to defend ourselves before you in this matter. If we are thrown into the blazing furnace, the God we serve is able to save us from it, and he will rescue us from your hand, O king. But even if he does not, we want you to know, O king, that we will not serve your gods or worship the image of gold you have set up. (Dan 3:16-18)

The king was predictably furious, and ordered the fire to be made seven times hotter than usual. God chose to send his angel to rescue them, violating the king's law in the process. In the face of this kind of power, Nebuchadnezzar quickly changed his tune and said, "Praise be to the God of Shadrach, Meshach and Abednego, who has sent his angel and rescued his servants! They trusted in him and defied the king's command and were willing to give up their lives . . ." (Dan 3:28). Having witnessed the rescuing power of God, the heathen king was converted to the virtues of their civil disobedience!

Daniel, the Diet and the Den

When Daniel was told to eat the food and wine of the Babylonians, he saw it contradicted the Old Testament dietary laws. "But Daniel resolved not to defile himself with the royal food and wine, and he asked the chief official for permission not to defile himself this way" (Dan 1:8). Notice the sequence. Daniel first resolved not to obey the orders due to the higher authority of God's law. He then asked the human authority to withdraw his orders. A testing period was agreed upon. The official was pleased at the result, so he withdrew his order.

We learn two things from this story. First, it is sometimes possible to appeal to an authority and persuade him to withdraw his unscriptural directive. Second, if it is not possible, or the appeal is made but not heeded, we must not lose our resolve to obey God's law rather than the human authority. The fact that it is not always possible or wise to make the appeal in the first place is evident in the cases of the midwives, Moses' parents, Rahab, Obadiah, Jehosheba and others. In the case of abortion, Christians have made and should continue to make legal and earnest pleas to those in authority to change the laws permitting and facilitating the killing of unborn children. However, this does not mean that they must obey civil laws requiring them not to intervene for children about to be killed.

While Daniel lived in Babylon, an official law was passed that for thirty days no one could pray to anyone but the king. Daniel decided not to obey, nor even just to disobey in private. "Now when Daniel learned that the decree had been published, he went home to his upstairs room where the windows opened toward Jerusalem. Three times a day he got down on his knees and prayed, giving thanks to his God, just as he had done before" (Dan 6:10). Daniel could be clearly seen doing this from the streets. Consequently he was arrested and thrown to the lions. God endorsed his public civil disobedience through his intervention ("rescue," vv. 16, 20, 27) in closing the mouths of the lions.

Like Nebuchadnezzar with Daniel's three friends, King Darius was deeply touched by Daniel's actions. Perhaps he was genuinely converted through the humble but determined civil disobedience of a godly man.

Esther's Rescue of the Jews

Esther is a fascinating book as it pertains to our subject, since it hinges on three acts of disobedience to civil authority. The first, and least significant, is Queen Vashti's refusal to obey the drunken king and be paraded before his subjects (Esther 1:12).

The second is Mordecai's refusal to obey the king's command to pay honor to Haman. The Scripture records that "all the royal officials at the king's gate knelt down and paid honor to Haman, for the king had commanded this concerning him. But Mordecai would not kneel down or pay him honor" (Esther 3:2). Day after day Mordecai was asked, "Why do you disobey the king's command?" But he stubbornly "refused to comply" (v. 4).

The third and most important act of civil disobedience came when Mordecai learned that Haman had persuaded the king to issue a decree to destroy all the Jews. He sent a messenger to Esther with a copy of the decree, "to urge her to go into the king's presence to beg for mercy and plead with him for her people" (Esther 4:8). The message she sent back to Mordecai said, "All the king's officials and the people of the royal provinces know that for any man or woman who approaches the king in the inner court without being summoned the king has but one law: that he be put to death. The only exception to this is for the king to extend the gold scepter to him and spare his life" (Esther 4:11).

Mordecai's response was to the point. "If you remain silent at this time, relief and deliverance for the Jews will arise from another place, but you and your father's family will perish. And who knows but that you have come to royal position for such a time as this?" (Esther 4:14).

There was no question what the no-trespassing law meant, or what the punishment was for breaking that law. Realizing that Mordecai was right,

Esther knew she must disobey the law and risk her life to save the lives of the Jews. Esther then asked Mordecai and the other Jews to fast and pray for three days. She said "When this is done, I will go to the King, *even though it is against the law*. And if I perish, I perish" (Esther 4:16). Esther did break the law, the King did grant her forgiveness for the capital offense of trespassing in his royal court, and the Jews' lives were saved.

Several things from this passage are significant to the issue of rescuing. First, Esther knew that what she was doing was absolutely against the law, but she nevertheless had a moral obligation to do it. Second, she had to do what she did even if her trespassing in the royal court brought severe consequences. Third, the compelling reason to do this otherwise unthinkable act of civil disobedience was *to save innocent human lives from destruction*. Fourth, Esther did not take this act of civil disobedience lightly, but went into it humbly, prayerfully, and uplifted by the prayers and fasting of the spiritual community.

Esther violated the law for the purpose of saving lives. She did so as God's representative and the representative of the spiritual community. God blessed her efforts, and innocent lives were saved. Even if her efforts had been unsuccessful, her actions were right and pleasing to God.

The Magi's Disobedience to Herod

Herod the king ordered the Magi to "go and make a careful search for the child. As soon as you find him, report to me . . ." (Mt 2:7-8). Herod's word was law, not only in Judah, where he gave the directive, but in Galilee and the rest of Palestine. The Magi were foreigners. But this does not change the fact that while inside Herod's jurisdiction they were legally obligated to obey his word.

The Magi were warned in a dream not to go back to Herod. So they went back to their country by another route. They disobeyed Herod's command, and gave him no information about the Messiah. Whether they understood the reason or not, the warning in the dream and the consequent civil disobedience was intended to buy time for the infant Jesus. When the Magi had gone, an angel of the Lord appeared to Joseph in a dream and told him to take little Jesus and Mary to Egypt. This saved the child's life from the hands of Herod, who would have legally but immorally put him to death.

Apostles, Angels and Lawbreaking

The Roman government granted the Jewish Sanhedrin full authority in religious matters.[2] They were able to legally arrest people and put them in jail (Acts 5:19). When they "commanded them not to speak or teach at all in the name of Jesus," Peter and John replied, "Judge for yourselves whether it is right in God's sight to obey you rather than God. For we cannot help speaking about what we have seen and heard" (Acts 4:18-20).

But when the Sanhedrin exercised their legitimate authority and told them not to preach the gospel, Peter and the apostles did so anyway. When told, "We gave you strict orders not to teach in this name," Peter and the apostles said, "We must obey God rather than men!" (Acts 5:29).

Between these two commands of the authorities, the apostles had been put in jail. "But during the night an angel of the Lord opened the doors of the jail and brought them out. 'Go, stand in the temple courts,' he said, 'and tell the people the full message of this new life' " (Acts 5:19). Here we see God's angels not only commanding civil disobedience, but doing it themselves through breaking the apostles out of prison.

Angels also violated the law by freeing Peter from prison after his arrest by Herod Antipas, and Peter violated the law by leaving and failing to return himself to the custody of the authorities (Acts 12:6-11). Peter said, "The Lord sent his angel and rescued me from Herod's clutches and from everything the Jewish people were anticipating" (Acts 12:11). He was rescued from death. Herod had already executed the apostle James and clearly had the same intentions for Peter (Acts 12:1-4).

Scripture includes other examples of civil disobedience of godly people. David hid from Saul, and Elijah hid from Ahab and Jezebel. Both of these acts were attempts to save their own lives.

Summary: Biblical Reasons for Civil Disobedience

What do we learn from these examples of civil disobedience? First, civil disobedience by godly people is clearly documented in Scripture. Second, in some cases God directly orders civil disobedience (e.g., Jeremiah, the Magi). Third, in a number of cases God after-the-fact condones and rewards civil disobedience as an act of obedience to him (e.g., the midwives, Moses' parents, Rahab and Daniel). Fourth, the contexts show that in a number of cases the civil disobedience was godly and right, even if this is not explicitly stated (e.g., the men of Israel saving the life of Jonathan, Obadiah saving the lives of the prophets, Jehosheba saving the life of Joash, and Esther saving the lives of the Jews).

In nearly every case the ultimate motive was to obey God. The immediate motives differ from case to case, but they fall into definite categories. Scripture clearly indicates that there is justification for civil disobedience in *at least* the areas affecting worship, evangelism and the sanctity of human life.

Worship and Evangelism

The command to worship false gods was violated by Shadrach, Meshach and Abednego. *The prohibition of praying to the true God* was violated by Daniel. *The prohibition of worshipping God in a particular way, place and time* was violated by the whole nation of Israel.

The prohibition of preaching the gospel was violated by Peter and the other apostles. The authorities wanted particularly to restrict public evangelism of a group or the masses, but the principle at stake would surely apply to private or personal evangelism as well.

Evangelism and edification are accomplished not only through sermons and gatherings, but also through Christian literature, especially the Bible. So it seems logical that the believer be permitted to violate the command of the state that declares it illegal to possess or distribute Bibles or other Christian literature.

Christians are commanded not to give up meeting together with fellow Christians (Heb 10:25). So the prohibition or severe restriction of church gatherings would also appear to be worthy of civil disobedience. This would be true even when the restriction is issued on the pretense of "zoning regulations" or "building codes," as is often the case in some places.

We must also ask if there is still broader application to the teaching of all Christian truth. For instance, a government might allow a church to "preach the gospel" but not allow it to take a public position on a moral issue, or to encourage activism on that issue. Since taking positions on moral issues and the teaching of the "whole counsel of God" are also required of the Christian by God, would there not be room here for civil disobedience?

The government of Nazi Germany gave considerable latitude to the church in preaching the gospel. But are we to obey God over men only when it comes to the *preaching* of the gospel, or also when it comes to the *living* of the gospel? If it includes the latter, then the door is opened to disobeying government in numbers of important areas, including church discipline, selection of church leaders, and how we raise our children.

The Sanctity of Human Life

The bulk of the biblical examples of civil disobedience do not relate to the matters of worship or evangelism. They focus directly on the issue of the sanctity of human life and the responsibility of God's children to deliver innocent human beings from being killed. As should be clearly evident from the many biblical examples we have studied, civil disobedience is biblically justified in both the refusal to take innocent human lives, and intervention to prevent innocent human lives from being taken.

The command to take innocent human lives was disobeyed by the Hebrew midwives. They utilized deception to avoid Pharaoh's reprisal on themselves and on the children they had illegally allowed to live (Ex 1:19). Moses' parents and sister also refused to kill the infant Moses. Then they went a step further. They denied others the opportunity to kill him by keeping his existence or whereabouts unknown. As we have seen, both Testaments commend them for what they did.

The prohibition from saving innocent human lives was disobeyed by Rahab who rescued the spies from the authorities of Jericho, the men of Israel who rescued Jonathan from King Saul, Obadiah who rescued the prophets from Queen Jezebel, Jehosheba who rescued the infant Joash from Queen Athaliah, Esther who rescued the Jews from the King's law, the wise men who rescued Jesus from Herod the Great, and the angel who rescued Peter from Herod Antipas.

In each case the people rescued from death were innocent. In each case the person they were rescued from had legal authority to have them killed. In each case the people doing the rescuing had not themselves been commanded to kill the innocent. In every case but one (the wise men) those rescuing did so through direct, physical and nonviolent intervention on behalf of the one about to be killed.

We might also include Jeremiah who tried to save the lives of Israelites, the angel who warned the wise men to disobey Herod and Joseph to flee, as well as Joseph himself who fled from Herod with Mary and Jesus. We could add David who fled for his life from King Saul, Elijah who fled for his life from Ahab, and Peter who fled for his life from the prison opened by the angel. In each case the motive for civil disobedience was to save an innocent life, either another's or one's own.

Hence, Scripture endorses in at least some cases each of the following life-saving interventions:

1. *Civil disobedience to save the life of God's representatives,* whether spies, prophets or apostles. Examples include Rahab, the men of Israel who rescued Jonathan, Obadiah, the angel who saved Peter, God or his angel who saved the three Hebrews, and God who saved Daniel.

2. *Civil disobedience to save the lives of God's chosen people.* Examples include Jeremiah and Esther.

3. *Civil disobedience to save one's own life.* Examples include David and Elijah.

4. *Civil disobedience to save the lives of infants.* Examples include the midwives, Moses' parents and sister, Jehosheba, the Magi, Joseph and Mary, and the angel(s) who directed the Magi and Joseph.

The Overall Perspective

In summary, we have cited seventeen cases of civil disobedience that are either explicitly said to be approved by God, or in their contexts are clearly condoned by Scripture. Of these, three cases involving six people (Daniel, his three friends, and Peter and John) are civil disobedience for purposes of worship. The remaining fourteen cases involve at least a few dozen people and probably far more, depending on how many midwives, "men of Israel" or Magi there were. This is not to mention all the others who must have been aware of and involved in the protection of Moses, David, Elijah, the prophets, Joash, and Peter, or the millions involved in the exodus.

Some did their civil disobedience individually, such as Daniel who prayed alone. Others did it in concert, such as the midwives, three friends of Daniel, and the men of Israel who rescued Jonathan.

Some acts, such as the intervention for Jonathan's life, were one-time commissions of civil disobedience. Many involved ongoing civil disobedience, such as the hiding and protection of Moses for three months by his parents, then years of cover-up by them as well as Pharaoh's daughter. Daniel prayed not only when he was caught, but continued till his life was saved and the unjust law was revoked. Obadiah's civil disobedience to save the prophets' lives went on for some time, and the cover-up and protection of Joash by Jehosheba and others went on six years. Likewise, the apostles repeatedly violated the command not to speak in Christ's name or to preach the gospel.

In some of these cases, such as Daniel and his friends and the apostles, the civil disobedience was done publicly. Jonathan's life was saved by the men in open intervention, and the lives of the Jews were saved by Esther through open trespassing before the king. But the interventions for the lives of the Hebrew children, spies, prophets, Joash and Jesus, as well as David and Elijah's efforts to save their own lives, were done privately or secretly. Some, such as the three Hebrews, did not try to escape punishment for their civil disobedience. Others covered up, used trickery and fled to escape unjust punishment. (Hence Scripture does not teach that the believer should necessarily accept every legal consequence of civil disobedience.)

It is significant that in these cases of illegal lifesaving there is no indication of violence. Whether private or public, the actions were done quietly and peacefully. The midwives didn't take up arms, Rahab didn't poison the officers searching for the spies, Obadiah didn't try to assassinate Jezebel, Jehosheba didn't cut the throats of the palace guards to get Joash, the apostles didn't set fire to the Sanhedrin's meeting place. We are not even told that the soldiers lifted their swords to threaten Saul when they intervened for Jonathan. There is a great deal of bloodshed recorded in Scripture, some directly commanded by God. It is therefore all the more significant that these particular cases of illegal interventions to save the innocent were *not* violent.

God's Word gives definite indications as to when civil disobedience might be necessary. But no strict instruction is given as to the particular form it is to take or the methodology to be used. But examples show it is normally to be nonviolent.

Christ, the Law and Human Welfare

Jesus modeled a spirit of submission to human authority. Yet there are definite and significant exceptions to his obedience to human laws. Certainly, he had no legal right to interfere with legitimate business, knock over tables, make a whip and chase the moneychangers out of the temple (Jn 2:13-17). What these businessmen were doing was perfectly legal. But it was morally wrong. What Jesus did was perfectly illegal, but morally right. The same is true when Jesus broke the Roman seal on his tomb in his resurrection. This was an act of civil disobedience for which we can all be thankful.

Jesus often violated the Jewish laws related to the sabbath and incurred the wrath of the religious authorities. Once the Lord's disciples picked some grain to eat on the sabbath. He pointed out that David and his companions had human needs that justified their eating food that was specifically forbidden by law. Indeed, Jesus directly defends their actions even though he says they did what was "not lawful for them to do" (Mt 12:3-8). After defending the breaking of the law for the good of human welfare, he stated, "The Son of Man is Lord of the Sabbath." This placed divine law above current laws, whether religious or civil.

On another sabbath Jesus asked the Pharisees, "Which is lawful on the Sabbath: to do good or to do evil, to save life or to destroy it?" (Lk 6:9). He then healed a man on the sabbath. They were again furious at his willingness to disobey laws that they held sacred, even when doing so was for the welfare of precious human beings.

Some of the Pharisees drew the conclusion that anyone who disobeys human laws is unspiritual. Some people today also hold this belief. They concluded, "This man is not from God, for he does not keep the Sabbath" (Jn 9:16). It didn't seem to occur to them that there might be a higher law he was operating by when he violated the sabbath laws.

Christ once healed a woman crippled for eighteen years. But, instead of rejoicing that she was healed, the religious leaders were outraged. "Indignant because Jesus had healed on the Sabbath, the synagogue ruler said to the people, 'There are six days for work. So come and be healed on those days, not on the Sabbath' " (Lk 13:14). Notice how Christ, in his undiplomatic response to this high religious authority, focuses on the human need of this woman:

You hypocrites! Doesn't each of you on the Sabbath untie his ox or donkey from the stall and lead it out to give it water? Then should not this woman, a daughter of Abraham, whom Satan has kept bound for eighteen long years, be set free on the Sabbath day from what bound her? (Lk 13:15)

A short time later, again on a sabbath, Jesus was at the home of a prominent Pharisee, and "was being carefully watched" by the religious authorities. Seeing a man suffering from dropsy, Jesus turned to the authorities and asked, "Is it lawful to heal on the Sabbath or not?" (Lk 14:3). They didn't answer, and he healed the man. "Then he asked them, 'If one of you has a son or an ox that falls into a well on the Sabbath day, will you not immediately pull him out?" (Lk 14:5).

There is a summarizing principle in Christ's own words. "The Sabbath was made for man, not man for the Sabbath" (Mk 2:27). We must not limit this principle only to the sabbath. The timeless principle is "human law was made for human welfare, not human welfare for the law." Any good law is designed for the protection of people, not to deprive them from protection.

Christ operated on the principle that laws were made for the welfare of people. Therefore, to him laws should not be placed above the welfare of people. Normally laws are of help to people. But in those rare instances when they hurt people rather than help them, we must not put legalism over human welfare. The "do no work on the sabbath" law can sometimes be like a "no trespassing on private property" law. Neither law should be allowed to stand in the way of doing something vital to human welfare, such as healing a suffering person.

Jesus rebuked the Pharisees for getting caught up in good but secondary points of law. He said to them, "But you have neglected the more important matters of the law—justice, mercy and faithfulness . . . You blind guides! You strain out a gnat but swallow a camel" (Mt 23:23-24). We must be careful not to strain out the gnat of trespassing while swallowing the camel of dying children.

We are like the Pharisees, not Jesus, when we put law over love and life. When we put legalistic observances over the welfare of people, we violate the original purpose of the law. We turn the law into an instrument of cruelty rather than compassion, of indifference rather than love. We must be careful not to follow the Pharisees, who were obsessed with being sure they did nothing "against the law," while they contributed to the murder of the inno-cent Son of God (Mt 27:6).

We must realize that in breaking the Jewish sabbath laws, Jesus was clearly disobeying the written and spoken laws of the religious authorities. Like imperfect civil government, imperfect religious government still has authority, and no doubt Jesus followed that authority whenever he could. In fact, a first-century Jew would have considered obedience to religious authority even more important than obedience to civil authority. Yet Jesus disobeyed this authority, breaking religious laws that all good Jews observed. He did so not indiscriminately and without reason, but *only when a higher law of human life and welfare was at stake.*

Most of Christ's lawbreaking was a violation of religious law, though his clearing of the temple violated civil law as well. Ultimately, however, he was executed for his violation of civil law. John Stott reminds us, "People don't sufficiently realize or remember that Jesus was actually condemned to death on a political charge. In the Roman Court he was condemned to death for sedition because he made himself a King and the Romans and Jews said, 'We have no king but Caesar.' "[3]

Indeed, in order to die on the cross on our behalf, Jesus had to be a violator of Roman law, for only the Roman government had the authority to execute prisoners by crucifixion. Later, the followers of Jesus would be executed for violating the civil law that required that they affirm Caesar as ultimate author-ity. So also Jesus was executed because he would not deny that he was the King, the ultimate authority over all men.

In his life and even his death, Jesus is the ultimate example of peaceful, humble intervention in disobedience to human authority to rescue those who would otherwise suffer and perish. On the cross Christ put himself between us and Satan, between us and hell. He delivered us from a horrible death, granting us eternal life.

As Jesus rescued needy people from suffering and death, and rescued us from eternal death, so we are to "rescue those being led away to death" (Prov 24:11). When we were in weakness and desperate need, Jesus rescued us from Satan, the wicked one. Likewise, we as his followers are to "rescue the weak and needy; deliver them from the hand of the wicked" (Ps 82:4).

5
The Laws of Man
& the Laws of God

*We give you a throne upon
condition you swear by Him
who made heaven and earth,
that you will govern us
according to God's law.*
Samuel Rutherford

C hristians are normally to obey the laws of the government under
which they live (Rom 13:1-7; Titus 3:1; 1 Pet 2:13-17). Romans 13 is
the most complete statement on this subject and deserves our close
attention.

Everyone must submit himself to the governing authorities, for there is no
authority except that which God has established. The authorities that exist
have been established by God. Consequently, he who rebels against the
authority is rebelling against what God has instituted, and those who do
so will bring judgment on themselves. (Rom 13:1-2)

We must put ourselves in the historical context of the New Testament to
understand the effect this statement would have on the original readers. In
coming to Christ the Roman Christians confessed "Jesus is Lord." Simultaneously, they boldly refused to recite the words of unconditional loyalty to the
state: "Caesar is Lord." That is why they were facing suspicion and increasing
oppression from the government. Within only a few years of the writing of
Romans, Nero would launch a campaign of persecution against them, which

would recur in waves over the next two and a half centuries.

So, if Christ alone is Lord and therefore Caesar is not Lord, how can Paul build a case for obeying government? He does so for several specific reasons. First he says, "For rulers hold no terror for those who do right, but for those who do wrong. Do you want to be free from fear of the one in authority? Then do what is right and he will commend you" (Rom 13:3).

Paul says the Christian should obey a government *because that government fulfills the reasons for which God has established it.* That is, it rewards righteousness and punishes evil. By restraining evil, government preserves society from the kind of sweeping judgment of God brought about through the flood (Gen 9:5-17).

Similarly, the apostle Peter says, "Submit yourselves for the Lord's sake to every authority instituted among men." He then describes these authorities as those "who are sent by him to punish those who do wrong and to commend those who do right" (1 Pet 2:13-14). No government is perfect, but a good government will fulfill this basic role of punishing evil and rewarding good.

"When men have a dispute, they are to take it to court and the judges will decide the case, *acquitting the innocent and condemning the guilty*" (Deut 25:1). This is the God-ordained role of human government. But what happens when government reverses its God-ordained role? What is God's posture toward civil laws which protect evil-doing and punish righteousness? "Acquitting the guilty and condemning the innocent—the LORD detests them both" (Prov 17:15).

Authority and Responsibility

Paul says, "Do what is right and he [the one in authority] will commend you." Why? "For he is God's servant to do you good" (Rom 13:4). Government is God's servant, God's representative, God's instrument of justice to carry out divine law in human affairs.

We typically emphasize the *authority* implicit in the fact that government is God's servant. But we must not overlook the *responsibility* it entails. For when one thinks of a servant he does not first think of authority, but responsibility. *A servant has no inherent authority, but only a derived authority.* His ultimate worthiness to be obeyed by others is determined by the degree to which he accurately represents his master. Any human government, called by Paul "God's servant," gains its authority from properly representing and carrying out the will of its divine master.

When Paul warns against disobeying government, it is with the assumption that the servant-government is in fact doing what Paul says it is ordained to do. That is, to protect the innocent and prosecute the guilty. We need not speculate that this is Paul's assumption, for he explicitly states it.

Paul calls government God's servant to represent his will and justice to the people of a society. Their obedience to the laws of that servant is obedience to God. This is true unless the servant prostitutes his very purpose for existence by violating the expressed will of the master. For example, he may command disobedience, or attempt to prevent obedience to the laws of God.

The state is the representative of God to society in the same sense that a babysitter is the representative of parents to their children. God delegates authority to the state just as parents delegate authority to the babysitter. But God does not give *unconditional* authority to the state any more than parents give *unconditional* authority to the babysitter.

The babysitter is given a wide range of discretionary options in the exercise of the authority granted. Nevertheless, the commands to the children must exist within the parameters of the moral standards of the parents. When the parents go out the door and say, "Children, obey the babysitter"—just as Paul says, "Christians, obey the government"—this does not mean they are to comply if she tells them to drink alcohol, watch an R-rated movie, or smoke pot. Neither are they to stand passively by as she beats up on them, sexually abuses their siblings, destroys the furniture, or sets the house on fire.

Parents are, by definition, *always* a higher authority than the babysitter. The babysitter has no *inherent* authority, only delegated authority. This does not undermine or minimize the fact that 99 per cent of the time a babysitter should be obeyed. The babysitter has been granted authority by a higher authority, the parents. The children must respect their sitter whether or not they agree with the rules.

Nevertheless, there are rare occasions when the babysitter violates what the children know to be the standards of their parents. In such a case, the chil-

dren should *not* comply with her orders, but instead follow what they know
to be the moral standards of their parents. Indeed, if the parents find that
the children have violated their household standards, they will not only rep-
rimand the babysitter, but will discipline the children for disobeying them.
The fact that they were obeying the babysitter does not lessen their moral
responsibility to do what their higher authorities, their parents, have taught
them is right.

Francis Schaeffer stated,

> God has ordained the state as a *delegated* authority; it is not autonomous.
> The state is to be an agent of justice, to restrain evil by punishing the
> wrong doer, and to protect the good in society. When it does the reverse,
> *it has no proper authority.* It is then usurped authority and as such it becomes
> lawless and becomes tyranny.[1]

Schaeffer further maintained, ". . . any government that commands what
contradicts God's Law abrogates its authority. It is no longer our proper legal
government, and at that point we have the right, and the duty, to disobey it."[2]
Speaking of civil disobedience to the state, he added, "All we have been saying
is relevant for the present moment, and especially in such areas as abortion."[3]

Government and Human Welfare

Both in its inception in Genesis 9, and again in Romans 13 and 1 Peter 2,
we see that the primary purpose of the state is to promote the welfare of all
human beings by protecting them from the evil actions of other human
beings. Old Testament law was so conscious of the welfare of human life that
it required houses to be built in such a way that people wouldn't be killed by
falling off roofs (Deut 22:8). The law provides specific protection for the lives
of children (Lev 20:1-5). It likewise protects the handicapped (Lev 19:14; Deut
27:18). It states categorically, "Do not do anything that endangers your neighbor's life" (Lev 19:16). The law commands that pains be taken to provide for
widows, aliens, elderly, poor people and others who could be easily taken
advantage of (Lev 19:10, 32-33).

All governments and their laws properly exist to protect the weak and
vulnerable from exploitation by the strong. That was certainly a major emphasis of the original government of the United States. As Thomas Jefferson

put it, "The care of human life and not its destruction is the first and only legitimate object of good government."

R. C. Sproul states,

One of the chief tasks of government is to protect, honor, preserve, and defend human life. When the state legitimizes abortion, it arouses protest from the church, not because it is failing to do the church's mission, but because it is failing to do the task for which God instituted government in the first place. When the state sanctions abortion, it uses the sword (or the scalpel) for evil rather than for good.[4]

The Problem of Balance

In response to a question about rescuing unborn babies, a well-known Bible teacher made this unqualified statement on his radio program: "All we can do, all the Bible ever did, all the prophets and apostles ever did, is call to the sinner to turn from sin. And there's no justification for civil disobedience."[5] He cites Romans 13 and 1 Peter 2 to back up this position.

Similarly, a well-known theology professor examines Romans 13 and states, "No exceptions are listed . . . that would justify civil disobedience."[6] After going to Titus 3:1 and I Peter 2:13-17, he says, "Again no exceptions are indicated either because of the type of government or because of the conscience of the believer. . . . in summary, the direct teaching of Scripture seems to require complete civil obedience on the part of Christians."[7]

Despite his absolute statement above, he does go on to acknowledge the existence of the cases of Peter in Acts 5, the three Hebrew children in Daniel 3, and Daniel himself in Daniel 6. He then says, "The only exception seems to be if the government forbids his worshipping God."[8]

The author fails to mention a dozen or so other cases in which civil disobedience is used to rescue innocent people from death. These include the Hebrew midwives, Moses' parents, Rahab, Obadiah and Esther. There are more of these cases, in fact, than those in which worshipping God is forbidden. Of his three examples, only Daniel was actually forbidden to worship God. Daniel's friends were told to worship a false god besides their own. The apostles were allowed to worship who they wanted, but not to publicly proclaim their faith in Jesus. Nonetheless, by acknowledging even one solitary exception, this theologian admits that Romans 13 is not absolute, and that there is a time when a Christian can and even must disobey civil government.

Why, then, does Paul list no exceptions? The reason is simply that Paul is not trying to make a completely balanced statement in Romans 13. God trusts us to compare Scripture with other Scripture. We are to prop up true but paradoxical statements against each other in order to find the right balance. When Paul told Timothy "drink a little wine for your stomach," he didn't have to add "but not so much that you get drunk." Timothy knew that. Bible students know that. As Jesus didn't list any exceptions to not resisting evil and to turning the other cheek, so Paul lists no exceptions to obeying government. But any Bible student knows a number of such exceptions exist.

Stephen Charles Mott points out that the historical context of both Romans 13 and 1 Peter 2 is the question of Christian freedom.[9] Indeed, Paul wrote Romans from Corinth, where the church was dominated by an unhealthy spirit of arrogance and independence. Their tendency was to not submit to others but to flaunt their freedoms by appealing to higher knowledge and insight as a Christian (e.g., 1 Cor 8). That this same sort of tendency was a concern to Peter is suggested by the caution he gives in the middle of his exhortation to obey the authorities: "Live as free men, but do not use your freedom as a cover-up for evil" (1 Pet 2:16). In other words, yes, you are free in Christ, and yes, Christ is your ultimate authority, but don't use your freedom to "do your own thing" and disobey human authorities based merely on your own personal whims and preferences.

Furthermore, Paul was writing to a Roman church feeling the heat of persecution. The Roman Christians could easily become resentful and even rebellious to the government of Rome. Historically, we know that many of the Roman Christians jumped at the chance to affirm Christ and deny Caesar. The greater the persecution, the greater their resolve, and the more the lines were drawn. Paul saw that in such a context Caesar could too easily be regarded as the enemy. But for the most part, Roman law was just and worthy of obedience. It was only in rare cases that Christians should disobey. For example, the law that commanded sacrifice to Caesar or the law that forbade intervention for the abandoned infants left to die outside the city gates. Paul did not have to mention those exceptions. All his readers knew them.

In writing Romans 13, Paul is walking into the wind, and when you walk into the wind you must lean forward. You must state your case as strongly as possible to make your point. Paul is resisting his readers' tendency to disrespect government and to unnecessarily disobey government. So he is stating his case in his strongest terms.

In addition, we cannot overlook the fact that this letter to the Roman churches would be widely circulated throughout Rome and would no doubt fall into the hands of officials in the Roman government. Why list exceptions to obeying government and thereby unnecessarily provoke suspicion and retaliation?

The historian Suetonius, writing in the early second century A.D., noted that Emperor Claudius (A.D. 41-54) had expelled the Jews from Rome because "the Jews constantly made disturbances. . . ."[10] Luke tells us of the same incident. In Acts 18:2, Aquilla and Priscilla were among those expelled. Christians were still viewed as a Jewish sect, even more troublesome than Judaism itself. While Judaism was a *religio licita,* a legal religion, Christianity was on the verge of becoming a *religio illicita,* an illegal religion. This happened within a few years after Romans was written.

Paul was a Roman citizen who fully recognized the benefits of a healthy relationship with the government. He often appealed to his rights and freedoms as a citizen of Rome (Acts 16:37-38; 22:25-29; 23:27). For the sake of the freedom to preach the gospel, Paul wanted to make sure that the Christian movement was not viewed by his government or fellow citizens as a rebellious and insurrectionist group.

Paul advocates obedience in that 99 per cent of the time where government law does not violate the law of God. Why deal with the other 1 per cent, well known to his readers? This would unnecessarily provide the enemies of the Faith a basis of accusation and persecution of the church.

Romans 13 and Rescuing
One of the most common objections to rescuing that I hear is, "There's no room for civil disobedience in Romans 13."

Suppose we were to invite the apostle Paul into our discussion and ask him, "Now, Paul, we notice that in Romans 13 you don't list any exceptions to obeying government. Does that mean you are saying there *are* no exceptions, that you are teaching unconditional obedience to human government?"

Paul would probably ask us to repeat the question, thinking he must have heard it wrong. Once he understood, he would be horrified. The very question incorporates a blasphemy, one which every Christian should immediately recognize. The heart and soul of the Christian faith is that Jesus is Lord, and that he *alone* commands our ultimate and unconditional obedience. Paul would probably say, "How could you dream that I would think such a thing— God forbid!" He might also add, "Has it ever occurred to you that I write most of my letters from prison? How do you think I get put in prison if not for disobeying laws?!"

Romans 13 either teaches absolute obedience to human law or it does not. We cannot have it both ways. We cannot approach the rescue question from the posture that Romans 13 allows no exceptions, then turn around and admit that in certain areas there really are exceptions after all. These exceptions include scriptural precepts and examples, historical examples and real life situations. Once we acknowledge that it does *not* teach absolute and indiscriminate obedience to civil laws we must disqualify Romans 13 as the final court of appeals. It must take its place *alongside* the rest of the Bible rather than be put *over* it.

To argue that Romans 13 and other "obey government" passages do not say believers can trespass at abortion clinics is merely to state the obvious, but prove nothing. Neither do they say Christians can violate civil laws that require killing the handicapped and elderly, hiring a homosexual pastor, or taking a mark on their hands before they can buy or sell.

The issue then is not "should we believe Romans 13?" Of course we should. But we should also believe the rest of the Bible. And the rest of the Bible must be taken into account in the interpretation of any passage, including Romans 13. Furthermore, we must not forget that Romans 13 itself contains statements that qualify what kind of government is to be obeyed and why.

How can the Bible make statements like those in Romans 13, 1 Peter 2 and Titus 3, then also advocate civil disobedience when the laws of man and God are in conflict? Indeed, how could Paul and Peter write these passages when they themselves would end up being executed by the Roman government for violating civil law? Were they hypocrites, who believed one standard but lived by another?

Perhaps an example will help us understand. In his book *Ethics*, Dietrich Bonhoeffer stated, "Government has the divine task of preserving the world, with its institutions which are given by God, for the purpose of Christ.... *Everyone is subject to an obligation of obedience towards government.*"[11] Here is an unqualified statement, based on and closely paralleling those of Paul and Peter. Yet, when Bonhoeffer wrote these very words he was illegally concealing them from the German police! Some parts of the book were confiscated by the Gestapo in 1943, the rest was found hidden in various places after his execution. Bonhoeffer's writing of the book was itself completely illegal, even if he hadn't concealed it. Hitler's Reich Chamber of Literature had forbidden him from writing any work intended for publication, because he had refused to sign on as a Nazi propagandist and had not filed for an exemption.[12]

Like Paul and Peter, Bonhoeffer could wholeheartedly say, "We are obligated to obey the government," yet simultaneously disobey it when it violated divine law. To them, this was not a matter of moral contradiction, but moral consistency.

Evil Governments and Evil Laws

God's absolute authority is affirmed throughout Scripture. "I am the LORD and there is no other" (Is 45:6). He is the King of kings, who "sets up kings and deposes them" (Dan 2:21). The ultimate authority of Christ over all the universe is repeatedly emphasized (e.g., Mt 28:20; 1 Cor 15:27; Eph 1:22; Rev 1:5). But can human authorities try to usurp the ultimate authority of God? Of course they can. In fact, that is exactly their tendency (Ps 2). Nebuchadnezzar and Herod provide graphic examples of the fate of human kings who set their word and will above God's (Dan 4; Acts 12:21-23). We must not be naive about the capacity of human government to do evil, and to function as an arm of the evil one.

"For any government deliberately to deny to their people what must be their plainest and simplest right ... would be to deny their trust. *I do not believe that such a government anywhere exists among civilized peoples.*"[13] These words were spoken in November 1937 by British Prime Minister Neville Chamberlain. The government he refused to believe would deny the basic rights of people was the government of Nazi Germany. His inability to believe human government could grossly pervert its God-ordained role kept England from acting to stop Hitler for several years, and nearly resulted in the destruction of Chamberlain's own country.

In an interview concerning civil disobedience, John Stott says,

> Romans 13 needs to be balanced by Revelation 13. The State which in Romans 13 is the minister of God, has become, in Revelation 13, the minister of the devil, that is the beast of the earth, which is commonly understood as the persecuting power of the state.
>
> What Romans 13 says is that the power exercised by the State has been delegated to it from God, and that this power derived from God is to be used for two broad purposes, one is to punish evil and the other is to promote good. And when the state fulfills its God-given vocation of promoting the good and punishing evil, then indeed, we are to submit to it respectfully and thankfully. But the question is, what happens when the state uses its God-given power to promote evil and to punish the good. Then, of course, it is so misusing its God-given power that we have to oppose it. . . .
>
> Of course, civil disobedience is a biblical doctrine. . . . the principle, as I see it, is that we are to submit to and obey the state right up to the point where obedience to the state would involve us in disobedience to God. At that point we have to obey God and disobey the state.[14]

In Revelation 13 we see the beast who comes from the abyss, in the form of a human head of government. His power is from the "dragon," his throne the throne of Satan, his authority the authority of hell. This proud and blasphemous beast slanders God and the saints, and sets up a government that is not a servant of God but a substitute for him. Under his government a second beast initiates civil laws, including the law that no one may buy or sell without the mark on his right hand or forehead (Rev 13:15-17). Such laws will seem to make sense politically and economically, but will result in tragedy for all who obey them. This eventual reality graphically illustrates the need for Christians to carefully scrutinize what laws they obey, rather than automatically obeying them all.

Everyone will recognize the authority of the beast and his government, *except* the true followers of Christ (Rev 13:8). *Christians will be recognized as such by their refusal to obey certain civil laws;* non-Christians, by their obedience to them. It is a chilling thought to consider that some people may take on themselves the mark of the beast out of a trained sense of religious duty to blindly obey government.

The government of Antichrist has been effectively foreshadowed in the governments of Stalin, Hitler, Mao Tse-tung, Pol Pot and Idi Amin, to name but a few bloody tyrants of our own century. The most notable aspect of each of these governments was its wanton disregard for innocent human life.

Does Our Government Command Evil?

One of the most frequently expressed objections to rescuing is that abortion is not required by the government, and therefore no one is being commanded to violate Scripture. A large pro-life church believes rescuing is wrong because "*Roe* vs. *Wade* neither requires abortions nor prohibits them, but makes them permissible with certain restrictions."[15]

A popular Bible teacher stated on his nationwide radio program,

It [rescuing] is really a convoluted perspective because the government of the United States does not mandate abortion. Nothing in our government mandates abortion. None of you is forced to have an abortion. No one is forced to have an abortion. That is an individual choice. The government . . . leaves some of those moral things to the discretion of people. So when you enact civil disobedience you are penalizing the government for something that is really not their authorization. Those things are being done by individuals.[16]

Certainly it is good that our government does not require people to get abortions. But what if it allowed, not required but only allowed, wife-killing? Would we breathe a sigh of relief and say, "Violating the law to rescue wives from murder is a convoluted perspective because the government of the United States does not mandate wife-killing. No one is forced to kill his wife. That is an individual choice. So, when you enact civil disobedience to save a woman from death, you are penalizing the government for something that is really not their authorization. Those things are being done by individuals."

Substitute "five-year-old children" or "elderly" or "handicapped" for wives and the point is the same. Once again, we see that despite our expressed beliefs to the contrary, we treat the unborn as less human or less valuable than born people.

The impression given by these Christian leaders is that our laws are really neutral, since they neither compel nor prevent abortion. But would we call a law that permitted rape a neutral law? Would we console ourselves that the government "leaves rape and other moral things to the discretion of people"? Civil law in our country does in fact actively allow, actively protect, and thereby actively encourage abortion. This is why the number of abortions dramatically increased once abortion was legalized.

One Bible teacher said, "In our situation today we face not a law that commands, but a law that simply permits."[17] A law that "simply" permits *what*? The killing of innocent children! The phrase "simply permits" is designed to console us about the fact that abortion is not required. But what consolation is that to the victims?

Furthermore, the fact is that the law does *not* "simply permit" abortion. It actually *prohibits intervention* to save lives at the very place they are being taken. It actively *facilitates* abortion, in that it forcibly removes those who would peacefully prevent it. It fines such people, puts them in jail, and awards their money to abortion clinics, in order to assure that child-killing can continue.

The fact that we are not forced to get abortions does not settle the moral issue. It is rare that laws directly command people to do what is evil. In a republic such as our own they almost never will. More often they will command people to *allow* evil, to not interfere with evil, to not intervene for innocent lives. In other words, governments order sins of *omission* much more often than sins of *commission*.

The law did not require that the German people kill Jews. The law only required that they stand passively by while others killed them. Likewise, our law "only" requires that no one be able to go to the killing place and stand between the baby and the knife. Some object to comparing Nazi Germany and the United States, which were two very different countries. But the point of the comparison is not the intent of the governments, but the reality of the victims. True, Nazi Germany and the United States are not comparable as governments. But it is no consolation to 4,500 innocent victims a day that they are being killed in the greatest republic the world has ever known.

Scripture doesn't say, "Anyone who knows the evil he shouldn't do and does it, sins." That is obviously true, but the Bible says something more: "Anyone, then, who knows the good he ought to do and doesn't do it, sins" (Jas 4:17). This means we cannot say, "No one requires me to sin by killing my child, therefore I am not morally obligated to save the lives of children being killed by others." God doesn't simply tell us not to kill, he also tells us to rescue those about to be killed. If it is right to intervene for the innocent, then a law that forbids intervention seeks to prevent people from doing what is right.

Natural Law

Law is found, not made. A physicist does not create the laws of physics, he discovers and applies them. A good lawmaker does not truly make law. He discovers Law, with a capital "L," and applies it in the form of laws, with a lowercase "l." The Greek philosophers believed that there was a natural law that God has placed on the hearts of all men. The Bible teaches the same (Rom 2:14-15).

"Natural law" may be distinguished from "revealed law" (Scripture), but it is not contradictory to it. Even if a government or individual is unaware of revealed law, the built-in natural law written on the conscience should tell him that such things as murder, stealing and adultery are wrong. Of course, revealed law is the most authoritative law, but both revealed and natural law are considered divine law because of their divine origin.

St. Thomas Aquinas distinguished between divine law and human law, as had Augustine and Origen before him.

> Laws enacted by men are either just or unjust. If just they draw from the eternal law, from which they derive the power to oblige in conscience. . . . and if a human law is at variance in any particular with the natural law, it is no longer legal but a corruption of law.[18]

In 1644 Samuel Rutherford wrote *Lex Rex: Or The Law and the Prince*. His thesis was that the law is king, that natural or divine law must be put above every human law, whether civil or religious. If the king or the highest church leader disobeys the law, he is to be disobeyed. The Parliament of Scotland met to condemn Rutherford for this "treason," and he would have been executed had he not died first.

Rutherford argued that Romans 13 indicates that all power is from God and that government is ordained and instituted by God. The state, however, is to be administered according to the principles of God's law. Acts of the state which contradicted God's law were illegitimate and acts of tyranny. Tyranny was defined as ruling without the sanction of God.[19]

Whose Law?

Whenever we use the term *law* we need an adjective. Are we talking about *divine* law? Or are we talking about civil or religious law invented by men? Unless the two are synonymous we must not use them interchangeably or serious confusion will result. For instance, one church leader seeks to disprove the legitimacy of rescuing by quoting Proverbs 28:4: "Those who forsake the law praise the wicked, but those who keep the law resist them." Similarly, he quotes Proverbs 28:9: "If anyone turns a deaf ear to the law, even his prayers are detestable." He then asks, "How can Christians pray in unity and with clear conscience for more people to join in breaking the trespassing laws for rescuing?" Finally, he appeals to Proverbs 29:18: "Where there is no revelation, the people cast off restraint; but blessed is he who keeps the law."[20]

The man drawing these conclusions is a godly brother, committed to the Scriptures. But the problem with his approach is that every time he reads the word *law* he is thinking of *civil* law or man's law. However, the law actually referred to in the texts is *divine* law or God's law.

Proverbs 8:13-16 explains the proper relationship between divine wisdom and civil law. It is by taking their cues from the all-wise God, who hates evil, that "rulers make laws that are just" (v. 15). Civil laws are properly derived from divine law. Hence, when Proverbs speaks of not turning a deaf ear to the law, it is speaking of divine law, the eternal law of God, revealed in Scripture. One may obey evil civil laws and thereby turn a deaf ear to God's law and come under his judgment. Or, one may disobey evil civil laws and come under man's judgment, but in the process obey God and come under his approval.

It is obedience to *God's* commandments, to *God's* law, that is the focus of Scripture from beginning to end.[21] It is precisely because of this pervasive emphasis on the ultimate authority of the laws of God that the biblical writers rarely qualify their directives to obey human authority, whether parents, husbands, masters, church leaders, or governments. They do not have to qualify them because *the entire Word of God qualifies them.* The heart and soul of the Christian faith, evident throughout Scripture, is that Jesus is Lord. Therefore *no one but him and no law but his* is ever to be automatically obeyed.

Conclusion

It is the purpose of Romans 13 to state a positive principle, not to deal with the exceptions to that principle. But the rest of God's Word clearly demonstrates *these exceptions do in fact exist,* and must be taken seriously by all who would follow the Lord. These exceptions include not only the many examples of civil disobedience but the central themes of divine law and the lordship of Christ.

Charles Colson summarizes it this way:

God has ordained government to preserve order, prevent injustice, restrain sin, and promote justice. That is the purpose of government. In so doing, government is God's delegated agent.

But once government promotes disorder or so abuses human rights that it undercuts the dignity of humanity, or when government becomes an instrument for the taking of innocent human lives, then the Christian has a higher duty, which is to obey God's law and not man's.[22]

6
Which Authority Do We Obey?

I die the King's good
servant, but God's first.
Sir Thomas More, before
his execution by Henry VIII

*O*ne of the most fascinating and disturbing psychological studies ever conducted is recorded in Dr. Stanley Milgram's *Obedience to Authority.*[1] Milgram and his colleagues solicited volunteers in newspaper advertisements. The participants who came to their Yale laboratory included postal clerks, high-school teachers, salesmen, engineers and a variety of laborers. In each experiment there was a "teacher" who asked questions and a "learner" who answered the questions. Under the instructions of a supervisor, the volunteer teacher administered an electrical shock to the learner for each wrong answer.

The original studies have since been replicated numerous times. In each case, the teacher believes that the learner is a volunteer just like himself, and that the shocks are real and steadily increasing in intensity. The learner is, however, an actor and there are no real shocks at all. The actor convincingly begins his response to the bogus shocks with mild protests, later moving to panic and frantic screaming, then finally unconsciousness due to the supposedly increased intensity of the shocks. The experimenter is the authority figure, who encourages the volunteer to continue inflicting more and more intense pain, despite the protests and cries of his victim.

Dr. Milgram states, "The aim of this investigation was to find when and how people would defy authority in the face of a clear moral imperative."[2] The most surprising aspect of the study is that over 60 per cent of those tested went far beyond the posted level of "Extreme Intensity Shock" and even "Danger: Severe Shock," despite the cries and convulsions of the victim. Why? Simply because whenever they hesitated, as most of them did at the victim's very first complaints, the authority figure prodded them on with statements like "Please continue," "The experiment requires that you continue," and finally "You have no choice, you must go on." At no time was there a physical threat or any external means of control of the experimenter over the teacher/volunteer. It is also remarkable that of the minority who did stop inflicting the pain at some point, almost all did so only after a great deal of protest and apparent pain on the part of the victim.

The study has been validated and redone in a variety of ways with the same results. These studies prove, and history has demonstrated, that ordinary people are capable of extraordinary indifference to human suffering. Furthermore, they will often actually inflict that suffering on others *when they do it in obedience to authority*.

The study demonstrated "behavior that is unthinkable in an individual who is acting on his own may be executed without hesitation when carried out under orders.... It is the extreme willingness of adults to go to almost any lengths on the command of an authority that constitutes the chief finding of the study and the fact most urgently demanding explanation."[3]

Rebellion, Obedience and Moral Responsibility

Many people will disobey authority if it is directly harmful to themselves. But the average person is extremely prone to obey authority even when it is terribly harmful to others to do so. But how can any decent person justify this? "The essence of obedience consists in the fact that a person comes to view himself as the instrument for carrying out another person's wishes, and he therefore no longer regards himself as responsible for his actions.... the disappearance of a sense of responsibility is the most far-reaching consequence of submission to authority."[4]

These were chilling statements for me to read, for they describe exactly the mentality that some Christians have expressed to me regarding obedience to husbands, parents, religious leaders and civil government.

So strongly did the study affect Dr. Milgram that he draws a conclusion out of keeping with the normal objectivity of laboratory studies: "Obedience to authority, long praised as a virtue, takes on a new aspect when it serves a malevolent cause; far from appearing as a virtue, it is transformed into a heinous sin."[5]

But didn't these people in the study, people like us, know that their obedience was wrong? "If people are asked to render a moral judgment on what constitutes appropriate behavior in this situation, they unfailingly see disobedience as proper. But values are not the only forces at work in an actual, ongoing situation."[6] Among these forces are the desire to cooperate, the avoidance of conflict, the concern about how one is perceived, the fear of displeasing the authority, and the fear of being punished in any number of ways for disobeying the authority.

Opponents of civil disobedience, including rescuing, often say that disobeying civil authority is a natural act of rebellion which we must guard against. This is certainly true when disobedience is to our personal advantage. But there are times when obedience to civil authority is to our own advantage, yet *goes against God's law and the good of others*. At such times the danger we must guard against is automatic obedience to human authority.

Every act of obedience can simultaneously be an act of disobedience. When I obey God, I am simultaneously disobeying Satan and my sinful nature. When I disobey Satan or my sinful nature, I am simultaneously obeying God. Hence, there is no inherent virtue in obedience, nor inherent vice in disobedience. It all depends on *who or what* we are obeying or disobeying.

The tendency of sinners is to disobey *divine* authority. As we disobey divine authority, we will obey some other authority, even if it is our own will. A person may rebel against God by obeying an ungodly authority. Indeed, disobedience to divine authority can be conveniently hidden behind obedience to human authority. The greatest evils of human history, including most massacres and holocausts, have been perpetrated in the name of obedience to human authority. Hence, we cannot say that "all obedience to authority is good." It depends on who the authority is, and what he is telling us to do.

The question of which command we obey and which we violate is better framed, *"Whose* command do we obey and *whose* command do we violate?" This puts the emphasis not on the content of the command, but its source. Is it from God or man? There is a grave ethical problem that arises when we confuse legality and morality. If life-saving is a moral obligation only when it is legal, then it is legality that determines morality. If an illegal act is immoral, then logic says that whatever is legal is also moral. Why was it right to stop an abortion twenty-five years ago? Because abortion was illegal or because abortion was immoral? Is the unborn child of today less worthy of intervention than the child of twenty-five years ago? The law says yes. Christian morality says no.

The Role of the Spectator

We could wish that Milgram's study would have included the presence of a spectator. It would have been interesting to see how much the victim would have to suffer before the spectator would actually intervene for him by interfering with the torture. In real life there is an essential role played by the spectator, who passively permits atrocities against the innocent. His failure to intervene for the victim makes him an enabler to the active participant.

Despite their mistreatment of the victim, some subjects in Milgram's study consoled themselves with the thought that at least within themselves they knew they were decent people.

What they failed to realize is that subjective feelings are largely irrelevant to the moral issue at hand so long as they are not transformed into action. The attitudes of the guards at a concentration camp are of no consequence when in fact they are allowing the slaughter of innocent men to take place before them. Similarly, so-called "intellectual resistance" in occupied Europe—in which persons by a twist of thought felt that they had defied the invader—was merely indulgence in a consoling psychological mechanism. Tyrannies are perpetuated by diffident men who do not possess the courage to act out their beliefs. Time and again in the experiment people disvalued what they were doing but could not muster the inner resources to translate their values into action.[7]

Milgram states that the "I'm really on the right side" coping mechanism of the participant is equally useful to the spectator for the same reasons. How many Christians today fuel the holocaust of the unborn by our passive consent, yet imagine we are all right because, after all, we do earnestly feel that abortion is really wrong?

When human authority punishes disobedience, as it normally does, the subject will always come up with reasons to justify his obedience. One reason is provided for him when authority figures convince him the victim is really subhuman and does not deserve to live. Milgram points out,

> For a decade and more, vehement anti-Jewish propaganda systematically prepared the German population to accept the destruction of the Jews. Step by step the Jews were excluded from the category of citizen and national, and finally were denied the status of human beings. Systematic devaluation of the victim provides a measure of psychological justification for brutal treatment of the victim.[8]

The application to the unborn is obvious. For a decade prior to 1973 the propaganda was preparing the American population to accept the destruction of the unborn. Relabeled *fetuses* and *embryos* and *zygotes* rather than children, they were systematically devaluated and dehumanized.

Another major factor in an atrocity is how visible the victim is to the ones either causing or ignoring his pain. "When the victim is close it is more difficult to exclude him from thoughts. He necessarily intrudes on the subject's awareness, since he is continuously visible."[9] Because there is no window to the womb, and because society refuses to look at the actual pictures of children torn apart from abortion, we delude ourselves. We fool ourselves into thinking that this is not really murder. Or we call it murder but don't take risks to prevent it, as we would the murder of other human beings, particularly our family or friends. After all, we would have to disobey authority to save these children from death, and (we tell ourselves) we must always obey authority.

In his study Milgram continually warns against what he calls the "agentic state," where a "person's moral judgments are largely suspended" because of his perceived duty to obey authority no matter what. Christians are to be servants of God. We are *his* agents, actively making moral judgments in light of his overriding moral law. We are not to become the passive agents of other authorities, suspending our moral judgments and actions to blindly follow men instead of God.

Which Court Is Supreme?

To teach absolute obedience to God is to properly train a Christian's conscience. To teach absolute obedience to human authority will desensitize a Christian's conscience. It is, in contrast to Romans 12:2, to teach conformity not to Christ, but to the current social norms that influence civil laws. Civil laws, after all, are not written in stone like the tablets of Sinai. They are written on paper that can be changed by the whim of courts or congress who are primarily influenced by the current drift of society.

Bernard Nathanson, a leading obstetrician and gynecologist who was once a prominent New York abortionist, tells an enlightening story in his book *Aborting America*. He asked a congressman how it was that a 1970 New York state law had set "viability" at twenty-four weeks, permitting abortions prior to this stage of development. His point was that every physician at the time knew for a fact that babies earlier than twenty-four weeks were viable. The congressman explained that most doctors put viability at twenty weeks, but that old English common law put it at twenty-eight weeks. So, the congressman said, "We split the difference." Nathanson, now an outspoken opponent of abortion, can't help but add, "And that, children, is how laws are made."[10]

Nathanson, and I with him, marvel at the totally arbitrary basis of laws affecting the lives of millions of human beings. Though it can be illustrated in many ways, the difference between the unchanging laws of heaven and the arbitrary laws of earth has rarely been more apparent than in the 1973 case of *Roe* v. *Wade*. That decision declared that state governments were no longer permitted to do what God designed them to do—protect the innocent and vulnerable. Rather, the personal opinions of seven men stripped unborn human beings of their legal right to live.

Bob Woodward and Scott Armstrong's *The Brethren* is a well-researched and compelling account of the inner working of the United States Supreme Court

from 1969 to 1975. It is an eye-opening and sometimes startling examination
of the subjective and arbitrary workings of this nation's highest court. In one
case, for instance, a justice admits to his clerks that he is choosing to vote in
a way he knows is wrong. Why? Because he hopes that by siding with another
justice in this case, he would win his vote in another. He did this knowing
full well that this "vote trading" would result (because of the 5-4 split) in
depriving a possibly innocent man of a new murder trial and condemning
him to spend the rest of his life in prison.[11]

The authors detail the incredible influence of the court clerks, who selectively expose the justices to materials and articles they deem important. When
Judge Blackmun asked one of his clerks (who was pro-abortion) to do his
research related to the upcoming *Roe* v. *Wade* case, the clerk nightly locked
up his work, for fear that another of Blackmun's clerks (who was pro-life)
would try to influence the judge's decision the other way.[12] Blackmun's three
daughters favored abortions, at least early ones. Blackmun's wife actually
"told one of his clerks, who favored lifting the restrictions [on abortion], that
she was doing everything she could to encourage her husband in that direction. 'You and I are working on the same thing,' she said. 'Me at home and
you at work.' "[13]

The arbitrary nature of these influences makes one pause to consider.
Harry Blackmun was the driving force behind the entire *Roe* v. *Wade* verdict.
Though six other justices voted with him, it was known all the way as Blackmun's case. How might the fate of twenty-six million babies, or at least the
vast majority of them, been different if Harry Blackmun's daughters or wife
or clerk (or teachers and boyfriends and others who influenced each of these)
had been against abortion instead of in favor of it?

The clerks in most chambers were surprised to see the Justices, particularly
Blackmun, so openly brokering their decision [on abortion] like a group
of legislators. . . . There was something embarrassing and dishonest about
this whole process. It left the court claiming that the Constitution drew
certain lines at trimesters and viability. The Court was going to make a
medical policy and force it on the states. As a practical matter, it was not
a bad solution. As a constitutional matter, it was absurd. The draft was
referred to by some clerks as "Harry's abortion."[14]

On July 3, 1989, sixteen years later, Harry Blackmun wrote his position, this time the minority position, on the landmark *Webster* v. *Reproductive Health Services* case. Blackmun spoke of "the chill wind blowing" that could result in the total overturning of *Roe* v. *Wade* and the return of the rights of states to regulate or even outlaw abortion. But the real chill wind blew back in the early seventies, when the fate of the lives of millions of innocent human beings was determined not on the basis of natural or divine law, nor even on the basis of constitutional law, but on the basis of personal preference.

Another Judge, Another Perspective

In 1982 in Grand Rapids, Michigan, the Honorable Randall J. Hekman, Juvenile Court judge, was petitioned to grant permission for a pregnant thirteen-year-old to obtain an abortion. In direct opposition to the law of the land, which said women cannot be denied an abortion, Judge Hekman refused to allow her the abortion. He further refused to assign the case to another judge. In the interim the young girl changed her mind and, relying upon her mother's advice and help, bore her child. Hekman was severely criticized in the press and by judicial colleagues. The child is now in grade school and is presumably more supportive of the judge's decision!

In a letter to the editor of a Grand Rapids newspaper, Hekman explained his refusal to comply with the legal process. The following is part of that letter:

Are there ever instances in which, for the sake of justice, judges should disobey the law? Or do we want our judges always to behave like mindless bureaucrats who dutifully process cases oblivious to the demands of ultimate justice?

What if the law requires a judge to order the execution of a person known to be totally innocent? What if a judge is required by law to order Jewish people to concentration camps or gas chambers because the law says that Jews are non-persons? What if a judge, sitting on a case involving a runaway slave, disagrees with the Supreme Court's 1856 decision in which black slaves were ruled to be nothing more than chattels? Are these not all instances in which judges should take a stand against unjust laws for the sake of doing that which is ultimately right? ...

Ten short years ago, a judge in Michigan would be guilty of a felony crime if he encouraged, much less ordered that a pregnant girl obtain an abortion. Then, in 1973, the Supreme Court ruled that all state laws making abortion a crime were unconstitutional. In one day, that which had been a reprehensible crime became a sacred right protected by the Constitution itself.

. . . in considering whether to order the demise of an unborn baby, judges are required to engage in the mental fiction that the baby is a nonentity. . . . When faced with this issue, a judge should courageously do what is ultimately right and just. [15]

Law-abiding Citizens

It was not the job of Ptolemy, Copernicus and Galileo to set the earth in orbit around the sun, but simply to recognize that was the way God had done it. Likewise, it was not the job of Justice Blackmun and the rest of the Burger court to determine law for the unborn. Their job was merely to discover and apply the already-existing law of God regarding the unborn. By inventing law when they should have discerned and applied law, they violated the very basis upon which their legitimate authority was established.

Imagine a group of physicists voting 7-2 that the law of gravity is out of date and no longer applies. People are told they now have the right to jump off buildings without being hurt. What has changed? Nothing. Sure, there are more people jumping off buildings, but the law of gravity still applies. Why? Because it is a constant reality, unaffected by the decisions of men. It was not voted into existence by men, and cannot be voted out of existence by them. Morality is forged in heaven by the vote of One, not on earth by the vote of the majority.

Changes in civil law have changed nothing in the moral realm. The unborn are still human beings created in God's image, deserving of full protection. Abortion has been decriminalized on earth, but not in heaven. Judgment for this criminal act has been postponed, but not eliminated.

We must define our terms when we speak of the importance of being a "law-abiding citizen." This is a virtuous label whenever those laws are good or even neutral. But to be "law abiding" in the case of a particular law that commands evil that God has prohibited or prohibits good that God has commanded, is to abide by human law at the expense of divine law. "Law-abiding citizens" were responsible for the horrible injustices and human suffering of the holocaust.

Many of the doctors, judges and Nazi officers at the Nuremberg trials justified their atrocities by saying, "I was just obeying orders." This was so pervasive that defendants were instructed to stop saying it. "I was just obeying orders" was irrelevant—it was simply not an acceptable defense. They would have to come up with something else or be found guilty.

What the courts said at Nuremberg they said again in 1968 at the trial of Lieutenant William Calley and company. These men were held accountable for the "My Lai Massacre," where three hundred unarmed Vietnamese civilians—mostly women, children and old men—were herded into ditches and murdered. The courts have said consistently in such cases, "You have a moral obligation to disobey your legal orders when you have been told to do what is morally wrong. Furthermore, if you stand passively by and let others do the dirty work, you are also morally culpable."

Less than thirty years after Nuremberg and five years after the trial of Lt. Calley, American parents and doctors were given legal authority to kill innocent unborn children. At the same time, American Christians were given legal orders not to physically intervene at the killing places in an attempt to prevent the violent child-killing we call abortion. We must each answer the question of whether "I was just obeying orders" is any more legitimate a defense now than it was then.

Giving God and Caesar Their Due

When asked about paying taxes, Jesus pointed out Caesar's image on a coin, and said, "Give to Caesar what is Caesar's, and to God what is God's" (Mt 22:21). The first half of his statement answered the question, but the second half put Caesar in his place. For whoever Caesar may be, he is *not* God.

Those who advocate general or indiscriminate civil disobedience fail to give Caesar his due. Those who advocate unconditional or undiscerning civil obedience fail to give God his due. Supreme loyalty and absolute obedience rightly belong only to God, and therefore must be given to him only, not to Caesar.

The issue of civil obedience and disobedience is ultimately an issue of lordship. Who is God, and who isn't? Christ put himself before the human authorities of family (Mt 10:16-22; 32-37) and government (Mt 22:21). Even the church can end up putting man's authority before God's. The religious leaders of Jerusalem made their ultimate betrayal of their Creator when they turned their backs on Jesus and said, "We have no king but Caesar" (Jn 19:15).

Two things are constantly happening in this struggle between our allegiance to God and to Caesar: first, *our* temptation is frequently to render to Caesar a great many things that should be rendered only to God; and second, *Caesar's* temptation is always to want to be God and thereby claim our total allegiance. And in a world where those two temptations often coincide, saying Yes to God and No to Caesar can become a very lonely business.[16]

Caesar has rightful authority in many areas. But what about the ultimate prerogative over the life and death of innocent people? What happens when government removes protection from innocent and vulnerable human beings? When it intervenes to protect those who kill these innocent beings? When it further intervenes to stop and to punish those who try to peacefully save those innocent lives?

Are these Caesar's prerogatives? Or in doing these things has he usurped the prerogatives of God? Is obeying Caesar's command to let the children die giving him his due—or is it giving him God's due?

7
The Law of Love

*Any man's death diminishes
me, because I am involved
in mankind; and therefore
never send to know for
whom the bell tolls;
it tolls for thee.*
John Donne

Scripture gives us many commands and principles. But it does not
state exactly how they are to be applied in every situation. God tells
me to rescue those who are being led to slaughter, but *how?* What
exactly should I do?

The biblical examples show me that civil disobedience can be appropriate
when it comes to saving innocent human lives, including the lives of children.
But the situation I face will rarely be an *exact* parallel to those examples of
Scripture. There is need for an ethical yardstick, a guiding principle to help
us properly apply the teachings of Scripture to the situations we daily confront.

God has given us just such a guiding principle. He calls it "the law of love."

Love Your Neighbor
In Leviticus 19 the people of Israel are told to make provision for the poor
and alien through leaving the gleanings of the field for them to harvest. God's
people are told to not steal, not deceive one another, defraud or rob our

neighbor. We are not to withhold wages, and we are strictly told not to take advantage of the handicapped: "Do not curse the deaf or put a stumbling block in front of the blind" (Lev 19:14). We are not to pervert justice, show partiality, or do anything that endangers another's life.

God summarizes these commands in a single statement: "Love your neighbor as yourself" (Lev 19:18). Here, buried in the midst of this series of commands, is what rises to be the second most important command in all of Scripture, inseparable from the first.

Jesus was asked, "Teacher, which is the greatest commandment in the Law?" He replied, "Love the Lord your God with all your heart and with all your soul and with all your mind. This is the first and greatest commandment" (Mt 22:37). But he did not stop there. He immediately added the quote from Leviticus 19, "And the second is like it: 'Love your neighbor as yourself.' *All the Law and the Prophets hang on these two commandments*" (Mt 22:39-40).

While Scripture does not address every given situation in any place and time, Jesus *does* give us a twofold guiding ethical principle that can be applied in every situation. Love God with abandonment, and love your neighbor as you love yourself. That central principle is the very heart and soul of Scripture, so much so that all the rest of the Bible is said to orbit around it and be subordinate to it.

Jesus concurred with the statement that loving God with all your heart and loving your neighbor as yourself "is more important than all burnt offerings and sacrifices" (Mk 12:33). The law required offerings and sacrifices. Yet God places the law of love even above obeying other important commands.

What does it mean to love our neighbor as ourself? It means to show the same care for others as we show for ourself. A husband is to love his wife as he loves his own body (Eph 5:28). How do we love our body? Not by looking in a mirror and admiring it. Nor by making public statements about how wonderful our body is. We simply feed and care for it (Eph 5:29). To love ourselves is to take actions for our self-preservation. Because we love ourselves we jump out of the way of a speeding car. If we love our neighbor as ourselves, we will also pull our neighbor out of the way of a speeding car.

James called this "the royal law" (Jas 2:8). It is the law that reigns over all laws. The golden rule is an extension of the same principle. It says, "Do to others as you would have them do to you" (Lk 6:31). Do for others the same you would do for yourself in their circumstances, *and* do for others the same you would wish them to do for you in the same circumstances.

When we focus on this overriding ethical imperative, seemingly complex dilemmas suddenly become much more clear. "Should I tell this person everything that's really wrong with this car I'm trying to sell him?" The answer becomes a simple matter of "if I was buying a car from someone, would I want him to tell me everything that was wrong with it before I decided whether to buy it?" The answer is "of course," and so the answer to my ethical dilemma is surprisingly simple. "Of course I should tell him what's wrong with the car." The question is no longer gray, but black and white. The law of love cuts through the fog and shows me the right action to take.

Putting to Test the Law of Love

Suppose you are a slave who has been beaten daily, whose wife has been raped, and whose children have lived in constant terror of their "master," the plantation owner. You are fleeing for your life and theirs, hoping to reach Canada where you can live in freedom. The question is, what would you do for yourself? Would you try to escape? Would you resist the attempts of others to kill you and your family? Would you try to find food and shelter?

The second question, the golden-rule question, is *what would you want someone else to do for you in this circumstance?* Would you want them to give you food and shelter? Would you want them to hide you from those who would take you back to certain misery and probable death? Or would you like them to close the door in your face, or lock you up and call the police to take you back to slavery and abuse?

Once again the answer is obvious. "Well, *of course* I would want them to give me food and shelter, and to help my family. I wouldn't want them to ignore my plight or turn me in." The "of course" is pivotal because the law of love operates on this "of course." As a matter of course, love others as yourself, take care of others as you would have them take care of you in the same circumstances. Stand up for others as you would want them to stand up for you in the same circumstance. This is the law of love, the royal law of loving your neighbor as yourself.

Yes, an escaped murderer would also want aid. However, in the case of morally innocent people our responsibility remains clear. We should do for the innocent what we would want done for us in the same situation. If you were a Jew living in occupied Europe and the Nazis were coming for you, what would you want others to do? Would you want them to say "I pity you" or "I'll pray for you," then obey the German laws by surrendering you to the authorities? Would you want them to ignore you and do nothing to help you? Or would you want them to take you into their homes and try to save you from death? Once again, the answer is obvious; it is self-evident. The law of love cuts through all the pros and cons, all the philosophical arguments. Do for another what you would want someone to do for you in the same circumstance.

Suppose you are a baby again, living in your mother. You are about to be taken to an abortion clinic. There a white-coated "doctor" will insert steel instruments into your living space, instruments that will literally cut you to pieces or suck off your arms, legs and torso. You will feel terrible pain, withdraw in horror, and die in frantic misery.

The law of love asks, "In such a circumstance, what would I want others to do for me?" With my death imminent, would I want them to go to church and not think about me? Would I want them at that very moment to gather in a public square and say how wrong it is to kill people like me? Would I want them right then to write a letter to a congressman about me? Or, would I want them to actually come down to this clinic and stand between me and the abortionist, who will otherwise surely inflict this horrible and painful death on me?

Would I want them to give my mother a chance to hear the truth that I am a real person? Would I want them to beg her to let me live? Would I want them to delay my mother's entrance into the clinic, giving me a chance that for any number of reasons she won't reschedule the appointment?

Once again, the answer to all these questions is obvious. The law of love is rarely easy to do, but it is usually quite simple to figure out. What would we want someone to do for us as we were about to be killed? The law of love says, "do the same for others about to be killed."

Of course, it could be argued that if I were an unborn child I would want someone to do *more* than peacefully stand between me and the abortionist. Nevertheless, we must surely agree that I would not want him to do anything *less* than that.

I do not want to be misunderstood here. If I was scheduled to be killed today, I would very much want sermons to be preached and letters to be written on my behalf. Such actions are *vital* and may result in the saving of many lives in the future. It is just that today I need someone to actually intervene for me before I die. Future babies may be saved from death because of current pro-life efforts. Our petitions and votes and letters and phone calls are an act of love for thousands or millions of future children. This is wonderful and essential. But my killing is on the appointment calendar *today*. Who is there who will love *me now?* Yes, many should be working to prevent abortion in the future. But is it not equally certain that someone should be intervening for my life today?

Which Law Do I Break?

In his critique of rescuing, one pastor states, "The Bible unquestionably teaches that the Christian should help victims when doing so is legal."[1] But what if it is not legal? The pastor does not seem to realize an important point. In cases where helping victims is illegal, there are always two conflicting ethical demands. One will be met and one unmet no matter what we do. One demand is to love your neighbor by saving his life. The other demand is to obey civil law. One of these ethical demands *must* be placed over the other. The question, then, is not *should we disobey an authority?* but *which authority shall we disobey—man's or God's?*

When seen in light of the law of love, the question becomes much weightier than "should I disobey a trespassing law?" The question is, "Should I obey the law of love?" Or to put it another way, *"Which law* should I violate, the law of love or the law of trespassing?" I will be a lawbreaker either way. My only choice lies in which law I obey and which I break. According to Scripture, is the law of love a higher law than others? The answer is clearly yes (Mt 22:37-40; Mk 12:33).

The law of love is the law of God. The law of trespassing is the law of man. Of course, 99.9 per cent of the time the law of trespassing is in complete harmony with the law of love, and in fact it usually facilitates it admirably. But that's beside the point when it comes to the 0.1 per cent. We must not disobey the law of love to obey a law that in other cases is good, but in this case will cause the death of innocent children.

If the lake is clearly posted "no swimming," but I see a child drowning in it, I do not debate the ethics of violating the "no-swimming" law. The law of love tells me to jump in, swim to the child, and save his life. By jumping in I am not saying that the "no-swimming" law is bad. I am saying that in this case it is transcended by a higher law, the "royal law of love." Someone may tell me, "Yes, but by breaking the no-swimming law you have set a precedent that may encourage others to go swimming even when there is no life to save." I may be able to argue that this is not so. But if it is proven true I must finally say, "I'm sorry, but the law of love does not allow me to sacrifice one innocent human life just because others may misunderstand my actions or use them to justify their own."

If I notice that a house is on fire and that people are inside, I do not slow down when I see the "no trespassing" sign outside the house. I figure that no one will care anyway, but even if someone does care, I don't. What I care about right now are human beings created in the image of God. Suppose someone tells me, "If you go in there and try to save those lives, you'll be arrested, fined, and maybe sued. You could lose all your possessions." It still does not matter. The law of love reigns supreme. When Esther decided to trespass to save the lives of the Jews, she said, "If I perish, I perish." The possible negative consequences don't change the issue. After all, there are innocent lives at stake, and I am supposed to love them.

A woman in our church told me of a baby whose mother was on drugs and whose behavior was clearly endangering the life of this child. This woman and the baby's grandmother went together and asked if they could take the child. The child's mother refused. After an ordeal in which it became clear that the child was suffering and could even die, this woman took the child and checked into a motel, to protect his life. The next day she was told by the authorities that she was guilty of kidnapping. Providentially, the child's mother had a change of heart, released the baby, and didn't press kidnapping charges. But even if she had, this woman told me, "I don't care if the law called it kidnapping. I'm glad I did it. And I would have gone to jail to protect that child."

This woman had probably never violated the law in her life, certainly not in such a dramatic way. But the law of love compelled her to act as she did. She didn't "try" to break the law. She only tried to act in love. The law being broken was incidental. This woman was not protesting the laws against kidnapping. She was simply saving one precious human being from death, as well as saving another human being from committing a terrible crime.

Loving the Others, Not Just the Baby

"But what about applying the law of love to the pregnant women and to the clinic personnel?" Love acts in the best interests of the other. What is in the best interests of a pregnant woman? We could stand passively by and say nothing, or we could intervene for her child. We could use our body and our words to say, "That's a living person in you, and we ask you to let your child live."

If you knew your next-door neighbor was about to kill his child, wouldn't the loving thing to do be to try to intervene to stop him? What is loving for the child is also loving for the one about to kill the child. What kind of "love" stands by while people destroy another life and their own life by becoming killers?

The law of love will also motivate us to provide money, housing, baby clothes, adoption services, legal help, counseling and a myriad of other forms of support to the pregnant woman. Love will compel us to share the gospel with her. The one thing love will *not* do is stand back and let her become the killer of her baby.

As for the abortionist, one could argue that there is a greater responsibility to care for a victim of a crime than the perpetrator of the crime. Nonetheless love dictates that we do not want the abortionist to commit another murder. Love does not stand idly by when innocent people are being killed, *or* when people are storing up for themselves guilt, judgment and personal destruction. There are other ways to show love to abortionists. My wife recently spent an hour sharing Christ with the manager of the largest abortion clinic in our state. This is love. But to say by our inaction "kill babies if you want to" is not love.

But Who Is My Neighbor?

If we understand what it means to love our neighbor as ourselves, there is still a way we can attempt to get around its command. We can exclude some human beings from the category of "neighbor." In Luke 10 an expert in the law repeated to Christ the two great commands. Jesus said to him, "You have answered correctly. Do this and you will live" (Lk 10:28). Then the Bible says, "But he wanted to justify himself, so he asked Jesus, 'And *who is my neighbor?*' " (Lk 10:29).

Notice that the man did not try to get around the first command about loving God with all his heart. This apparently did not present a problem to him. After all, he was a teacher of the law. He no doubt did all the things that worshippers of God did at that time. He offered sacrifices, prayed, studied, went to synagogue, tithed, everything. But he wished to justify his own actions on the command to "love your neighbor as yourself." The important word is *neighbor.*

In asking the question this man was seeking *a narrow-enough definition of the word* neighbor *to absolve himself of responsibility for some classes of human beings.* That way he could justify his lack of loving intervention on their behalf.

In reply, Jesus told him the story of the good Samaritan (Lk 10:30-37). A man was beaten by robbers, stripped of his clothes and left half dead. A priest—not a heathen or tax-collector—saw the man, but passed by him on the other side of the road. A Levite—not a drunk or a prostitute—saw him and also left him to die. The priest, the Levite, and the expert in the law all would have despised the Samaritan who found the man next. But the Samaritan exercised the law of love by taking care of the man. The passage is filled with verbs of action. For example, the good Samaritan "went" to the man "bandaged" his wounds, "poured" on medicine, "put" the victim on his own donkey, "took him" to an inn, and "took care of him" through the night. The next day he "took out" two silver coins and "gave them" to the innkeeper. Then he said, "Look after him and when I return I will reimburse you for any extra expense you may have."

The story occurs in a Jewish area, and the victim is assumed to be a Jew. His own people, his own religious leaders, ignored him and left him to die. On the other hand, a despised Samaritan becomes Christ's moral example.

He makes great sacrifices in order to save the life of a person he doesn't even know, and who is part of a different "class" of humanity.

Christ's message here is clear. When you really love people, you don't ask if they're enough like you to warrant intervention to save their lives. You don't ask whether it's inconvenient or expensive. You simply do what needs to be done to save the life. The law of love leaves you no option. Love intervenes. The person who loves protects and rescues from harm the one whom he loves.

So, Jesus asks the expert in the law, "Which of these three do you think was a neighbor to the man who fell into the hands of robbers?" (Lk 10:36). The expert in the law replies, "The one who had mercy on him." Jesus says, "Go and do likewise." The Lord doesn't allow us the luxury of making up our own definition of "neighbor." *Every human being in need is my neighbor,* whether he be of a different race, religion, gender, age or size. The bottom line is the command to actively love—go and *do*.

Is the Unborn My Neighbor?

We are in danger today of falling into the same error that the expert in the law fell into when he attempted to exclude certain people from his definition of neighbor. That class of human beings called the unborn can be considered "unneighbors." They can either be overtly declared inhuman, *or* be treated as if they are not human by failing to do for them what one would do for other humans.

For instance, after granting that one could give shelter to an escaped slave, a Bible teacher adds this qualification: "The one in danger, however, must do the fleeing and make the request for deliverance . . . these conditions do not exist in the abortion clinics of our day."[2]

This is a curious and arbitrary distinction that allows us to answer the question "Who is my neighbor?" in a way that excludes unborn children. Where in the Bible do we find that one's capacity to flee and request deliverance is a basis for deserving deliverance? Suppose it would have been illegal to give medical help to the Jew on the road to Jericho, as it *was* in fact illegal to give medical help or other assistance to a Jew in the Warsaw Ghetto, in occupied Poland. Would the good Samaritan have left him in the ditch saying,

"But Lord, he didn't flee from the danger or request deliverance of me"? *Of course* he didn't flee and request deliverance. He couldn't, because he was physically incapable, being unconscious and half dead. *Of course* the unborn children don't flee and request deliverance. They can't.

The Hebrew babies didn't flee or request deliverance of the midwives, nor did baby Joash flee or make a request of Jehosheba. This position ignores the law of love, which is not contingent on the physical ability to flee or to request deliverance. In fact, a person who is incapable of these things is all the more vulnerable, all the more needy and worthy of intervention. This stipulation that "the victim must request deliverance" is strongly reminiscent of the technicalities developed by the lawyers and Pharisees to justify their lack of love for some classes of humanity.

Many who are pro-life appear oblivious to the inherent contradiction in saying on the one hand that unborn babies are human beings, and on the other hand that one should never break the law to save their lives. Pro-choice columnist B. D. Colen describes a scenario in which the reader is a Pole living near Auschwitz in 1943. He asks, "Are you morally obligated to save what lives you can? Of course you are."

Clarifying that he himself does *not* believe abortion is murder, Colen goes on to say, "Those taking part in Operation Rescue say they believe abortion to be murder, and I'm sure that many of them do." He then draws this conclusion based on what he considers to be inescapable logic—"Anyone who believes that abortion is murder has a moral obligation to join Operation Rescue. How can they not?"

Colen then says,

How is the person who considers abortion to be murder any different from the Pole who knew what was going on at Auschwitz? If the Pole was morally obligated to attempt to save lives, isn't the person who opposes abortion under the same obligation? . . .

No, the question being asked about Operation Rescue shouldn't be, "Why are these people doing this?" Rather, it should be, "Why has it taken them so long to get to this point? Where have they been?"

. . . It seems to me that, at this point in time, Operation Rescue is clearly where the rest of the anti-abortion movement should be. . . . Clearly, the high ground in the anti-abortion movement has been captured by those involved in Operation Rescue.[3]

I do *not* agree that all who are pro-life need to be active in rescuing. I only wish to show that even a pro-choice non-Christian recognizes that if one believes the unborn are human beings, then he is morally compelled to treat them as such when it comes to saving their lives. If he would defend breaking the law to save a born person, then he must affirm the moral right for others to do so to save the unborn child. To do otherwise is to make the unborn an inferior class of humanity to which the law of love does not apply. It is to say, "The unborn is not my neighbor."

The God Who Intervenes

The concept of loving intervention is woven throughout Scripture. To illustrate this major theme, I will use a small sampling of passages using the English word *rescue*.

God is by nature a rescuer, one who intervenes for his oppressed and endangered people. "I have come down to rescue them from the hand of the Egyptians" (Ex 3:8). "Praise be to the LORD who rescued you from the hand of the Egyptians and of Pharaoh" (Ex 18:10). "So the LORD rescued Israel that day" (1 Sam 14:23). King Darius describes God as a God who "rescues and he saves . . . he has rescued Daniel from the power of the lions" (Dan 6:27).

God's people often give testimonies of how he has rescued them, especially from men of violence who have threatened their lives (2 Sam 22:18, 20, 49). "He rescued me from my powerful enemy, from my foes, who were too strong for me" (Ps 18:17).

In their vulnerability and weakness, God's people pray to him to rescue them. "Guard my life and rescue me" (Ps 25:20). "Turn your ear to me, come quickly to my rescue" (Ps 31:2). "Rescue my life from their ravages, my precious life from these lions" (Ps 35:17). "Rescue me, O LORD, from evil men; protect me from men of violence" (Ps 140:1). "Listen to my cry, for I am in desperate need; rescue me from those who pursue me, for they are too strong for me" (Ps 142:6).

God promises to intervene for his endangered people. "He will rescue them from oppression and violence, for precious is their blood in his sight" (Ps

72:14). "I have made you and I will carry you; I will sustain you and I will rescue you" (Is 46:4).

When he rescues, God often utilizes his emissaries. After being delivered from prison, Peter said, "Now I know without a doubt that the Lord sent his angel and rescued me from Herod's clutches" (Acts 12:11). More often, though, God does not use his angels but his *people* to rescue those about to be killed. "By my servant David I will rescue my people Israel from the hand of the Philistines" (2 Sam 3:18). "So the men rescued Jonathan, and he was not put to death" (1 Sam 14:45). "But when they were oppressed they cried out to you. From heaven you heard them, and in your great compassion *you gave them deliverers, who rescued them* from the hand of their enemies" (Neh 9:27). These deliverers were people who sensed God's call to intervene for those in need of rescue.

These passages and countless others make clear that Christians are not to look at people in desperate need and conclude, "God will rescue them himself if he wants to." As long as we are able to do so, we are to assume that *we* are the instruments God intends to use to rescue the needy.

The saddest passages are those that tell of a situation in which there was "no one to rescue you/them" (Deut 28:29; Judg 18:28; Hos 5:14). Among these is the girl who was raped when there was "no one to rescue her" (Deut 22:27). Other passages are strongly suggestive of the plight of the unborn child. "They will tear me like a lion and rip me to pieces with no one to rescue me" (Ps 7:2). "They have become plunder, with no one to rescue them" (Is 42:22).

Christ is the ultimate rescue model. He came "to rescue us from the hand of our enemies" (Lk 1:74). "He has rescued us from the dominion of darkness" (Col 1:13). He "rescues us from the coming wrath" (1 Thess 1:10). Peter tells us "the Lord knows how to rescue" (2 Pet 2:9).

Christ extends to us the responsibility to rescue, to deliver, to intervene, to love on his behalf. Christ stretches the command "love your neighbor as yourself" to its ultimate limits when he says, "My command is this: Love each other *as I have loved you*" (Jn 15:12). Here the standard of our love for self is overshadowed by the standard of Christ's love for us.

There is no speculation as to the nature of this love. The Bible shows us exactly how Christ loved us. It was not a theoretical love. It was not a distant love that said, "I love people, what a pity they're going to hell," and left it at that. It was a real love, a love that acted, a love that intervened, a love that didn't merely talk but was willing to take the greatest risks and the most severe consequences. It was a love that saw the desperate plight of people and determined to take the drastic steps to rescue them from destruction.

The Poor and the Unborn
There is a whole class of people in the Bible corporately referred to as the "poor." They include any person who is downtrodden, helpless, neglected, abused, and without sufficient resources. They are society's innocent victims, the weak and powerless who are taken advantage of by the strong and powerful. The poor include the widows and the orphans, that is, those who have no protector, no advocate. God is known as the rescuer of the poor, who delivers them from the hand of the wicked who would destroy them (Job 29:12; Ps 35:10; Jer 20:13).

The theme of intervening on behalf of the weak and vulnerable, of protecting the unprotected from the abuses of others, is central to literally hundreds of passages. It is one of the most dominant themes in the entire Bible. Typical of these passages is Proverbs 31:8-9 which states, "Speak up for those who cannot speak for themselves, for the rights of all who are destitute. Speak up and judge fairly; defend the rights of the poor and needy." The Old Testament prophets boldly spoke forth God's commands to care for the poor (Is 58:7; 58:10-11). Jesus came to preach the good news to the poor, the captives, the blind and oppressed (Lk 4:18-19). Though poor himself, Jesus made a regular practice of giving to those even poorer (Jn 13:29). He also repeatedly commanded care for the poor (Lk 14:12-14).

Special offerings to help the poor were commonplace in the early church (Acts 11:27-30; 24:17). Galatians 2 shows the apostles placed caring for the poor above almost all other issues. "All they asked was that we should continue to remember the poor, the very thing I was eager to do" (Gal 2:10).

James was particularly insistent that no one is godly unless he takes action on behalf of the poor (Jas 1:27; 2:14-16). His concern was that our beliefs and words do not help the needy, but only our actions.

A. W. Tozer said this about our tendency not to act on our beliefs:

So wide is the gulf that separates theory from practice in the church that an inquiring stranger who chances upon both would scarcely dream that there was any relation between them. . . . Christians habitually weep and pray over beautiful truth, only to draw back from that same truth when it comes to the difficult job of putting it in practice. . . .

It appears that too many Christians want to enjoy the thrill of feeling right but are not willing to endure the inconvenience of being right. So the divorce between theory and practice becomes permanent in fact, though in word the union is declared to be eternal. Truth sits forsaken and grieves till her professed followers come home for a brief visit, but she sees them depart again when the bills become due. They protest great and undying love for her but they will not let their love cost them anything.[4]

All the truth we know about the unborn children will not save them from death. Furthermore, it is action that gives credibility to beliefs. It is intervention, sometimes costly intervention, that gives credibility to our words about the unborn. It was said of King Josiah, "He defended the cause of the poor and needy, and so all went well. *Is that not what it means to know me?* declares the LORD" (Jer 22:16).

Sheep, Goats and Loving Intervention

Speaking of the poor and needy, Jesus stated, "I tell you the truth, whatever you did for one of the least of these brothers of mine, you did for me" (Mt 25:40).

This passage takes us beyond "Love your neighbor as yourself," beyond "Love your neighbor as Christ loves you," to "Love your neighbor as you love Christ." This means that you do for your neighbor in his need exactly what you would do for Christ in his need. In fact you cannot do anything for a needy person without doing the very same to Christ.

The term "least of these" describes the have-nots, the hungry, thirsty, homeless, physically disabled, sick, persecuted, weak and defenseless. These are the most in need of protection and love, regardless of status, size or age.

Jesus spoke these words to Jews who would have been aghast at the very thought of murdering their young. That was something only the heathens did.

But had he spoken to us today, I have no doubt that he would have specifically included the unborn. "I was in the womb, about to be killed, and you intervened to help me." Or, "I was in the womb, about to be killed, and you did not intervene to help me."

Unborn babies meet all the qualifications to be put in the category of Matthew 25. They are helpless, weak, fatherless, vulnerable, innocent, despised, neglected, and victimized by the powerful and unprincipled.

According to Jesus, the issue in the Day of Judgment will not be what we *thought* about the poor and weak and defenseless and needy. It will not be what we *said* about them. Judgment will be according to what we actually did or didn't *do* to intervene on their behalf and help them. If we take the words of Matthew 25 seriously, then he who feeds the hungry feeds the hungry Christ, and he who intervenes to rescue the unborn is rescuing the unborn Christ. It is unfortunate if doing any of this requires that we break a human law. But no human law can absolve us from the moral responsibility to follow God's law by intervening for him in the form of his needy ones.

If that were the baby Jesus being taken in to the abortion clinic to be mercilessly slaughtered, what would you do? Then do it. For inasmuch as you do it for one of the least of these, you do it for him.

How Do We Love the Unborn?

So how, specifically, can we love the unborn? To follow the analogy of the Good Samaritan story, there are a number of things we can do. We can protest beatings and robbery. We can educate the church and society against beating and robbing. We can write letters and lobby to get lights installed from Jerusalem to Jericho, so there will be less beatings and robberies. We can organize "Robbers Anonymous," provide "crisis centers" for those feeling pressured by circumstances to beat and rob others, and thereby save some victims and some people from committing crimes. We can organize days of prayer for victims of beatings and robbery.

All of these are good, some of them are *very* good. But some of us—not all, for there are other vital ministries too—need to go out on the road, on behalf of the whole Christian community, and actively physically intervene for the victims who are getting beaten and robbed *today*. The law may say people are free to choose to beat and rob. Many people in society may say, "I am not necessarily pro-beatings, but I am pro-choice when it comes to beatings." Those who administer the beatings may be highly educated professionals. The police may pull us away from trying to stop the beatings. But none of these things lessens our responsibility to help the victims. For with all the variables, social sensitivities, and pros and cons about civil disobedience, *the law of love never lets us forget the victim.*

Conclusion

While in England my wife and I spent an unforgettable morning with a pastor and his wife, Phil and Margaret Holder. We discovered that Margaret had been born in China to missionary parents who were with China Inland Mission. In 1939, when Japan took control of Eastern China, thirteen-year-old Margaret was taken prisoner in a Japanese internment camp. There she remained, separated from her parents for six years.

Margaret told us of one very special person in the camp, a godly man she called "Uncle Eric." He tutored her in chemistry, and was deeply loved by her and all the children in the prison camp. "Uncle Eric" turned out to be none other than Eric Liddell, "The Flying Scot," hero of the movie *Chariots of Fire.* Liddell was the man who shocked the world by refusing to run his Olympic race because it was scheduled on Sunday.

After the Olympics, where he won a gold medal in a different race, Liddell had gone on to be a missionary in China. When war broke out, he sent his pregnant wife and children to safety, hoping to follow later. Meanwhile he stayed to help others. Because of his loving and sacrificial actions, he would never see his family in this world again. "I remember," Margaret told us through tears, "the day that Uncle Eric died."

Margaret then spoke with awe and delight of the "care packages," the barrels of food and supplies parachuted down from American planes near the end of the war. One day, not long after the bomb was dropped on Hiroshima, Margaret and the other children were lined up as usual to count off for roll call (they would often have to stand in line for hours in the bitter cold). Suddenly a plane flew over low. They saw the markings—it was American! Then they saw it circle and drop more of those wonderful barrels of food. But as the barrels came near the ground the prisoners realized that this time something was different. In Margaret's words, "The barrels had legs!" They were soldiers—the sky was full of American soldiers!

Margaret and the others, including the several hundred children, rushed out of the camp, past the speechless Japanese guards who offered no resistance. Out of their prison for the first time in six years, they ran to the soldiers—who by now were raining down everywhere—throwing themselves at them, hugging and kissing them.

When Margaret and the other children had wondered if anyone really knew they were there, if anyone out there really loved them, the packages from the sky had rekindled their hope. But the day they really knew they were loved was the day *when people actually came to rescue them.* No doubt many letters had been written and phone calls made, and that was good. But that day at great personal risk and sacrifice the soldiers had physically arrived on the scene and delivered them. To the children, those soldiers were nothing less than angels sent from God.

Doesn't *every* little child about to be killed need someone sent by God to rescue him?

8
Civil Disobedience in Church History

In Germany they came first for the Communists, and I didn't speak up because I wasn't a Communist. Then they came for the Jews, and I didn't speak up because I wasn't a Jew. Then they came for the trade unionists, and I didn't speak up because I wasn't a trade unionist. Then they came for the Catholics, and I didn't speak up because I was a Protestant. Then they came for me, and by that time no one was left to speak up.
Martin Niemöller

*I*n discussing the subject of civil disobedience to save unborn children, I am frequently struck with the number of Christians who are unaware of the heavy price of civil disobedience that Christians of conscience have continually paid throughout church history. They reject the concept of civil disobedience not primarily on biblical grounds, but simply because it is so utterly foreign to their thinking.

Having lost a sense of connection to our forefathers in the faith, we easily evaluate issues from a contemporary American Christian point of view rather than an historical global Christian point of view. As we will see in this chapter, the tradition of civil disobedience evident in the Scriptures continued on throughout the centuries. It forms a vital part of our Christian heritage.

In this chapter I will first give a broad survey of civil disobedience throughout church history. Then I'll focus on two great eras of tremendous relevance to our subject: the Christian resistance to slavery in nineteenth-century America, and the Christian resistance to the holocaust in twentieth-century Germany and occupied Europe. I will finish by applying these lessons of history to today's issue of intervening for unborn children.

The Early Roman Empire

In Thessalonica, Paul and Silas were hunted by their opposers. The Jews told the city officials, "These men who have caused trouble all over the world have now come here . . . . They are all defying Caesar's decrees, saying that there is another king, one called Jesus" (Acts 17:6-7).

The book of Hebrews details some of the persecutions of first-century Christians, which included imprisonment and the confiscation of their property (Heb 10:32-36). They were encouraged to stand fast by looking to the examples of those in Scripture and others who persevered despite severe persecution for their faith (Heb 11). Several of these examples of godly faith involved civil disobedience.

Peter and Paul were executed under Nero. The other apostles, with the possible exception of John, were put to death at various times and places. These martyrdoms began with James who was beheaded by Herod Antipas (Acts 12:2). We must remember that *it was not rioting mobs, but the established civil government, who killed the apostles and other Christians. The state imprisoned and tried them on their violations of civil law.*

Historian Roland Bainton says that the fundamental reason Christians were persecuted by Rome was because they followed a "malefactor crucified by the government of Rome [who] was declared to have an authority exceeding that of the emperor of Rome. The cult of Christ and the cult of Caesar were incompatible."[1]

Francis Schaeffer reminds us,

> The early Christians died because they would not obey the state in a civil matter. People often say to us that the early church did not show any civil disobedience. They do not know church history. Why were the Christians in the Roman Empire thrown to the lions? . . . From the viewpoint of the Roman State, they were in civil disobedience, they were civil rebels. The Roman State did not care what anyone believed religiously; you could believe anything, or you could be an atheist. But you had to worship Caesar as a sign of your loyalty to the state. The Christians said they would

not worship Caesar, anybody, or anything, but the living God. Thus to the Roman Empire, they were rebels. And it was civil disobedience. That is why they were thrown to the lions.[2]

Virtually every criticism leveled against rescuing and other forms of civil disobedience today was brought against the early church. For example, Bainton tells us about the public-image problem of the Christians that stemmed from a misunderstanding of their civil disobedience:

> The government branded them as unpatriotic and illegal. The philosophers called them stupid and irresponsible. . . . Celsus accused them of irresponsibility and declared that if all men were as they, the empire would be overrun with lawless barbarians.[3]

Foxe's Book of Martyrs details case after case of Christians standing before civil authority, refusing to bend in their commitment to worshipping and obeying Christ, and whenever necessary, disobeying the state in order to do so.[4]

Pliny wrote to the emperor Trajan (A.D. 98-117):

> This is the way I have dealt with those who have been denounced to me as Christians: I asked them if they were Christians. If they admitted that they were, I asked them again a second and a third time threatening them with capital punishment. If they still persevered, I ordered them to be executed. For I felt certain that whatever it was that they professed, their contumacy and inflexible obstinacy obviously demanded punishment.

> Trajan wrote back and affirmed Pliny's policy: "If they are denounced and found to be guilty, they must be punished, but with this restriction: If anyone says that he is not a Christian, and shall actually prove it by adoring our gods, he shall be pardoned as being repentant, even though he may have been suspect in the past."[5]

In the eyes of the state it was easy to "smoke out" true Christians. Those who would obey the civil law that required offering sacrifices to the emperor and the state were, by definition, not Christians. Those who refused to obey this law were Christians. It was as simple as that.[6]

In A.D. 202 the Roman government issued an edict that forbade conversion to Christianity. Not only was it civil disobedience to preach Christ, but *even to become a Christian*. Tertullian addressed the government on this point and said, "If you are saying that Christianity is illegal simply because that is your will, not because it really ought to be illegal. . . . If a law of yours has erred it is, I presume, because it was conceived by man; it certainly did not fall from heaven."[7]

When Origen (185-253) was only sixteen, his mother hid his clothes to keep him from going to the provincial court to publicly proclaim himself a Christian, because she knew it would result in his death.[8] Later Origen, by then a leading theologian of the church, articulated the distinction between human law and divine law. He said, "One may only obey the laws of the state when they agree with Divine law; when, however, the written law of the state commands something other than Divine and Natural law, then we must ignore the commands of the state and obey the commands of God alone."[9]

This distinction surfaced in the law that gave fathers absolute power over whether or not their children would live. Under Rome it was illegal to pick up, care for, or raise as your own the abandoned infants that were left to die outside the city gates. The Christians disobeyed this evil law, obeying the higher law of God by intervening to save the infants' lives.[10]

Under Diocletian's persecution in A.D. 300, it was declared illegal to have a Bible. Civil authorities regularly came to collect any illegal copies. The Christians violated the law by hiding them. In early fourth-century Africa, Christian literature was confiscated by the government. The believers routinely deceived the officials by giving them old and less important documents and hiding those of true value. Not only did they regard this as permissible, they believed that to turn over to the state illegal Christian writings was sin.[11]

In A.D. 385 the Emperor Valentinian decided to make a church available for use by a heretical group. Ambrose not only protested himself but recruited many other protestors, and successfully managed to nonviolently prevent the Emperor himself from misusing church facilities![12]

These were not isolated cases of civil disobedience, nor were they the kneejerk reactions of thoughtless zealots. Rather, they were deeply rooted in a theological persuasion that put God's law over man's. Augustine, the greatest theologian of early Christianity, maintained that "an unjust law is no law at all." Thomas Aquinas, the primary theologian of the Middle Ages, stated exactly the same.[13] Aquinas reasoned, "Laws may be unjust in two ways. First by being contrary to human good . . . secondly, laws may be unjust, through being opposed to the Divine good . . . laws of this kind must in no way be observed."[14]

The Protestant Reformers

William Tyndale (1490-1536) taught that the truths of Scripture had authority over both the state and the church. Partly for this "heresy," government authorities in England tried to capture him, but Tyndale evaded them for years. He was finally caught, tried as a heretic, and executed in 1536.[15] When Martin Luther posted his ninety-five theses on the cathedral door in Wittenberg he publicly affirmed that he would not submit to human authority that was misrepresenting God. At the Diet of Worms in 1521, he stood before not only the leaders of the church, but the highest civil authority, the Emperor himself. When asked if he would repudiate his books and their "errors" he replied,

> Since then Your Majesty and your lordships desire a simple reply, I will answer without horns and without teeth. Unless I am convicted by Scripture and plain reason—I do not accept the authority of popes and councils, for they have contradicted each other—*my conscience is captive to the Word of God.* I cannot and I will not recant anything, for to go against conscience is neither right nor safe. God help me. Amen. Here I stand, I cannot do otherwise.[16]

As I stood on the very spot in Worms where Luther made this proclamation, I was overwhelmed with emotion, profoundly touched by my heritage. On the same day I visited nearby Speyer where, several years after Luther's dramatic trial at Worms, a whole community stood against the established authorities. They said, in essence, "We insist on believing, teaching, and living what is right according to God's Word." It was there at Speyer that this band of rebels was first known as "Protestants." They were those who stood in *protest* against the prevailing laws and policies. Every Protestant today should remember the meaning of the label he bears. It is a testimony to a long heritage of standing for what is right against great odds, at significant cost, and in conflict with those in authority who have overstepped their God-given boundaries.

Luther made clear where he drew the line in his obedience to civil authority. In a letter to a government official he stated,

Dear Sir, I am in duty bound to obey you with my body and property. You may command according to your authority on earth. I will follow you. But if you force me to deny my faith and to destroy my books, I will not obey. For then you are a tyrant and are overstepping your authority. You are commanding something that you have neither the right nor might to do.[17] After he was condemned as a heretic and his teachings outlawed, Luther's friends kept him in hiding for ten months. Violating the Worms Edict, which carried both religious and civil authority, Luther busily wrote pamphlets and disseminated information and instruction. His illegal literature filled the countryside, and became the inspiration that fueled the Protestant Reformation.

Reformer John Calvin illegally sent ministers into France. They had false names and carried false papers, and if discovered were killed. Calvin's writings were outlawed in France, but were smuggled in with his knowledge and blessing. In his *Institutes of the Christian Religion*, Calvin made an eloquent and powerful statement of the proper relationship of human and divine authorities:

But in the obedience which we have shown to be due to the authority of governors, it is always necessary to make one exception, and that is entitled to our first attention—that it does not seduce us from obedience to him to whose will the desires of all kings ought to be subject, to whose decrees all their commands ought to yield, to whose majesty all their scepters ought to submit. And, indeed, how preposterous it would be for us, with a view to satisfy men, to incur the displeasure of him on whose account we yield obedience to men!

The Lord, therefore, is the King of kings; who, when he has opened his sacred mouth, is to be heard alone, above all, for all, and before all; in the next place, we are subject to those men who preside over us, but no otherwise than in him. If they command anything against him, it ought not to have the least attention, nor, in this case, ought we to pay any regard to all that dignity attached to magistrates, to which no injury is done when it is subjected to the unrivaled and supreme power of God. . . . As if God had resigned his right to mortal men when he made them rulers of mankind, or as if earthly power were diminished by being subordinated to its author before whom even the principalities of heaven tremble with awe.[18] Scottish Reformer John Knox stated that a civil ruler must view himself as "Lieutenant to One whose eyes watch upon him." He maintained, "Kings then have not an absolute power in their regiment to do what pleases them; but their power is limited by God's Word."[19] On this basis he stated that people had a moral duty to disobey human laws that contradicted the laws of God.

Francis Schaeffer reminds us that "in almost every place where the Reformation flourished . . . there was civil disobedience."[20] Schaeffer goes on to give pages of illustrations of this Christian civil disobedience in the Netherlands, Sweden, Denmark, Germany, Switzerland, Scotland, Hungary, France and Spain.

In the spirit of the reformers, in 1660 John Bunyan disobeyed the law of England by preaching without a license. He was arrested at a church meeting and put in a prison so damp that he said it was enough to "make the moss grow on one's eyebrows." There he converted his prison into a pulpit and wrote the greatest of all Christian classics, *Pilgrim's Progress*. He was told that he would be released if he promised not to further violate the law for which he was imprisoned, but he refused to do so.[21] He was arrested two more times for the same act of civil disobedience.

The Puritans
The Puritans, too, understood the need for civil disobedience in certain situations. William Perkins (1558-1602) wrote *A Discourse of Conscience* and *The Treatise of the Cases of Conscience*. He defended from Scripture the fact that the conscience cannot be ultimately bound by any civil law, but only God's Word. He viewed human laws as not inherently binding on the conscience, but only as far as "they are agreeable to God's Word, serve for the common good . . . and hinder not the liberty of conscience."[22]

One of Perkins's illustrations is particularly pertinent to the question of rescuing. He told of a fictitious city in time of war, where the magistrate commanded that the city gate not be opened. The purpose of this law was to protect the citizens from the enemy. But certain citizens ended up outside the city gate and were being pursued by the enemy. Consequently, a man opened the gate to rescue them. Has the man sinned? Perkins answers, "He has not: because he did not hinder the purpose of the law, but rather furthered it."

Since the proper purpose of civil law is the common good, one fulfills the purpose of the law by doing what is for the good of innocent people. Applying the argument of Perkins, since the purpose of a "no trespassing" law is to protect the welfare of people, rescuers fulfill the purpose of the law by protecting people even if they have to "trespass" to do it.

Christian Civil Disobedience and American Slavery

To be consistent, American Christians who believe there is no place for civil disobedience should not celebrate the Fourth of July. The American Revolution may or may not have been justified, but it was certainly a revolution. When they were regarded as unjust, the legal claims of England upon the colonies were actively resisted, first peacefully and later by active and widespread violence.

I do not, however, believe any revolution, including the American Revolution, should be used to justify civil disobedience. Many would argue on both sides as to whether or not such a revolution is biblically defensible. Nevertheless, apart from the revolution, American history is full of examples of Christians nonviolently and peacefully breaking civil law because of a conflict with biblical values.

For instance, in 1829 the state of Georgia enacted a law that the Cherokee Indians would have to give up their claim to their land. The law also ordered that missionaries to the Cherokees both recognize this law and secure a license to preach. If they did not, they were to leave the state. The Rev. Samuel A. Worcester and Dr. Elizur Butler refused to do either, and went to jail for it. They argued that their decision was a matter of "clear moral obligation—a question of right or wrong—of keeping or violating the commands of God...."[23]

Some of the greatest examples of Christian civil disobedience in American history relate to the issue of black slavery. There are close parallels between the black slaves of the last century and the unborn children of today. These examples, then, are particularly worthy of our attention.[24]

The Fugitive Slave Laws

A 1793 act of the United States Congress, called the First Fugitive Slave Law, made it a crime to give assistance to a runaway slave. This law applied not only in the slave states, but in the free states as well. Because some people had the compassion and courage to disobey this evil law, slave owners bitterly complained.

The slaveholders argued that the slaves were theirs and they had the right to do with them as they wished. They claimed that their personal rights and freedom of choice were at stake. They said that the slaves were not really persons in the full sense. They pointed out that they would experience economic hardship if they were not allowed to have slaves, and developed slogans to gain sympathy to their cause. They maintained that others could choose not to have slaves, but had no right to impose their anti-slavery morality on them. All of these pro-slavery arguments should sound familiar to anyone who has listened to the modern pro-abortion rhetoric.

This point of view was given credibility, as well as legal support, in the Dred Scot Decision of 1857. The Supreme Court determined in a 7-2 decision that slaves were not legal persons and were therefore not protected under the Constitution. In 1973, one hundred and sixteen years later, the U.S. Supreme Court, by another 7-2 decision, would determine that unborn children also were not legal persons and therefore not protected under the Constitution.

Prior to Dred Scot, in 1850 the Second Fugitive Slave Law made the crime of intervening on behalf of a slave even more serious. The penalty was a fine of $1,000 (a great deal of money in that time) and imprisonment up to six months, as well as civil damages to the slave owner of $1,000 per slave. This parallels the damages sought by abortion clinics when their source of income is diminished by rescuing. At that time President Fillmore declared that resistance to the Fugitive Slave Law was an act of treason. It was both illegal and un-American to rescue slaves. Many churches were also split over the issue.

The Underground Railroad

This was the moral climate that gave birth to the Underground Railroad. The Underground Railroad was actually a system of contacts, consisting of compassionate and principled Americans, who at great risk to themselves provided food, shelter and protection to slaves running from the tyranny of their masters. The Underground Railroad had its own maps, secret routes and passwords. It consisted not of criminal types, but of the most religious and moral citizens.

Though his position made it difficult to publicly endorse the Underground Railroad, President Abraham Lincoln had this to say about the Fugitive Slave Law:

It is a very strange thing, and not solvable by any moral law that I know of, that if a man loses his horse, the whole country will turn out to help hang the thief; but if a man but a shade or two darker than I am is himself stolen, the very same crowd will hang the one who aids in restoring him to liberty. Such are the inconsistencies of slavery, where a horse is more sacred than a man; and . . . if one man chooses to make a slave of another, no third man shall be allowed to object.[25]

The Underground Railroad gave an opportunity to many common and normally law-abiding citizens to show unusual heroism in the face of an evil law and the intolerable abuse of human beings. One such person was Calvin Fairbank, who saved a black family of three, then served five years in prison for doing so. Not long after being released, he helped a female slave escape from Kentucky, and was put back in prison another fifteen years. His fiance faithfully waited the full twenty years to marry him.[26] Fairbank set aside his own convenience and forfeited a normal life in order to rescue four defenseless black people.

When Quaker Thomas Garret was criminally convicted for helping slaves, and fined to the point of bankruptcy, he said to the court, "Judge, thou hast not left me a dollar, but I wish to say to thee, and to all in this courtroom, that if anyone knows of a fugitive who wants a shelter and a friend, send him to Thomas Garrett and he will befriend him."[27]

In 1860 Maria Child addressed the legislators of Massachusetts on the subject of "The Duty of Disobedience to the Fugitive Slave Act." Referring to the fact that the slave owners claimed they could "prove" the slaves belonged to them, she boldly cried, "Show me a bill of Sale from the Almighty!" Maria went on to quote from Bishop Gregory of Asia Minor, who fifteen hundred years earlier had said this:

> Who can be the possessor of human beings save God? Those men that
> you say belong to you, did not God create them free? . . . are your fellow-
> men to be bought and sold, like herds of cattle? Who can pay the value
> of a being created in the image of God? The whole world itself bears no
> proportion to the value of a soul, on which the Most High has set the seal
> of his likeness. This world will perish, but the soul of man is immortal.
> Show me, then, your titles of possession.[28]

Deliberately deciding to live right on the line of the Underground Railroad,
for thirty-three years Levi Coffin and his family opened their hearts and
homes to over a hundred slaves each year. Called in before an Ohio grand
jury, Coffin later recalled his defense of his actions:

> I had read in the Bible when I was a boy that it was right to feed the hungry
> and clothe the naked, and to minister to those who had fallen among
> thieves and were wounded, but that no distinction in regard to color was
> mentioned in the Good Book, so in accordance with its teachings I had
> received these fugitives and cared for them. I then asked [the prosecutor]:
> "Was I right, Friend, in doing so?"
> He hesitated and seemed at a loss how to reply. I continued:
> "How does thy Bible read? Was it not as I have said?"
> "Yes," he answered, "it reads somehow so."[29]

Christian ministers were actively involved in the Underground Railroad. Jonathan Blanchard (1811-1892) was the founder and president of Wheaton
College. He was a strong voice against slavery, and stated that if a law is
wrong, it should be disobeyed by Christians.[30] Evangelist Charles Finney's
Oberlin College, with its Oberlin church, was a well-known station on the
Underground Railroad, so much so that the Ohio State legislature tried to
close down the school.

Charles Beecher, brother of Harriet Beecher Stowe, defended the Underground Railroad from his pulpit. He and other pastors who took similar
stands were severely criticized for doing so. They were often reminded that
as pastors they should set an example by obeying the law. But they believed
that they would set a higher example through obeying a higher law. Here is
part of a sermon on the Fugitive Slave Laws, for which Beecher was expelled

from his ministerial association:

The men that refuse obedience to such laws are the sure, the only defenders of law. If they will shed their own blood rather than sin by keeping a wicked law, they will by the same principle shed their blood rather than break a law which is righteous. In short, such men are the only true law-abiding men. For they never break a law, except when they see that to keep it would be to violate all law in its very foundation, and overturn the very government of God; while *those men who clamor for blind obedience to all law—right or wrong—are striking at the throne of God* . . .

In conclusion, therefore, my application of the subject is—Disobey this law. If you have ever dreamed of obeying it, repent before God, and ask His forgiveness.[31]

Christian Civil Disobedience against the Nazis

On April 1, 1933, Adolf Hitler called a national boycott of all Jewish businesses. The boycott was honored by most German citizens. "After three days the boycott ended. Hitler had learned what he wanted to know: no one would stand up for the Jews."[32]

On the very day the boycott began, a group called the "German Christians," which included a number of well-known church leaders and theologians, held their first national rally in support of Hitler and the "new Germany."

Fortunately, however, there were other Christians such as those in the Young Reformation Movement. Among them were Martin Niemöller and Dietrich Bonhoeffer. They opposed the Nazis, who were using the law as a tool to accomplish their ends, including usurping the independent powers of the church. Bonhoeffer's own ninety-year-old grandmother "walked resolutely through the cordon of storm troopers and Nazi youth" that blocked entrance to a store owned by Jews. She did her shopping and walked out without being stopped. It was the extraordinary courage of ordinary people like her that temporarily restrained the holocaust.[33]

A Compromising Church

In September 1933 the German Evangelical Church elected Hitler's puppet to leadership. They submitted to the decree that all Jews by race, as well as those married to Jews, would be disqualified from church office. Considering it to be a biblical responsibility to government, they also passed a ruling that pastors take an oath of loyalty to Hitler and the government of Germany. An outraged Bonhoeffer urged that all pastors resign from a church that was selling out to the state. Meanwhile, Niemöller formed the Pastors' Emergency League, which was joined by 2,300 pastors who pledged to be bound in their preaching "only by Holy Scripture and the Confessions of the Reformation."[34] Niemöller pointed out in his sermons that Jesus, a Jew, was our Lord and the center of our faith.

Niemöller and several other clergymen were granted a meeting with Hitler. The Führer ranted and raved, questioning their loyalty to the state. When Niemöller explained that he was concerned for the people of Germany, Hitler shouted, "I will protect the German people. You take care of the church. You pastors should worry about getting people to heaven and leave this world to me."

When it was time to leave, and the pastors were trembling in the face of Hitler's rage, Niemöller felt compelled to make one last statement: "A moment ago, Herr Hitler, you told us that you would take care of the German people. But as Christians and men of the church we too have a responsibility for the German people, laid upon us by God. Neither you nor anyone else can take that away from us."[35]

Miraculously, Niemöller walked out of Hitler's office. Several of the other clergymen were outraged that he had risked their welfare, and that of the church, by this untimely reminder to Caesar that he was not God.

The tragedy is that many pastors heeded Hitler's warning. They did forget about the welfare of the German people, especially the Jews, and focused on the harmless "business of heaven." Their religious exercises involved no personal risk for them precisely because they constituted no threat to the evil laws and policies of Hitler's government. The church stayed safe—and in the years to come ten to twelve million Jews, gypsies, handicapped, sick and elderly would be murdered. Another result was that the German church would lose its credibility with its people and the entire world.

The Monday after the meeting with Hitler, the Protestant bishops of Germany issued a statement of unconditional support for Hitler and the government of Germany. We must understand that Germany was a country with a constitution, a judicial system and a parliament. The stripping away of the rights of the Jews was perfectly legal, just as the stripping away of the rights of the unborn by the U. S. Supreme Court was and is legal. Both were legal, neither was moral. Both flew directly in the face of the clear teachings of Scripture and the common decency of any civilized nation. As such, neither deserved the respect and obedience of any citizens, least of all Christians.

The German laws depriving the Jews of rights were obeyed by the German Christians out of fear, and the result was the murder of millions. We in America must also ask ourselves if we have respected and obeyed laws that have contributed to the murder of over twenty-five million innocent babies.

"Peace to the Church"
Niemöller refused to recognize laws that robbed Jews of their rights, when a higher law, from a higher lawgiver, had given them those rights. One of the church bishops, speaking for others, addressed the gathering of the Free Synod in Berlin, pleading for "moderation" and "conciliation." "We are trying to bring peace to the church," he said, "and this Jewish question can only make us seem like the greatest troublemakers in Germany."

Niemöller responded to the bishop's concerns by asking, *"What does it matter how we look in Germany compared with how we look in heaven?"*[36] But this did not settle the issue. The bishop replied, "But the business of a synod is the church. We cannot pronounce judgment on all the ills of society. Most especially we ought not to single out the one issue that the government is so sensitive about . . ."

Tragically, "the majority of pastors thought laws about Jews were a state matter."[37] Niemöller issued a prophetic warning to his fellow pastors. "We shall be obliged to say more," he said, "and it may be that our mouths will only be really opened when we have to undergo suffering ourselves."

When Niemöller proposed that they publicly read in their churches a bold memorandum standing up for the Jews, one brother anticipated the response of some of the Christian leaders: "They will say we should stick to the issues of the church and leave the politics to the state." Niemöller replied, "The Jews are our issue!"

When Bonhoeffer was asked his opinion, he said, "I think we must not worry what people think. We must be the church and speak as Christ. And the words of Proverbs . . . remain relevant, 'Open your mouth for the dumb.' " Out of 18,000 churches, only a few hundred read the proclamation.

Soon thereafter, Niemöller was arrested and imprisoned. When a chaplain who hadn't heard of his arrest stumbled upon the well-known leader in jail, he asked in shock, "But brother, what brings you here? Why are you in prison?" Niemöller's reply was to the point: "And, brother, why are you *not* in prison?"

Unable to be silent and passive as innocent people were murdered, Bonhoeffer became a leader in the German resistance. He ran an illegal seminary, and between 1936 and 1945 there was never a time where some of his students were not in prison. He wrote and hid his manuscripts illegally, being unapproved by the state as a writer. Bonhoeffer was finally arrested in 1943. Two years later, within weeks of Germany's surrender, he was hung.

Dietrich Bonhoeffer's book *The Cost of Discipleship* is a well-known Christian classic. Bonhoeffer knew firsthand the cost of standing up against man's laws to defend the law of God, and the innocent people protected by that law. Had he been silent and passive, he could have, like most of the Christians in Germany, survived the war. But he was fighting in another war, serving another Commander. To the laws of that Commander, not to the laws of Germany, Bonhoeffer was faithful.

Lifesaving Efforts in Occupied Europe
Meanwhile, other Christians spread across occupied Europe were also doing what they could to save the lives of Jews. In his fascinating book *The Warsaw Ghetto: A Christian's Testimony*, Wladyslaw Bartoszewski tells of his work in Warsaw, where half a million Jews were forced into an incredibly small living space.[38] Giving food or water to a Jew, even if he would die without it, was punishable by death. Anyone found harboring Jews was executed. But Bartoszewski and his friends organized not only to supply Jews with food and shelter, but to falsify birth certificates, baptismal certificates, identification papers and forge work permits. All of this was, of course, illegal. It also managed to save the lives of about ten thousand people.

Many readers know the story of Corrie ten Boom and her family, recorded in *The Hiding Place*. At great risk they disobeyed the law by building a false wall in their Holland home and hiding Jews to protect them from the concentration camps. When their rescue operation was discovered, they too were hauled away. Having intervened for the Jews, they were considered worthy of the same fate as the Jews. Ironically, the ten Booms were strongly criticized by a pastor who objected to such activities. Holding a Jewish baby in his arms, Mr. ten Boom told the pastor, "You say we could lose our lives for this child. I would consider that the greatest honor that could come to my family."[39]

The most remarkable account of World War 2 resistance I have ever read is recorded in Philip Hallie's *Lest Innocent Blood Be Shed*.[40] It tells the story of André Trocmé, a Presbyterian pastor who convinced his congregation in the French village of Le Chambon to house, care for and transport Jews fleeing for their lives.

Trocmé oversaw what Hallie calls a "rescue machine," a network of ordinary Christians who were willing to disobey civil law and risk their lives to save those of another country and religion.

The actions of the Christians in Le Chambon were in clear violation of the laws of France. They forged false identity cards for the Jews and shuffled them from house to house. Trocmé refused to divulge the names of Jews or of those participating in rescues.

Some church leaders were critical. One superior told Trocmé to cease the rescues, fearing they were "endangering the very existence not only of this village but of the Protestant church of France!"[41]

Like Niemöller, Trocmé refused to stop despite criticism from other Christians. He was now disobeying not only civil but religious authority. But he and his church persevered in what they believed was right. As a result, "Le Chambon became the safest place for Jews in Europe."[42] Over a period of about four years, 2,500 Jews were rescued.

Speaking of the dual commands to love God and to love the neighbor as yourself, Hallie—himself not a Christian—captures the heart and soul of the church at Le Chambon:

It was this strenuous, this extraordinary obligation that . . . Trocmé expressed to the people in the big gray church. The love they preached was not simply adoration; nor was it simply a love of moral purity, of keeping one's hands clean of evil. It was not a love of private ecstasy or a private retreat from evil. *It was an active dangerous love* that brought help to those who needed it most.[43]

Moral Clarity and the Passing of Time

It is easy to admire from a distance the early Christians who stood up for what they believed was right, opposing perhaps the most powerful human authority in history, the government of Rome. It is likewise easy to admire Martin Luther, Levi Coffin, Maria Child, Martin Niemöller and the church at Le Chambon. The real question is, however, are we willing not only to *admire* them, but to *imitate* them? We laud their example, but will we actually follow it when it comes to intervening to save the lives of innocent human beings?

Furthermore, while we may be shocked at the Christians who criticized the life-saving actions of these people simply because they were illegal, we must ask ourselves if we too have criticized our brothers and sisters in Christ for breaking the law in their attempts to nonviolently save the lives of innocent unborn human beings.

The fact is that many moral actions now regarded as good were opposed by churches at the time. This raises the question, what actions are Christians now opposing that will one day be recognized as having been right?

Those who put laws made in the image of man over lives made in the image of God are eventually seen as guilty of what Bartoszewski, in *The Warsaw Ghetto*, variously labels "the sin of inaction," "indifference," "cowardice" and "small-mindedness."

Time has a way of changing our perspective. The United States was largely outraged by the civil disobedience of Susan B. Anthony. In 1872 she was arrested for unlawful voting and refusing to pay the fine. A hundred years later our nation honored her actions by putting her image on a silver dollar. The nation was similarly offended at the appalling civil disobedience of Martin Luther King, Jr., a Christian minister. Twenty years later his name was memorialized by a national holiday. How many of us would disagree with Charles Beecher's sermon about obeying the higher law of God to help the slaves? Yet, when he actually preached the sermon it lost him his membership in the ministerial community. It is now clear to most of us that he was right all along. But at the time, immersed in and conformed to the norms of that society, what would we have thought? What would we have done?

I suppose most of us think we would have stood for what was right, that we would have stood with Maria Child and Calvin Fairbank even if it meant breaking the law. But are we actively and sacrificially intervening for innocent children being torn to pieces daily in our own cities? If not, what makes us think we would have rescued Jewish babies in occupied Europe, where it could have cost us not just some public embarrassment, not just some possible jail time, not just some possible lawsuits, but our very lives?

Niemöller published a group of sermons entitled *Christus ist mein Führer,* or *Christ Is My Führer.* The clear implication, "Hitler is not my Führer," escaped no one, least of all Hitler. The distinction between Christ as Lord and civil authority as lord was an important one—important enough that it cost Niemöller seven years in Dachau. But the significance of this distinction was not recognized by most Christians at the time. And the result was what we know today as the holocaust.

9
Rescuing As a Form of Civil Disobedience

Must the citizen ever for a moment, or in the least degree, resign his conscience to the legislator? Why has every man a conscience, then? I think that we should be men first, and subjects afterward. It is not desirable to cultivate a respect for the law so much as for the right.
Henry David Thoreau

One may well ask: how can you advocate breaking some laws and not others? The answer lies in the fact that there are two types of laws: just and unjust. I would be the first to advocate obeying just laws. Conversely, one has a moral responsibility to disobey unjust laws.
Martin Luther King, Jr.

*T*he modern concept and expression of civil disobedience has been primarily shaped by three men—Henry David Thoreau, Mohandas Gandhi, and Martin Luther King, Jr. It is important to emphasize that these men did *not* invent civil disobedience. We saw in chapter four that disobedience to civil laws on the grounds of conscience and higher law is firmly rooted in the Scriptures. It was practiced thousands of years before Thoreau, Gandhi and King. And as the previous chapter demonstrates, the Christian community throughout the centuries, including our own, has when necessary practiced civil disobedience on the individual, familial and congregational levels.

What Gandhi and King did was develop and popularize a particular form and methodology of civil disobedience. They did this in a way that promoted widespread participation by others. They extended civil disobedience beyond the individual, familial and congregational levels, to the community and national levels. Furthermore, as required by the large-scale nature of their actions, they adopted certain guidelines or rules of conduct for these united public expressions of civil disobedience. Their intent was to protest and draw attention to certain injustices, with the hope of influencing public opinion and social change. Much of the social and legal changes they sought did in fact materialize. Of course, this does not mean that their philosophy or methods were necessarily right, only that they were somewhat effective.

I want to emphasize that my personal belief in the legitimacy of civil disobedience is *not* based on the writings or experiences of Thoreau, Gandhi or King. Though it is instructive to examine what they did, I believe one can take issue with them and still advocate civil disobedience for a number of other reasons, including to save the lives of innocent children. The primary foundation for this belief is the Scriptures. The secondary foundation is the history of the church. These have both been previously examined. An examination of these recent proponents of civil disobedience is useful primarily for information and understanding, not as a basic defense of rescuing.

Thoreau and Gandhi

In 1846 Henry David Thoreau was arrested in Massachusetts for refusing to pay his poll tax. He refused on the grounds that the tax essentially sponsored slavery and the Mexican War, both of which he believed were immoral. At one point Thoreau also aided at least two fugitive slaves, violating the Fugitive Slave Act. However, Thoreau's relatively isolated acts of civil disobedience would have been long forgotten were it not for his famous essay *On the Duty of Civil Disobedience*.

Though it is uncertain that he was a Christian, Thoreau did believe in the concept of natural law and that a man's conscience should be ultimately governed by God's law, not man's law. It troubled him that "there are thousands who are *in opinion* opposed to slavery and to the war, who yet in effect do nothing to put an end to them." He argued, "Under a government which imprisons any unjustly, the true place for a just man is also a prison."[1]

Many people think of Thoreau as a social reformer, but he was not. His experience as a protestor was brief, sporadic and individualistic. He was motivated as much by his own independence and resentment at the government's audacity as he was by social injustice. His most significant contribution to the modern practice of civil disobedience came from the fact that one day a young man named Mohandas Gandhi would read his essay and be deeply influenced by it.

After studying law in London, Gandhi went to South Africa where he lived until 1914. He became a key leader in the Indian community's fight for civil rights. It was there, influenced in part by Thoreau's essay, that he developed the principle of *satyagraha,* or nonviolent civil disobedience. This included publicly burning the registration cards that facilitated the injustices of South African racism.

When he returned to his native India, Gandhi became leader of the Congress Party and initiated a campaign of peaceful civil disobedience to the laws of the governing British authorities. Gandhi was arrested and imprisoned many times. Thousands of his followers were beaten and killed in peace marches, usually making no attempt to defend themselves. Their brave but costly efforts eventually led to India's independence after World War 2.

Gandhi was also heavily influenced by Christ's Sermon on the Mount. He interpreted the command not to run or to fight, but to turn the other cheek, as a means of passive resistance for the sake of righteousness. He abhorred violence, and was deeply hurt when others resorted to it, even for causes which he espoused. Gandhi felt that if people believed so strongly in morality and justice that they were willing to take abuse for standing up for it, then this would force society to re-examine its injustices, bow its head in shame, and finally implement legal and moral change.

Martin Luther King

Gandhi was a primary inspiration for the American civil rights movement, spearheaded by Martin Luther King in the fifties and sixties. King spoke of the "moral responsibility to disobey unjust laws." A Baptist preacher, he believed that the Christian gospel had clear social implications, and that racism, though reflected and promoted by civil laws, was inconsistent with the gospel. He believed that Christians should peacefully and nonviolently stand up for what was right, even at their own expense. In fact, the civil rights movement was born and nurtured within the context of local Christian churches.[2]

Because of his civil disobedience, which included "sit-ins" where Blacks were not legally permitted, King was arrested over thirty times. King's insistence on nonviolence distinguished him from other Black leaders such as Malcolm X and Stokely Carmichael. He was criticized for his refusal to establish justice through violence and retaliation, but King believed the way of Christ was the way of firm but peaceful insistence on what was right. He agreed with Gandhi that the willingness of people to suffer for what was right would eventually bring about change. King once stated to his adversaries, "We will wear you down by our capacity to suffer." While his personal life at times left much to be desired, King's sincere goal was to bring the biblical principles of love and justice to every member of society, despite color, gender, age or any other distinguishing characteristic. In 1983 Martin Luther King's birthday was declared a national holiday, making him the only nonpresident to have received that honor.

But the verdict on King was quite different when he was actually doing those things for which the nation was to reward him twenty years later. The irony of this struck me as I was released from Portland's Justice Center after spending a two-day jail sentence for rescuing innocent babies. When I walked out on the street and looked back at the building in which I had been imprisoned, there in large letters on the cornerstone was this quote: "Injustice anywhere is a threat to justice everywhere." Underneath was the date 1963, preceded by the name of the man who said it—Martin Luther King.

What irony that twenty years earlier King himself was considered a doer of injustice because he broke civil laws. Indeed, at the date those very words were said King was being locked up in places just like this one that was now proud to put his quote on its cornerstone! Now the very legal system that prosecuted him recognized that King had been right and the law had been wrong. The law has changed, and so (for many Americans, at least) has the verdict on King's civil disobedience. The verdict has also changed on those who defended the laws that King broke. They were law-keepers; King was the lawbreaker, yet it is *his* name, not theirs, that is now on the cornerstone of a building dedicated to upholding the law.

What Is Civil Disobedience?

Opponents of rescuing fall into two categories when it comes to rescuing's parallels to the civil rights movement. Those who are against the civil rights movement say rescuing is more of the same. Those who are now for the civil rights movement (which includes many Christians who at the time were against it) say rescuing is completely different. In short, some criticize rescuing because they suppose it is the same thing done by King, while others criticize it because is not the same thing. Civil disobedience must be defined for purposes of discussion, but the definitions vary. I will define it as I use it in this book. *Christian civil disobedience is a peaceful act of violating civil law. It is done out of a sense of conviction or moral necessity, compelled by a biblically and morally sensitive conscience that knows it is ultimately accountable to God and his law.*

One of the characteristics of civil disobedience, which makes it distinct from lawlessness, is its attempt to try to maintain respect for the law even while breaking it. Esther had great respect for King Ahasuerus and for the law. Yet she violated the sacred "no-trespassing" law because of an even higher respect for the lives of innocent people. She did this without losing her respect for the king *or* his law. No doubt she would never violate that law again unless it was demanded by a need to save the lives of the innocent, or by some equally compelling moral imperative.

In his "Letter from a Birmingham Jail," Martin Luther King stated, "One who breaks an unjust law . . . to arouse the conscience of the community over its injustice, is in reality expressing the highest respect for the law."[3]

Stephen Charles Mott agrees. "Civil disobedience," he says, "seeks to bring law and morality into greater congruence, and this congruence underlies respect for the law."[4] He adds, "Civil disobedience, stepping into the breaches of constitutional order, gives justice a second chance."[5]

Civil Disobedience vs. Revolution

Civil disobedience is not ordinary lawbreaking. If you rob a bank and shoot someone, you have disobeyed civil law, but you have not done an act of "civil disobedience." Everyone knows the difference between Martin Luther King on the one hand, and Bonnie and Clyde on the other.

Civil disobedience is not revolution. Revolution is violent and sweeping in its implications. Civil disobedience is the breaking of a specific law in a context of general respect for the law. Revolution is not the attempt to change an unjust law by breaking it. Revolution is an attempt to break the government behind the law. Martin Luther King's civil disobedience did not aim for the overthrow of law. He wanted the reform of certain laws, as well as the implementation of laws which were being neglected. He sought to call the existing government to task and help it be a better government, not to replace it with another government. When civil disobedience accomplishes this end, it may actually preserve government by saving it from the judgment of God that is bound to fall upon unchecked injustice.

One Christian seminar teacher has told pastors across the country that rescuing is the same sort of activity that characterized the French Revolution.[6] The French Revolution was a violent movement of godless rebels who shed the blood of thousands of innocent people for their own benefit. Rescuing, in contrast, is a nonviolent peaceful movement of committed Christians to save innocent blood from being shed, not for the selfish benefit of the rescuers, but at their own expense. It is hard to imagine a more unfair and inaccurate comparison.

Some argue that there is no place for individuals to initiate civil disobedience. They argue against rescuing, but defend the American Revolution on the basis of Calvin's concept of lower magistrates being able to declare war on the higher magistrates when their laws become unfair and burdensome.[7]

But what do we do with all the biblical examples of individuals and small groups disobeying government? And is there not an irony in the idea that we cannot disobey our government in a specific area of evil until it becomes necessary to join the lesser magistrates in declaring war against it? Perhaps if we would selectively disobey evil laws we could exercise enough moral influence that the government would not have to become sufficiently immoral to justify revolution.

In this light, civil disobedience is not anarchy, but a selective attempt to implement a justice and compassion that society has turned its back on. A true state of anarchy exists when people are given a free hand to kill children for their own private reasons. Is it anarchy to peacefully oppose such a moral nightmare? If this is a well-ordered society, at whose expense is it well-ordered? The rescuer is not seeking to *remove* moral sanity—it has already been removed. He is seeking to help *restore* it.

John Jefferson Davis states,

> The true "disturbers of the peace" are those who have perpetuated fundamental injustices, rather than those who attempt to call attention to them, even at the risk of losing their personal freedom. In the biblical outlook, fundamental *justice* is a weightier value than the preservation of merely external order and peace.[8]

Rescuing acknowledges the purpose and legitimacy of government. It is not clandestine. It is not violent. I know of no rescuer who has turned to burglary, embezzlement, or drug-dealing because he has gotten used to breaking the law. On the contrary, rescuers are and remain model citizens, patriots, and strong contributors to the moral fiber of their communities and nation.

Civil Disobedience As an Agent to Change Laws

Though the primary purpose of rescuing is to save lives, part of its effect as a form of civil disobedience is to draw attention to the injustice of killing innocent children. This, in concert with petitions, ballot measures, elections and education, can stimulate society to consider changing the laws to once again protect the unborn. Laws that are unchallenged remain unchanged. History demonstrates that evil laws must usually be repeatedly broken by good citizens before they are changed. In 1941, U.S. Supreme Court Justice Harlan F. Stone stated, "The law itself is on trial quite as much as the case which is to be decided."[9]

I have heard Christians say, "A change of law would mean nothing. Just as many people would still get abortions." This seriously underestimates the power of law to mold thought as well as action. When slavery was abolished, people gradually began to think differently. The civil rights movement brought about further changes in law, and once the laws were in place and enforced, people really did begin to think differently. Martin Luther King said, "Morality cannot be legislated but behavior can be regulated. Judicial decrees may not change the heart, but they can restrain the heartless."[10]

Stephen Charles Mott speaks of the "educative factor" in law:

> Law . . . communicates a standard of right which can function through the

superego. Law can legitimate morality. Law also has a conditioning factor. Virtues are habits, and habits are formed by doing similar acts over a period of time. . . . One can promote public behavior by encouraging the desired values legally.[11]

The saying "You can't legislate morality" is a half-truth, and a dangerous one. Before abortion was legal in this country there were abortions, but the number skyrocketed once it was legalized. The laws that had once restrained evil now encouraged it. Daniel Callahan has said,

A change in abortion laws, from restrictive to permissive, appears—from *all data* and in *every country*—to bring forward a whole class of women who would otherwise not have wanted an abortion or felt the need for one. . . . Women can be conditioned (and are in many places) to want and feel the need for abortions. . . . Evidence from those countries where abortion-on-request has been long available (Russia, Japan, Hungary, for instance) shows that the subjectively-felt stress that leads women to seek an abortion is socially influenced. Civil law does not regenerate, but it does have power to reform. [12]

Our goal is not to legislate morality, but to have moral legislation. We must unapologetically strive for laws to protect the unborn. Rescuing can be part of this process in that it makes a strong public statement that some citizens really believe the unborn are human beings.

The Methodology of Civil Disobedience

I heard one Christian leader say that true or legitimate civil disobedience requires a public display of protest, involves total submission to all legal consequences, and requires a high likelihood of success in changing attitudes and laws. On this basis he declared rescuing did not qualify as legitimate civil disobedience. But on what grounds did he determine this definition? Perhaps from his understanding of the practices of Gandhi and King, but certainly not from Scripture.

The biblical examples of disobeying the law because of conscience demonstrate a wide variety of situations and considerations, which cannot be pigeonholed to follow exact guidelines. In many cases, for instance, civil disobedience was not public, and there was not a submission to legal consequences, because it was kept secret (e.g., the midwives, Rahab, and Obadiah). Success did not seem particularly probable with the midwives, Rahab, or Esther, and seemed humanly impossible with Daniel, his three friends and the apostles. They did what they did not merely because they were confident it would work, but because they believed it was right. The Bible neither prescribes nor prohibits organized public efforts of civil disobedience. It seems logical that what one is compelled to do based on his individual conscience may also be done on a larger scale in concert with those of the same conviction. The collective conscience of a group of Christians can be manifested in a collective way, as it was when the men of Israel together intervened to peacefully rescue Jonathan from Saul's unrighteous law that otherwise would have resulted in his death.

Rescuing has utilized some methodology similar to that employed in the civil rights movement. This includes the practice of the "sit in" or peaceful group protest at a certain location, disrupting "business as usual" when that business is violating fundamental human rights. Rescuing, however, must be judged on its own merits. It may appear to be no different than a sit-in or protest, but it may in fact be motivated by something very different. The fact that it utilizes certain methods may only indicate that coincidentally those are the necessary or most effective methods to accomplish its purpose.

One theologian condemns rescuing on this basis:

> The methodology of such demonstrations has been borrowed from non-Christian and revolutionary sources. From one end of the Bible to the other, no warrant can be found for this methodology. To use ungodly means is a way of saying that God's grace and power are insufficient resources for Christian action. It means abandoning Christ for the methods of His enemies.
>
> Such methodology can be effective, but not for the triumph of grace. When the leaders of the people wanted to force Pilate's unwilling hand, they assembled a mob to demonstrate before Pilate and to shout down all protest, screaming, "Crucify Him." (Mk 15:13)[13]

Brushing aside the hideous parallel between saving babies and calling for the murder of Christ, on what scriptural basis does the author conclude that peaceful nonviolent intervention for the innocent made by a group of Christians is ungodly? We could point out that "from one end of the Bible to the other" there is no indication that a group of Christians *cannot* act on their consciences and live our their biblical convictions in concert. In doing so they might not be "abandoning Christ" but instead be obeying him!

One Bible teacher says, "Humanism is the philosophic basis for most civil disobedience." [14] He is probably right. But humanism was not the philosophic basis for the civil disobedience condoned in Scripture, nor for most of that practiced throughout the history of the church. Just because a humanist may violate the law to save a life or defend a right does not necessarily make it humanistic or wrong for a Christian to do so. Even if one totally disagrees with India's (or America's) historical fight for independence, or with the civil rights movement, this does *not* in itself invalidate rescuing.

Does Rescuing Qualify As Civil Disobedience?

One theologian states, "Operation Rescue does not meet either the biblical or U.S. historical standards for civil disobedience."[15] As we saw earlier, the biblical standards clearly *do* allow, and in some cases may even demand, violating the law to try to save the lives of innocent human beings. Whether rescuing meets the "U.S. standards for civil disobedience" is another question. What are these standards? Who determined them? If such standards exist, in what way does rescuing not meet them? And even if it does not, what should we think if it meets the biblical standards but not the U.S. standards?

We have to be careful of the circular reasoning involved in giving civil disobedience a certain definition simply because Martin Luther King or someone else did it that way, and then saying that rescuing is wrong because it doesn't meet those "standards." Such definitions of civil disobedience are descriptive, not prescriptive. That is, they describe what some people *have* done, but cannot thereby prescribe what other people *should* do.

The same theologian states, "Because Operation Rescue *opposes* the right to abortion on demand, it differs from the civil rights movement of the 1960s, which *supported* the right of Blacks to vote and attend schools."[16] This is a purely semantical argument, without real substance. It could be said just as accurately that the civil rights movement *opposed* the right for Whites to discriminate against Blacks, whereas rescuing *supports* the rights of babies to live.

In fact, the civil rights movement, like the abolitionist movement a hundred years earlier, vehemently opposed the exercise of personal rights that much of society defended. It was solidly anti-choice when it came to this matter of racial discrimination. Whites historically had a free choice to own slaves and abuse them, and later to have segregated lunch counters if they chose to. After all, America was a free country. But the civil rights movement fought to take away that free choice from them, just as the women's movement fought to take away an employee's free choice to discriminate against women.

Every movement of oppression and exploitation—from slavery, to prostitution, to pornography, to drug dealing, to abortion—has labeled itself "pro-choice." Likewise, every movement of compassion, liberation and deliverance has been labeled "anti-choice" by the exploiters. In the cases of prostitution, pornography and drugs, it can be argued that the victim does indeed have some choice. But in the case of abortion, the victim has no choice. He is society's most glaring exception to all the high-sounding rhetoric about the right to choose when it comes to living one's own life as he pleases.

One Bible teacher says of rescuers, "Their idea of reacting to abortion as one would to any other kind of murder certainly does not have the depth or accuracy of Gandhi or King."[7] There is something disturbing about evangelical theologians and Bible teachers defending the civil disobedience of the civil rights movement, yet opposing rescuing. If it was legitimate to break the law to take away someone's choice of racial discrimination, why is it illegitimate to do so to stop someone's choice of an abortion? Is it really worse to keep someone from voting or going to a certain school, than it is to kill an innocent child? What is it about treating abortion as we would treat other life-taking that lacks "depth or accuracy" as compared to King or Ghandi?

It is compassion for the victim, not hatred for the victimizer, that motivates us. From the victim's point of view, would you rather have to go to a segregated and underfunded school, or be mercilessly hacked to pieces? I applaud the civil rights movement's emphasis on the rights of full racial equality. I highly value those rights. But I cannot consider them higher than a baby's right to live.

Is Rescuing Really against Civil Law?

The fundamental doctrines of American law are governed by such documents as the Declaration of Independence and the Constitution. This means that laws permitting and facilitating the killing of innocent unborn children are themselves essentially illegal. The Preamble to the Constitution says our republic was formed to "establish justice" and "promote the general welfare, and secure the blessings of liberty to ourselves and our posterity." Are not laws unconstitutional, therefore, if they violate justice and rob unborn children of their welfare? If rather than securing for our posterity the blessings of liberty, they result in the extermination of our posterity?

The Declaration of Independence states, "We hold these truths to be self-evident: That all men are created equal; that they are endowed by their Creator with certain unalienable rights; that among these are life, liberty, and the pursuit of happiness." All men are *created* equal, not merely born equal. The framers of these documents knew that life began in the womb, not outside it. Do these documents have any meaning to citizens forced with a choice between following them and following current civil laws which have stripped away the rights of life and liberty for innocent children? Even apart from the issue of obeying the highest law, God's Law, is it not possible to violate a civil law in order to remain true to Constitutional law?

Furthermore, a strong argument can be made that in many cases rescuing does not even violate current civil law. Many states have a "choice of evils" statute that allows a "necessity defense" to those who have supposedly broken the law. That is, there is actual legal justification for breaking a lessor law to fulfill a higher good. The law specifically allows this when a human life is in danger.

In my own state, Oregon Statute 161.200, titled the "Choice of evils," says that "conduct which would otherwise constitute an offense is justifiable and not criminal" when two conditions are met. The first is that "the conduct is necessary as an emergency measure to avoid an imminent public or private injury." The second is that "the threatened injury is of such gravity that, according to ordinary standards of intelligence and morality, the desirability and urgency of avoiding the injury clearly outweigh the desirability of avoiding the injury sought to be prevented by the statute defining the offense in issue. . . ."

The choice of evils law is intended, for example, to protect someone from being prosecuted for violating a trespass law to save a drowning child. It keeps a citizen from being guilty of "breaking and entering" when he kicks down a door to rescue people from a burning building. The threat to human life, and the immediacy of that threat, outweighs any damage caused by the trespass violation.

The issue, then, is whether in rescuing the trespasser's conduct is necessary to prevent an injury that outweighs the gravity of the trespass law and the rights it is intended to protect. The trespass law is designed to protect the human right of private property and the normal operation of business. Obviously, this is usually a good law, which is why most rescuers have never violated it for any other purpose.

But in keeping with the conditions of the ordinance, *is there an urgent human right or need at stake in this issue higher than the right of private property and business?* The answer comes down to whether or not an unborn child is in reality a human being, with worth and dignity and rights. If he is not, then the ordinance does not apply, and the "rescuer" is a lawbreaker. But *if* the unborn is indeed a human being, then the fact that this human being is about to be destroyed clearly outweighs the desirability of the trespass law. Thus, it fulfills the stated conditions of the choice of evils statute.

If taken literally, the choice of evils statute invites everyone who believes that the unborn are human beings to try to save their lives, even if this means having to break a secondary law to do so. Of course, most judges will not look at the scientific and common-sense evidence, but will fall back on previous court rulings and current popular opinion which regard the unborn as subhuman and devoid of rights. But isn't it the truth, not the judge's opinion, that is the Christian's primary concern?

There have been court cases where rescuers have used the "choice of evils" or "necessity defense" and been found innocent. For instance, a St. Louis Circuit Court Judge, in August 1989, found eleven defendants "not guilty," even though they had clearly "trespassed" and blocked access to an abortion clinic. Judge Gerhard cited a Missouri law very similar to Oregon's "choice of evils" statute, and then made a statement of which this is a part:

The overwhelming credible evidence in this case is that life begins at conception . . . This court finds that the credible evidence in these cases establishes justification for the defendants' actions. Their violations of the ordinances involved here were necessary as emergency measures to avoid the imminent private injuries of death and maiming of unborn children, which imminent deaths and maimings were occasioned through no fault of the defendants but occasioned by the operation of a lucrative commercial endeavor. The desirability of avoiding death and maiming of unborn children—persons—obviously outweighs the desirability of avoiding the injury sought to be prevented by the ordinances. The Court therefore finds the defendants [names stated] not guilty of the charges against them.[18]

Such rulings are, at this writing, uncommon, because they require a judge or jury who are willing not only to listen to the compelling evidence for the humanity of the unborn, but to acquit the defendants despite the criticism they will surely face. The fact that the courts, blinded by the "pro-choice" deception, will not often accept this defense, however, does not negate its validity. The crux of the whole issue is whether the unborn are real children.

While many Christians are arguing against the validity of breaking a trespass law to try to save those they claim to believe are human beings, it is significant and ironic that *even the state's own law says that when the lives of human beings are at stake, trespassing and other secondary offenses are in fact legally acceptable.*

The Limits of the "Choice of Evils" Defense

Having said all this, however, I do not take much consolation in the "choice of evils" law. Why? Because even if that law was not on the books, as it isn't in some states, it would not change the fundamental moral issue. If I would trespass to save a life because of the choice of evils statute, then what would I do if that statute was struck down? Or if I moved to another state that didn't have such a law? Would I then refuse to save lives? Would trespassing to save lives be right in one state and wrong ten miles away in another?

If rape was legal and I was visiting another state and saw a woman being raped, would I check around to try to find out if there was a choice of evils statute, or would I intervene to save her from being raped? The fact that over four thousand children are being killed each day may seem to no longer make it an emergency, but for each victim it is as terrifying as if he or she were the only one. The law of love tells me to intervene regardless of what civil law may say.

When all is said and done, despite the choice of evils argument, rescuing will normally be seen as civil disobedience. After all, civil law prevents tres-passing on private property, and prevents the interference with a legal busi-ness—and killing children prior to birth is a legal business.

Rescuing's Uniqueness As Civil Disobedience

Not all acts of civil disobedience can be lumped together. There are illegal nuclear protests, tax protests, environmental protests, animal rights protests, and human rights violation protests, to name but a few. Some Mormons have protested laws against polygamy through civil disobedience. For the Christian, the primary (though not exclusive) basis for evaluating any civil disobedience must be the clear and fundamental biblical rightness of the cause. Most civil disobedience is designed to make a statement, but rescuing is designed to save a life. Most civil disobedience looks down the road to eventual change, while rescuing looks at saving lives today. It is not just an attempt to state a con-viction but to implement a conviction. It is not just an attempt to say "babies are worth saving," but to save babies. It is not done primarily to procure eventual civil rights, but to act on someone's immediate right to live.

In most cases the people whose rights are being fought for will be well represented in an act of civil disobedience. Hence, it was mostly Blacks who were arrested in the civil rights movement, and mostly women who partici-pated in the suffrage marches and other women's demonstrations. In the case of rescuing, we have people who are standing for an entirely different group of people. The unborn are not in a position to defend their own cause or save their own lives.

Unlike many "protestors," rescuers are not primarily motivated by personal gain. It is not *we* who have been abused, it is not *our* rights we are standing for. No rescuers were aborted as children. In rescuing we have nothing to gain and everything to lose. In contrast, the unborn have nothing to lose and everything to gain. We do what we do to intervene and speak up for those who, though they can feel the horrible pain of abortion, cannot speak up for themselves (Prov 31:8).

10
What Really Happens at a Rescue?

We stand for those who have no voice.
Each precious child without a choice.
The will of God we must obey,
That they might see the light of day.
Chris Cowgill

No great cause ever achieved a triumph before it
furnished a certain quota to the prison population.
General William Booth

I once met with a group of pastors to discuss the issue of rescuing. Several of them made statements and asked questions that demonstrated a lack of understanding of what actually happens at a rescue. What concerned me was not that they had different opinions on rescuing, but that they *did not know the* actual facts. Therefore their evaluations of rescuing were bound to be inaccurate.

For instance, one of these pastors honestly and sincerely asked, "Instead of shouting at these pregnant women, have you ever thought of praying and singing, to show the love of Christ?" Those of us who rescue were speechless. Anyone who has ever been to one of our rescues knows that we don't shout at the women. We sign a pledge card in which we promise not to raise our voices. Even more significantly, the most central and basic components of our rescues are *praying and singing!*

Without ever having been to a rescue, this pastor assumed we didn't pray and sing. To him it was a simple matter of fact that rescuers shout at women. He needed to attend a rescue and a pre-rescue rally. This would quickly correct his misunderstanding. By attending a rally and rescue he could meet the participants and their leaders. He could talk to them if he wished, observe firsthand their attitudes and actions, and examine the covenant that the rescuers sign.

Where did these pastors get their impressions of rescuing? The media, where else? We should not miss the irony of this. These were conservative pastors, good men, sincere and well-meaning. Many of them had undoubtedly condemned from the pulpit the liberal bias of the news media. They knew that Christians are often unfairly and inaccurately portrayed as stupid, barbaric and offensive. Yet, to learn what brothers and sisters in Christ do at rescues, *they looked to the media they condemned.* Some of them had drawn their conclusions about whether rescuing is right based on the biased accounts of the pro-abortion media. As a result they may have dissuaded some of their own people from participating in, or sympathizing with, rescues.

Media Facts and Fictions

I have often been misquoted in the media. Usually, however, it has been due to carelessness rather than malice. But in abortion-related matters there is often an extreme bias. For instance, a pro-choice newspaper columnist in our area once wrote an article stating that rescuers had taken twenty people hostage at an abortion clinic. She said the rescuers held the people inside "shaking" and "crying," without food for seven hours.[1] Meanwhile the rescuers were "screaming" and "shouting" and "throwing themselves on cars." This was of great interest to me and my wife and daughters. We were at the rescue, and the story was false. These things simply did not happen. But, of course, in the minds of almost everyone—including Christians—who read our state's primary newspaper, they really did happen.

I was interviewed at one rescue by a newspaper reporter. We had talked at length, and I was pleased that all the rescuers were very calm and controlled, so he wouldn't have any grounds for a sensational story and would hopefully stick to the facts.

Later, however, one woman who was not with our group and did not come to rescue arrived on the scene and began shouting at the clinic personnel and one policeman. One of our leaders took her aside and begged her to stop. I immediately went to the same reporter and pointed out that the woman shouting was not with the group doing the rescue, and in fact we were actively trying to calm her down and get her off the premises. I specifically said, "Please don't give the impression that she's with us, because she isn't."

The article in the next morning's paper focused on this woman and her shouting and name-calling. It left the definite impression that she was not only with our group, but representative of our behavior. This isolated ten-minute incident, totally uncharacteristic of the rest of the five hours we were there, became the major focus of the story. Five hundred thousand readers would come away with a completely inaccurate impression of both the rescue and the rescuers.

A Minneapolis pastor told me of an incident at a rescue he observed firsthand. While rescuers were blocking access to an abortion clinic, news cameras arrived. A young woman then tried to make her way into the clinic and was peacefully prevented by the locked arms of the rescuers. She sobbed, right in front of the television cameras, "I'm just here for a pap smear—why won't you let me in?" Obviously, this made ideal footage to discredit rescuing.

A little while later, the pastor saw the same woman wearing one of the clinic's "escort" vests. She had been working for the abortion clinic all along! The entire drama had been staged and the woman was an actress, a phony. When the pastor pointed this out to the news crew, its members didn't care. They said, "We have our story." And they put it on the news that evening. Though they knew it was absolutely false, it served their purposes.

Why does this happen? Because the people who control the media, with some happy exceptions, are pro-choice. There are times when they do not simply report events as they actually happen. Often their reporting leaves impressions supporting their own points of view. Sometimes this is subconscious. Other times, they deliberately distort what actually happened in order to portray their own moral position as the right and intelligent one, and the pro-life position as vicious and ignorant. The degree of bias is demonstrated by the fact that the *Los Angeles Times'* editorial policy requires the use of the terms *pro-choice* and *anti-abortion,* and disallows *pro-life* or *pro-abortion.*[2] *Times* reporters have no choice but pro-choice.

It is tragic that the average Christian, even the average Christian leader, has formed conclusions about rescuing based on secondhand information. They need to actually go to the rescues and participate in the singing and praying, and see the sidewalk counselors calmly sharing the truth. They may not choose to join the rescue. Maybe they will be critical of rescuing, but at least they will have some firsthand knowledge of what they are criticizing.

This chapter provides a clearer understanding of what occurs at a rescue. It is an actual account of one rescue in which I participated. During the Friday night pre-rescue rally and the Saturday rescue I wrote down my observations and thoughts as they came. Every rescue is a bit different, but this one was fairly typical of others in which I have participated. For many readers this may be their first inside exposure to a rescue. Perhaps my account will answer some questions they have about rescues.

A Rescue Journal

The Pre-Rescue Meeting

It's the night before the rescue. I'm sitting at the meeting in an old church building. My wife Nanci and daughters Karina and Angela came with me, along with Kathy and Amy, my secretary and her nineteen-year-old daughter. There are about sixty of us here, including ten children. The lighting is poor, the PA system is ancient and scratchy. Two girls sing about the unborn. Another manually operates a slide projector, flashing powerful images to the cracked old screen up front. This is a change from my church, where the equipment is nice and most everything done in the services has a professional look. Nothing about this is slick or modern—but it doesn't matter. We're not in this to be slick or modern. We're in it to please God and try to save lives.

Most of the people are wearing blue jeans and plain clothes. There's a few teenagers, several young couples, but most of us are in our mid-thirties or early forties. There's an age gap among us. Not many here are in their late forties or fifties, but more are in their sixties or seventies.

Ron is up front leading the singing. He's Kathy's husband, Amy's dad. Ron is the friend from my church who got involved in rescuing the same time I did. Years ago we asked him and Kathy if they'd raise our daughters if we died. Their commitment to intervene for the needy on Christ's behalf has reconfirmed the rightness of that choice. Ron's also a great musician, a natural on the electric piano he's now playing. The songs he's leading are some of my favorites. "We Exalt Thee." "Bless the Lord." "Abba Father."

Now Julie, a petite blonde in her twenties, is telling us of her most recent stay in jail. She shared Christ with several women, and read her Bible with one of them. She also encouraged a pregnant inmate to get help and support in her pregnancy, rather than follow through on the abortion she'd been reluctantly planning. The girl appeared to have genuinely changed her mind—another precious life saved, and a mother saved from killing and guilt.

Julie's talking now about Joseph and how his imprisonment was used by God for good. Joseph said to his brothers, "You intended to harm me, but God intended it for good to accomplish what is now being done, the saving of many lives" (Gen 50:20). The verse applies not only to seeing God's sovereign plan but directly to what rescuing is about—the saving of lives. Julie was put in jail for trying to save lives, and in jail she was used to save more lives—physically, and hopefully spiritually as well.

This is so good for my girls to hear. They need to know that when their dad goes to jail God is in control, and will use him there to minister to others.

A pastor is up front now, sharing his impressions of a local television "face off" of pro-lifers and pro-choicers that several of us participated in last week. I was on the program also, and agree with his assessment. The moderator was fair, and the pro-life position came off well. They even showed a picture of a child whose life had been saved because Christians intervened at the abortion mill! That says it all. (And what a refreshing contrast to the usual media bias.)

Dawn, one of the rescue leaders, is reading to us from Hebrews 10:32-39. This is one of my favorite passages, about standing our ground, even when publicly exposed to insult and persecution. It talks about standing side by side with the mistreated, sympathizing with those in prison and joyfully accepting the confiscation of our property because we know we have "better and lasting possessions." With all the threats of imprisonment, larger fines and lawsuits, these are words we need to hear.

Ron is up front again, reminding us that our goal tomorrow is not to make a political statement, but to try to save lives, to buy time for the unborn and their mothers. Dawn passes out copies of the commitment to Christlike behavior. I remember a woman attending a previous meeting. She said, "I don't want to sign this card, in case the Spirit leads me to raise my voice or do something you might not consider Christlike." The leaders gently but firmly responded, "Well, if you don't sign the pledge card, we'd ask you not to come to the rescue." You need to be in top shape spiritually going into a rescue. Those who aren't right with God, those who haven't spent extra time in his presence and seeking his face, have no place in warfare this intense.

We also fill out a plain index card, so that if we're arrested they'll be able to keep track of who's been released and who hasn't.

Now it's role-play time. I'm one of six volunteers who demonstrates how to lock arms in front of the abortion clinic door and how to go limp when the police remove us from the door. After that everyone goes to a corner of the church, and this time they lock arms and several of us role-play as police officers. We drag a few people away just to get them used to it. It's really important that first-time rescuers are exposed to this, because it's so shocking when it actually happens.

We end with a powerful time of prayer. Nothing is quite so earnest as the prayers before a rescue. They are prayers from the heart, prayers of needy and nervous people, scared people who know they must find their strength in Christ. But this weakness we feel is to our advantage if properly responded to—God's power is made perfect in weakness, and his grace is sufficient for us (2 Cor 12:9). Courage is not the absence of fear, but the determination to do what is right in spite of our fears. In this time of prayer, God infuses courage into us.

Afterward the sidewalk counselors meet in one group, "crowd marshals" in another. Crowd marshals are experienced and character-qualified leaders who take charge of groups at various clinic doors. Sometimes there are six doors that have to be covered, and we want to be sure there's order, effectiveness and spiritual direction at each door. Another group of us meet to discuss our upcoming court appearances and the punitive measures we're likely to face this time. It's 8:45 now, and time to drive home, get to bed and get some rest. No matter what happens, tomorrow will be a long day.

The Rescue

Up at 4:50 A.M. This is my first day of vacation—what a way to start! I'm picking up our friend Theda at 5:30. Have to be at the meeting place by 6:00. It's raining steadily. Theda and I speculate on the way about which of the four abortion clinics we may be going to today. Each clinic brings back many memories of previous rescues, some bad, many good, all vivid.

About fifty of us have gathered now outside a downtown church. Many faces are familiar, but a dozen or so are new. The leaders give last-minute instructions, especially to those who couldn't make the meeting last night. We break up into groups of four to pray. My arms are on the shoulders of two women from our church. First rescue for one of them. She's very nervous. We all are. The prayer is deep and penetrating, sincere and from the heart. We all know that this is spiritual battle.

We've just been told where we're going. No one's told in advance, because abortionists have gotten on mailing lists and even come to rallies so they can prepare for our arrival. We pool rides and caravan from the church parking lot. People who don't know each other are already like old friends.

We drive to the parking facility near the clinic. No one's there but us at 6:30 A.M. on a Saturday. Up to the third level. I expect to wait till we get word that the abortion clinic is open. Once we waited up here two hours. But this time the clinic has already opened, the killing is starting early. We're out of the cars, down the stairs and out on the streets, about fifty of us. I move quickly to move to the front, as we go the three blocks to the clinic.

The clinic's on the ninth floor. Last time we were here the outside doors were locked before most of us could get in. We had to do our blocking on the outside entrance. That's tough, because then we have to try to screen people who are going in for legitimate reasons, haircuts and other appointments. This time we hope to get up to the ninth floor so we're blocking only the clinic.

We get in the front door. Seven of us grab the elevator. Most choose to take the steps because in the past the elevator has been shut down. This time it's

OK. We're the first ones up to floor nine, around the corner and to the clinic. It's a small office door, so I put my back to it and cover most of it myself. I'm surrounded by the other six. I hear the door locking on the inside—no need. We have no plans or desire to go inside, only to block access to the killing center. The clinic owner is in the hallway. She walks past us, but won't make eye contact. She's known for being calm, in contrast to some of the other clinic owners.

Seems like forever before the others come. Have they been cut off and forced out the building? Is it just going to be the seven of us? Not an encouraging thought. Here they come, huffing and puffing after nine flights of stairs. There are thirty of us now. We fill the narrow hallway. We can now cover a second door that also has access to the killing room. We start to sing. Stan, a brother from my church, reads a passage of Scripture. We're dressed for the cold, but it's very hot in here. Coats are coming off. It's tougher being inside than outside. You feel more vulnerable when you're away from the moral support of the singers and pray-ers and sidewalk counselors and other "nontrespassers" who are such an important part of a rescue. Also, when you're away from the public eye and there are no video cameras running, no one can see how you're being treated, so sometimes it gets rougher.

The clinic owner comes up to us. She knows we don't hurt anyone, so she's not afraid of that, but our calmness and confidence in the rightness of what we are doing unnerves her. She's different than most abortionists and clinic owners—her heart doesn't seem as hard. We pray for her often. Now she says, "I want you to understand that you're not just trespassing here. You're in violation of a court injunction that says you can't even come close to this building, much less come inside it. I can sue every one of you. In addition to putting you in jail, we can take your homes, your cars, and garnish your wages. Do you understand this?"

We nod and say nothing. No point in arguing. She knows why we're here. The statement we make by intervening for the unborn with our bodies is statement enough.

My wife actually owns my house, but these people might find a way to take it anyway. My car is twenty years and 200,000 miles old, so this is no big worry! My family and I have counted the cost of this before. I think of Hebrews 10.

I don't want to lose these things. But if I lost them in obedience to Christ, what a small loss it would be.

A Change of Plans

A surprise—one of our leaders tells us we're leaving the building to go block the outside doors after all. Apparently the clinic has a new strategy, and we won't be effective trying to block from up here. I don't understand, but I've learned to trust these leaders. They know what they're doing. Back down the elevator and out the front door.

The clinic owner is on the lobby phone as we walk out. She looks surprised, but not pleased. We immediately begin blocking the outside door. She suddenly pushes hard against the door to get out. Not necessary since we gladly move aside for anyone coming out, as well as police, building employees and anyone else (e.g., men and older women) coming in who is obviously not getting an abortion.

The clinic owner comes out and angrily says, "What if there's a fire in here?" Someone promises we'll move in case of fire. But I wonder, what if there *is* a fire? What's her point? That someone could be hurt? One thing is sure. Twenty or so human beings are scheduled to be killed in here today. Ironic that someone who kills for a living is concerned for the lives of other people just because they're bigger and older than the ones she kills every day. I don't hate her, or even dislike her. I do feel sorry for her—but even more for the mothers, and still more for the children.

As I look around at those rescuing with me I'm struck again with the diversity. We're plainly dressed. Most appear to be lower middle class. Wide age diversity, several nationalities. My back is against one of the four glass doors, so I'm looking toward the street. The girl in front of me has a beautiful voice. The brother next to me has on a "precious feet" pin, an exact replica of a ten-week-old unborn's feet. They're perfectly formed. I read that they are models of the feet of a child aborted right here in Portland.

I notice several passers-by talking with our people across the street. I can almost hear them ask, "What are these people doing?" I see their interested responses as our people share. Not only a pro-life position, but often the gospel is shared this way. I remember a few months ago at this same clinic, when a teen-age girl walked by and angrily challenged a few of us. We talked for some time. Later in the day I saw her with one of our women, blocking a door! I found out she had led her to Christ and had begun discipling her in her new faith in the five hours or so remaining in the rescue.

One of those in a support role is a local seminary professor—he's just read a psalm to us. He's a fine man. We've spoken several times since he started wrestling with this some months ago. Just a few weeks ago he and I were on a panel together, representing a "pro-rescue" position. And now I see someone else from our church who's come out to see what a rescue is about.

Tense Moments from Prior Rescues
So far it's been pretty uneventful. Usually a number of women are coming up to get abortions and the sidewalk counselors have opportunity to talk to them while we block the doors. But today the clinic has intercepted each woman and is cloistering them a few blocks away, probably to keep them from being exposed to our "subversive" influence—otherwise known as telling the truth. Presumably they will all come down together when the police create a corridor to usher them in the building. The action will all come at once then.

Most rescues haven't had any violence. At the last one, clinic personnel poured water on us from above. A few girls kept circling the block in their car, pulling over to scream obscenities at us. They shouted incredible accusations, like, "The only reason you want to save these children is so you can rape them." When their voices got hoarse and they ran out of dirty words (which took a *long* time), they came back with a carton of eggs and pelted us. I've learned from rescuing what it means to be a fool for Christ, sometimes hated and despised and scorned for trying to follow him.

Back to the present. A police wagon drives up. Are they going to arrest us this time? (They haven't the last few rescues.) A brother reads 1 Peter 3:13-17. Good reminder about being willing to suffer for what is right. There's a huge flagpole across the street. Someone leads in the pledge of allegiance. They end by saying, "With liberty and justice for all, born and unborn." Someone else leads in the "Star Spangled Banner." Ironic. These people are patriots. They would die for their country—unlike many of those who mock us and yell at us about freedom and rights. I think about how much I love my country—but I love God more. If we put the laws of our country above God's law, it will ultimately lead to the worst possible thing for our country—the devastating judgment of God.

More and more police are arriving, but they haven't started moving us yet. Seeing all these police arrive—there's about a dozen now—reminds me of one rescue where we were taken off to the police station in a bus. After dragging us all on the bus, the policeman at the front was very quiet. He cried as we sang. I wanted to talk to him, but there was no opportunity. Was this a brother in Christ who sings these songs on Sundays and was now asking himself how he could be arresting fellow believers for trying to keep babies from being killed? Was he wondering whether by arresting us he was facilitating the killing of those which, as a Christian and a rational person, he believes to be human beings? What a difficult position to be in. I prayed for him.

That time we were held just a few hours before we were booked and released. I was in a 6′ by 9′ holding cell with eighteen other men. I was literally being touched from all sides just as I was standing there. The air was thick and the room was hot. Someone joked, "Well, we've only got an hour's worth of oxygen, so we may as well die praising God!" We began singing and immediately it was like being in the throne room. The acoustics were unreal. The sound was almost deafening, but it made you want to sing louder. We sang for over half an hour.

We found out later that one of the police officers had turned up the monitor and that the whole police station was listening to us sing. One woman working at the front desk commented, "I've never heard such beautiful singing." That's another thing about rescues—you affect people you often don't even know about. Even if not a single child was saved—and usually a number are—there is influence on police, bystanders, judges, attorneys and fellow inmates.

Access to the Killing Place

More and more police. Something is about to happen. The woman next to me says she's a medical secretary for some obstetrician-gynecologists. After hearing their own descriptions of abortions they've done in their offices, she said, "I realized I couldn't stand before God, knowing what I know about abortion and not having tried to save those little lives." Once again I smile—or maybe wince—at the irony of the caricature of rescuers as "off the wall people." Some of the sanest, most down-to-earth people I've ever met are standing next to me doing this "crazy" thing—trying to save children's lives.

It's raining hard now. I'm pressed against the clinic doors, so I'm under some shelter, but some of our people are getting soaked. The seminary professor reads Psalm 34. I remember reading that at my first rescue. Never had it been so real to me—"the angel of the LORD encamps around those who fear him, and delivers them."

The clinic bouncer is getting agitated. He's a good 6′ 5″ and 280 pounds. He's supposed to be intimidating us, I guess. At $250 per abortion, they can afford to hire some muscle. Here comes the clinic owner again. She starts to read the injunction to us.

We've heard it all before. We just keep singing "Amazing Grace." She's infuriated. I don't feel smug, but grieved. I love this woman. I'll never forget seeing her several months ago, driving off with her own children, in a beautiful car paid for by the blood of other children. I'm sure she loves her kids. Maybe in some ways she's a good mom. What blindness is upon her. She is not the main enemy. She is his victim, and now his puppet. God, please cut the strings and save from the coming wrath this precious soul for whom the baby conceived in Nazareth came to die.

It's now almost nine o'clock. I put down my pen when the police started dragging us away thirty minutes ago. I remember the look of horror on a college girl from our church, watching from across the street. She'd heard that it can get rough, but couldn't believe the way bodies were being manhandled, even though no resistance was offered. She covered her eyes and the tears were flowing. The pain-compliance holds were especially tough this time. I was one of the last taken, and the officers were tired and angry by the time they got to me. One of them said, "You walk on your own or I promise you, I'll break your arm."

Like most of the others, I didn't walk—not out of belligerence or disrespect, but just to buy more time for the babies. If we all just got out of the way, it would give the moms less time to reconsider, and it would allow the children to be subjected to the knife or suction tube that much sooner. I involuntarily cried out at the pain—the worst I've felt at a rescue. Three fingers are numb. A television camera was right in my face. On TV, it may look like I was angry, but I wasn't—I was in pain.

After we were all cleared away and they created a chute, the police brought in about ten mothers with some boyfriends. We calmly said to the women such things as:

"Please let your baby live."

"Your baby has a heartbeat and brain waves."

"We will adopt or help you financially."

"God loves you and your baby."

A dozen of us, led by my friend Ron, stepped into the street to lock arms and "cap" the chute. Police pushed us from the back, clinic personnel from the front. I was thrown to the ground twice. The youthful grandmother next to me—all 100 pounds of her—was pushed so hard by a big policeman that her neck snapped back as she landed on a few of our fellow rescuers. One need not choose to be subjected to this in order to rescue. Everyone is free to make his own decisions.

It's a vulnerable feeling to be struck and to know you must not strike back. The helplessness of it all is a way of identifying with the helplessness of the unborn who is going to the slaughter. We go home and treat our scratches and bruises, and are fine a few days later. But the children are cut to pieces. That's where the identification ends. Our lives in this world go on. Theirs are snuffed out.

The mothers are inside. The officers now leave, all fourteen or so at once. Several of them are now friendly with us. One says, "I believe in what you're doing. I'm glad you're here." I think he means it, though it seems a little strange, since he was one of the roughest.

Since we weren't arrested, we reassume our position at the doors. Now it could get interesting. Sometimes the clinic escorts try to force their way through to bring in more moms and babies to the slaughter. I've even seen them use pain-compliance holds like the police. A few more mothers come up and can't get in. The sidewalk counselors are talking with them, explaining that their babies are people, showing them pictures of them at their current stage of development. We pray for these women and our counselors. We know from experience that if we weren't here blocking the doors many of them wouldn't stop to listen to the truth.

Fellow Rescuers

More singing and praying. People are starting to relax again. I notice "Doc," an eighty-four-year-old saint, who has his usual large two-sided sign in hand. One side of his sign says "Stop Murder/ Stop Abortion/ Save the Children." This is his statement to the public. But when the mothers come for their abortions, he turns the sign the other way for them: "Please let your baby live—We will help you." These aren't empty words. Many of us rescuers offer on the spot to pay the entire costs if women will only let their babies live. Then they can keep them or we will find a home for adoption, whichever they choose.

When I was on a secular radio talk show recently, a caller asked the question, "Once you rescue these babies, where are you for the next eighteen years of their lives?" The answer is often, "With these same children." The same day this question was asked me, one of our pastors and his wife had offered to adopt a rescue baby who was due within a month. Two other Christian couples also wanted the baby. Also on the same day, another of my fellow pastors at our church was adopting "unwanted" child number fifteen. At the time he had a total of eighteen children, including two with Down's Syndrome and others of a variety of races and handicaps. Then, for those who keep their babies and need help, we give housing, food, clothes, financial help, you name it.

My wife Nanci goes down to an abortion clinic every week to talk to the abortion-bound moms, and she says Doc is always there with his big sign, no matter which day. (Doc's in jail right now as I write this book, serving his tenth week with no release date in sight.) This quiet servant of God has been faithful in little, and in the kingdom he'll be put over much.

Now that we've reassembled at the doors I'm surrounded by different people. Next to me is a high-school boy in a letterman's jacket. With a neck that thick, he's got to be a football player or wrestler. I've seen him before. I ask and he tells me he's come from 300 miles away to stand with us. He says they're having their first rescue in his home town in a few weeks. He's really excited.

Some more moms come. The escorts immediately intervene and surround them, saying, "Don't listen to these people." They are right to feel threatened, because some women will choose not to get abortions when they're actually told the facts and see the pictures of the unborn. Just a few weeks ago my wife and a few others from our church were at one of the clinics. One woman they talked with read the literature. She came back the next day and told another sidewalk counselor that because of what she read she had decided to keep the baby rather than have an abortion. Praise God!

I notice one car that has circled the block several times. The young couple is just looking at us. I'm reminded again that many women won't face the confrontation at the door. And many won't be back again, but will end up having their babies. Just recently a woman told us she'd scheduled an abortion, then the night before she saw us on the news, blocking doors at the clinic. As a result she thought it through and decided to have her baby. She called to thank us!

I smile, thinking about the young couple I met the other day, a beautiful baby in their arms. Some months earlier they'd come for an abortion. They listened to a sidewalk counselor. They'd decided to let their baby live. And through the contact with Christians they'd come to a saving knowledge of Christ. Not only is the baby alive—she's growing up in a Christian home. If being part of this makes me a fanatic, it's a label I'm willing to bear!

Two women come out of the clinic now. Presumably, one's abortion is over. The rescuers are kind and gentle, and offer post-abortion counseling if she needs it. What's done is done. Now is the time to reach out and try to help.

I ask a rescuer in front of me how he got involved in all this. He said he'd heard Francis Schaeffer say years ago, "If we won't stand against abortion, we won't stand against anything." This made him decide to do something. After years of picketing, he was discouraged at the apparent lack of results, and felt like he had to do more. Rescuing was the answer.

I talk to another rescuer, a seventy-or-so gray-haired gentleman. I recognize him as one who was hit with billy clubs at an earlier rescue. I remember how concerned I felt, and how unbelievable it seemed that he was being beaten for peacefully trying to save lives. I ask him if there was any permanent damage. "Well," he says, "the old bones can't take it like they used to." But he doesn't complain.

An employee of another business in the building comes up to the door. When we're sure she's not here for an abortion, we move aside. "I'm pro-life. I'm all for what you're doing," she says. "Thanks," one of the group says. "Then could you please write a letter to the owner of the building asking him not to renew the lease to the abortionists?" She gives a blank look and a little shrug, and moves through.

Wrapping It Up

It's 11:15 now. We've been here five hours. The clinic is shut down and it's now clear there's no more appointments scheduled today. At 11:30 we gather to sing and pray one last time. We "debrief" a little, have a time of prayer and close by singing the doxology. There's a lot of hugging and handshaking afterward. The camaraderie from these rescues is so strong. Baptists, Charismatics, nondenominational evangelicals such as myself, and several Catholics. But everyone I've talked to loves Christ and is here for him. What a privilege to stand for my Lord, for the unborn, and to stand next to some of these precious saints.

Back to the parking garage. I'm feeling my blood sugar slip, and I need to stop for lunch. At a truck stop I have my first cup of coffee eight hours after waking. Theda and I discuss the day. She asks how I felt about it. From the standpoint of Christlike behavior and witnessing opportunities it was a good day, and it's always nice not to get arrested. From the standpoint of lives saved, there may not have been more than a few this time. But, then, if you or the baby you've adopted were one of the few, you'd feel it was worth it, wouldn't you?

I've been to rescues where we've shut down the clinic for the day and all killings were prevented. Not today. Blood was shed, innocent lives were taken. That's discouraging. But were we faithful to what he called us to do today? I think so. And there's no feeling better than deep inside sensing his "well done, my good and faithful servant."

When I arrive home my wife greets me with a big hug, and my two daughters are all over me. They won't let go of me, and want to know all about the rescue. My youngest says, "Daddy, we've been praying for you and the babies all day." I start crying. My heart is always more tender on a rescue day. A few lives as precious as my daughters were saved today. How could I be discouraged with that?

It wasn't an easy day, but it was a day well spent. A day invested in eternity. A day that I believe will count for something on the final day.

11
The Purposes & Results of Rescuing

It is not your purpose to succeed,
but to do right; when you have done so,
the rest lies with God.
C. S. Lewis

Rescuing is a united action in which people place their bodies in front of the entrances of an abortion clinic. The purpose is to prevent access to the clinic and thereby to save the lives of unborn children who would otherwise be killed shortly after their mothers enter the building.

Of course, mothers denied entrance still have the option of rescheduling an appointment at another time, at the same clinic or a different one. But the rescue accomplishes several vital things. First and foremost, it buys time for the unborn child. The child does not die *today*. Second, there is a good chance the child will not die at all. The mother might decide not to have an abortion, or to delay indefinitely rescheduling an abortion.

Perhaps the mother is moved or convicted by the intervention of these people. Perhaps there was something a sidewalk counselor said to her. Maybe she was touched by a picture of the unborn child, and the information about the child's development in her womb. Maybe she sees hesitations on the part of her boyfriend or mother who was with her when she was denied access to the clinic. Maybe she wonders about the motives of the clinic personnel who seem so eager for her to have an abortion. Perhaps she recognizes one of the people at the rescue who she knows to be an honest and caring person. Maybe she took seriously the offer of the rescuers to pay her medical expenses and help adopt the child. Maybe she didn't change her mind, but she just procrastinates rescheduling.

But for whatever reason, sometimes the abortion is canceled and other times indefinitely delayed. One abortionist complained that when his clinic was rescued 20 to 25 per cent of the women canceled their appointments and never came back.[1] I am told that Planned Parenthood has stated that 20 per cent of women who miss their initial appointment for an abortion, regardless of the reason, *do not come back to any clinic, and do not end up getting an abortion at all.*

Even if a woman reschedules her appointment, it might be another week or two before she can get back in. That may be enough time for something to really sink in, time to feel her baby move inside her, time to change her mind.

While many of the little ones may still be killed, the bottom line is that, because of the rescue, some innocent human lives are saved from a horrible death.

Who Are the Rescuers?

Who are these people who choose to rescue? Usually they are the most law-abiding citizens, who have never been arrested for anything else. In a society where many people cheat on their taxes, cheat on their spouses, and cheat on their employers, these people provide a strong moral model. It is their lifetime of commitment to obeying the law that makes this exception so striking.

Paul deParrie's *The Rescuers* tells the personal stories of thirteen people involved in the rescue movement—women and men, young and old, homemakers, police officers, a psychologist, a teacher—people from every walk of life.[2] The purpose is not to manufacture heroes, but to show the vastly different backgrounds out of which rescuers have come, to walk through the difficult decisions they have had to make, and to show how God has worked in and through them. The personal nature of these profiles will introduce you to a side of rescuing I cannot adequately portray in this book. They richly illustrates the warm human drama of personal intervention for the unborn.

Is Rescuing Effective?

Abortion clinics are in an awkward position. On the one hand they complain because rescuing is effective and they are losing many clients and a great deal of money. I have heard this in courtrooms where we are being sued by them for their huge losses of business due to our presence at the clinic.

On the other hand they often publicly deny that rescuing is effective, for fear they will encourage it. Clinic personnel routinely say to the media, "Every woman scheduled for an abortion today got one despite these protesters." That may be true on some days, but I have heard this said when I've known for a fact it isn't true, when anywhere from a half dozen to thirty women have left and not come back.

Some Christians, unfortunately, believe what the clinics say to the news media. They conclude that rescuing is ineffective, and that lives aren't really being saved. For instance, referring to a series of large rescues, a prominent theologian says, "It is questionable whether or not these demonstrations saved the lives of any unborn babies: the women seeking abortions simply went elsewhere."[3]

A Bible teacher, also arguing against rescuing, concedes that Proverbs 24:11 "definitely can have application to this cause, but only under one circumstance; that the trespassing activity directly rescues those being led to death when non-trespassing would not. I am not convinced that this circumstance exists."[4]

Still another Bible teacher states, "In reality very few babies are rescued, and the demonstrators are only protesting. The protesters may claim that they may stop a woman from an abortion that day, but this is a hollow claim."

These statements can be easily and objectively proven incorrect. These Christian leaders are believing exactly what the abortion clinics want them to believe. But it is simply a fact that rescuing saves lives—I've held such lives in my own arms!

Between May 1988 and May 1989 Operation Rescue, a national organization founded by Randall Terry, had 224 documented cases of babies whose lives were definitely saved through rescues.[5] This does not include lives saved in rescues unaffiliated with Operation Rescue, or the many situations impossible to follow up and document. The total number for that one-year period was almost certainly in the thousands, but even if "only" in the hundreds, isn't this still significant?

On a busy Saturday in our area there is one clinic that can do forty abortions. If a rescue closes the clinic for the day and 20 per cent do not reschedule an abortion here or elsewhere (using Planned Parenthood's figures), then that's eight lives saved. If the clinic is closed only half the day, then maybe it's four lives saved. If it's a smaller clinic or we're arrested early, maybe its "only" two lives saved.

Multiply that by six or twelve or twenty rescues a year in one area, then multiply again by over a hundred other places in the country where rescues are being regularly done.[6] The number may still be small compared to those killed, but what kind of price tag do we put on a few thousand children, a few hundred, or even a dozen? How many lives have to be saved to make lifesaving "worth it"? One life saved is certainly worth it from the point of view of the one life saved! If you or your child were one of the lives saved, would you view this as a "hollow claim"?

A friend of mine wrote this in a personal letter:

I was talking to a pastor a few weeks ago who said he was counseling a girl who just had an abortion. After much discussion and soul searching, she accepted Christ as her Savior. As she was getting ready to leave the pastor asked her, "What would you have done if you had seen people blocking the doors at the abortion clinic?" She said that when she got in her car to go to the clinic that morning, she said to herself, "If I see anyone holding a sign or any resistance at all to what I am going to do, I'll just drive past the clinic and keep the baby." Needless to say the "anyone" was not there and another little one was led to slaughter.[7]

Primary Goal, Secondary Objectives

The fundamental goal of rescuing is to obey and glorify God through attempting to save the lives of the children. Unfortunately—for whatever reasons—

many people don't seem to understand or believe this. One of the Christian leaders who doubts any babies are saved by rescuing says, "In 1988, another revolutionary ploy became the methodology of many churchmen, the demonstrations at abortion clinics designed to violate the laws of picketing and protest and ensure arrest for impeding access."[8]

Rescuing is called a *ploy,* a word with strong negative connotations, suggesting an antagonistic, contrived or even dishonest approach. Furthermore, the author thinks rescuing is merely a demonstration, that the goal is to break laws, and that rescuers actually desire to be arrested.

In actual fact, the goal of rescuing is not to break the law or to be arrested. Breaking the law is simply a side effect of accomplishing the goal to save lives. At the end of a rescue, if we have kept the clinic closed for the day and can go home without being arrested, we are absolutely delighted. We don't want to go to jail! Grandstanding is not the point. Intervening for innocent victims is.

In its statement against rescuing, the leadership of one large church says, "The real issue when properly framed is this: when, if ever, is civil disobedience an approved biblical alternative means of effecting moral, legislative, social or spiritual change?"[9]

This question assumes that the central point of rescuing is persuading society to change. But this isn't true. Rahab's main goal was not to change the laws of Jericho. Obadiah was not trying to bring Ahab and Jezebel to spiritual change. David was not trying to persuade Saul of anything by running away from him to escape murder. Sometimes the law must be broken to save an innocent life. *This* is the most fundamental issue in rescuing, not whether or not it can or will cause anyone to change.

Obeying God's Word

Scripture says, "Rescue those being led away to death; hold back those staggering toward slaughter" (Prov 24:11). "Defend the cause of the weak and fatherless; maintain the rights of the poor and oppressed. Rescue the weak and needy; deliver them from the hand of the wicked" (Ps 82:3-4). We are commanded to intervene for the fatherless and poor, those deprived of their basic human rights (Deut 10:18; 14:29; Ps 10:14; Is 1:17; 58:6-7; Jer 49:11). We are to practice the law of love (Jas 2:8). Do these passages not apply to unborn children? One author says, "Using Proverbs 24:11 the way Mr. [Randall] Terry does, Operation Rescue could sit-in to block the execution of convicted murderers who are, after all, being led to death and slaughter."[10] This misses the point, of course, because Scripture delegates to government the right and responsibility of capital punishment in the case of a convicted murderer. Proverbs 24 obviously refers to innocent people about to be wrongly killed. The issue is not intervention for guilty murderers but for innocent children.

Also objecting to using Proverbs 24 as a defense for rescuing the unborn, a pastor argues, "Every Bible student worth his salt knows that the Proverbs are occasional and don't apply to everybody in every situation. The danger every teacher must avoid with the Proverbs is the tendency to 'overextend' the proverb in application."[11]

I understand this assessment, but as a pastor who has studied and taught the Proverbs, I see an even greater danger. That danger is not that we would apply the Proverbs or the rest of Scripture too broadly, too diligently and too often, but that we would apply them too narrowly, too weakly and too seldom. If Proverbs 24:11 does not apply to the unborn facing imminent slaughter, who does it apply to? *Real* people? *Valuable* people? *Born* people?

I've heard several opponents of rescuing maintain that the true meaning of "rescue" in Proverbs 24:11 is metaphorical and spiritual rather than physical. But a careful study of the biblical usage of the original Hebrew word demonstrates this is not true. The Hebrew word *nasal* is used just over two hundred times in the Old Testament, and is often translated "deliver." The majority of the time it refers to an act of intervention to save a person or nation from actual physical enemies who are about to kill or harm them (e.g., Josh 2:13; 1 Sam 30:18). The Expository Dictionary of Bible Words states, "*Nasal* is a word that means 'to deliver or save.' It is usually used of a literal, personal deliverance from danger."[12]

In twenty-seven cases, including Proverbs 24:11, *nasal* is used as an imperative or command. It is a plea of desperation to rescue those about to be physically killed (Gen 32:11; Judg 10:15; Ps 59:1-2; 142:6-7). In one of these cases God says it is evil not to try to rescue the innocent person (Jer 21:12).

Most usages of *nasal* refer to a physical situation in which an innocent person is faced with imminent harm, often death. There is frequently a strong sense of desperation and immediacy. While some cases are figurative or "spiritual" rescues (Ps 34:4; 54:7; 56:13), the type of rescue required depends entirely on the nature of the situation. That is, if people are being "spiritually" oppressed, then they need to be spiritually rescued. But if they are in physical danger, then they need to be physically rescued.

If Proverbs 24:11 applies to all innocent people—and there is no indication it does not—then either the unborn are not innocent people, or it does in fact apply to them. If the plight of preborn children is a figurative or spiritual one, then they need to be figuratively or spiritually rescued. But the fact is their plight is physical. They are about to be physically torn to pieces. They are therefore in need of physical rescue. There is no way to spiritually rescue an unborn child about to be killed by abortion.

Most of our attempts to "rescue" the unborn, such as by influencing legislation and by crisis pregnancy counseling, are done prior to the arrival at the killing place. Technically, these are not really rescues, but pre-rescue preventative measures which, if effective, will make rescues unnecessary. Surely we will all agree it is *far* better to prevent the emergency of imminent death than to have to intervene once it occurs. However, once the child is actually about to be killed by abortion, all talk of other forms of rescue or pre-rescue becomes irrelevant. They either weren't done or they didn't work. What this child needs now is direct, lifesaving intervention.

Given the predominant use of the word *nasal* in the Old Testament, as well as the normal physical sense of "death," "staggering," and "slaughter," Proverbs 24:11 may be uncomfortable, but it is not unclear. If a murder is happening in proximity to us, and the authorities will not intervene to stop it, then we must intervene physically to save the life. It does not take a theologian to understand this clear and obvious meaning of the text.

While Proverbs 24:11-12 is quoted in reference to rescuing more than any other passage, the biblical argument for rescuing in no sense hinges on this one text. Neither does it hinge on Psalm 82:2-3, which is directly addressed to civil leaders, but has obvious application to all God's people as well. The dominant and pervasive theme of intervention can be seen by a study of passages containing words such as *rescue, help, save, defend,* and *love,* as well as *poor, weak, innocent* and *needy*. There are literally hundreds of commands to intervene for those in need, whose rights are being violated, and whose lives are in danger.*The biblical defense of rescuing is rooted in broad and central biblical themes developed in innumerable passages, not just a few isolated proof-texts.*

Identifying with the Children

While the main goal of rescuing is to obey God by saving lives about to be killed, rescuing has secondary objectives as well. These include identifying with the victims, making the public aware of the holocaust, appealing to the conscience of society, and eventually effecting change in the laws, so that once again the rights of the unborn children will be legally protected. Our actions also appeal to the consciences of abortion clinic staff. In some cases, people have been delivered from the darkness of child-killing through the influence of rescues.

Eight of my fellow rescuers in Portland were held in jail indefinitely until they would swear that they would not return to a local abortion clinic. All were held for sixty days, and four are still in jail as I write, after ninety days. One, from my church, has lost his job. None of them have been sentenced for what they did. Instead, they are being imprisoned to prevent their peaceful intervention at abortion clinics. Such treatment is not imposed upon common criminals, who are punished for what they actually have done in the past, not for what they might do in the future. This is one among many examples showing that the injustice of society against the unborn will be felt by those who intervene for the unborn. The closer to the babies the intervention comes, the more injustice it will receive.

Joan Andrews has been rescuing for many years and has spent a large part of her life in jail because of it. She makes this statement of rescuing's identification with the unborn:

> The closer we are to the preborn children, the more closely identified are we with them; the more faithful we are, we become more identically aligned with them. This is our aim. This is our goal: to wipe out the line of distinction between the preborn discriminated against and their born friends, becoming discriminated against ourselves; incurring the wrath

and enmity of the anti-child societal forces. Good! This is necessary. Why should we be treated differently?

The closer we are aligned with the preborn, the stronger the bond, the more we will be discriminated against, persecuted, rejected. The rougher it gets for us, the more we can rejoice that we are succeeding; no longer are we being treated so much as the privileged born but as the discriminated against preborn. And the gap narrows between born and preborn, as between "whole" and handicapped. We must become aligned with them completely and totally or else the double standard separating the preborn from the rest of humanity will never be eliminated. I don't want to be treated any differently from my brother, my sister. You reject him, you reject me.[13]

Joan Andrews knows what she's talking about. In a case that involved trespassing and unplugging a child-killing apparatus at an abortion clinic, the prosecution asked that Joan Andrews be given a one-year sentence. Instead, the judge imposed five years. The same day, in the same courtroom, the same judge sentenced two men convicted as accessories to murder to four years in prison.[14] Like the unborn she intervenes for, Joan Andrews is a victim of legalized injustice. Unlike them, however, Joan is still alive.

Unless the injustice of child-killing becomes embodied in the sacrifices of people that society cannot ignore, there will be no end to the deaths of the children:

The evil of slavery became intolerable because of the proximity of slavery itself to the lives and consciences of the citizenry. This proximity of victim to liberator, of injustice to justice, was not brought about so much through books and articles. It was brought about by those who in fact stood in to help the fugitive slaves, and thus the issue was raised, and thus the issue demanded resolution.[15]

Appealing to Society's Conscience

Rescuing keeps the holocaust of the unborn from being swept under the rug, both inside and outside the church. It puts the unborn child before the public eye. It raises the consciousness and pricks the conscience of the nation, community and church. It points the finger at the smoke rising from the

Auschwitzes and killing fields of our cities. It forces judges and police officers and ordinary citizens and religious leaders and church members to deal with what we do not want to deal with—innocent children are being daily slaughtered within miles of where we live.

Stalin, the master butcher who killed at least sixty million people, five times more than Hitler, said this: "One death is a tragedy. A million deaths is a statistic." The statistics have lulled us into forgetting that every number is a real human life. Rescuing reminds us of this. It forces us to deal with something we would rather deny or ignore.

In his classic, *Knowing God*, J. I. Packer sees this as part of the purpose in Daniel's civil disobedience:

> It is not that Daniel . . . was an awkward, cross-grained fellow who luxuriated in rebellion and could only be happy when he was squarely "agin" the government. It is simply that those who know their God are sensitive to situations in which God's truth and honour are being directly or tacitly jeopardized, and *rather than let the matter go by default will force the issue on men's attention and seek thereby to compel a change of heart about it—even at personal risk.*[16]

Mark Belz speaks of the effect on the national conscience of citizens illegally assisting the slaves in mid-nineteenth-century America:

> Inaction on the matter of the fugitives meant the continued bondage of black men, women, and children in great sections of the country. But that was not all. Inaction also meant bondage of the individual's conscience. It was not so much that slavery itself was burdening the consciences of the northern abolitionists. Slavery was not universal in the country. But the toleration of slavery was universal. And it was the national toleration of slavery, and indeed its universal advancement and protection by federal laws, that weighted down their consciences. The toleration of slavery, like a chain around a dog's neck, was slowly choking the conscience of the entire country. But as these few brave citizens patiently and persistently showed *de facto* solidarity with the slave, the conscience of the nation gradually became energized.[17]

Many pro-life leaders believe that our ultimate legal goal must be to adopt a constitutional amendment that once and for all declares unborn children worthy of protection. This way the fate of millions cannot be decided by the whim of a future Supreme Court or other authoritative but arbitrary group. As the fourteenth amendment came out of the overturning of the Dred Scott decision, and doomed slavery, so we need a human-life amendment that specifically protects unborn children and thereby dooms legalized abortion.

However, the rightness of rescuing cannot be judged on how effectively it changes laws alone. Those who disobeyed the slave laws and the fugitive slave act certainly wanted the unjust law to be changed. Still, their intention in any given case of disobeying that law was *not* to protest or change the law but simply to save the lives of the people the law was not protecting. It had an invaluable effect on eventual legislation, but it was lives, not laws, that were the immediate focus. Likewise, rescuing is intended to save lives in the short-term, but may also have the long-term effect of helping change laws, thereby saving many more lives in the future as well. The desire of every rescuer is to see a day in his country where civil disobedience is no longer necessary to save the children. We would be delighted never to have to rescue again.

If the President, Congress and Supreme Court, as well as local and state legislators and governors, were to sign a sworn statement that in six months abortion would be absolutely illegal, all pro-lifers would naturally be elated. Most would lay down their armor and cease their activities, for their goal would have been accomplished.

But for the following six months many pro-lifers would probably be amazed to see that rescues would continue. But *why*, when the battle has been won? Why keep fighting when the law has been changed? What would be left to protest?

Perhaps then people would believe us when we say we rescue to save lives. Because despite an eventual change in the law, the fact remains that *today*, right now, an innocent human life is about to be taken. The good Samaritan was not protesting robbery. We are not simply protesting abortion. We are trying to save innocent lives.

Other Results of Rescuing

We must not evaluate anything purely by its effectiveness on the human level. Something can be "successful" and be wrong, as it can be "unsuccessful" and be right. As Mother Theresa has reminded us, "God doesn't call us to be successful, but to be faithful."

On the other hand, we need to evaluate the fruits of rescuing. As stated before, lives are being saved and the plight of the unborn is receiving unprecedented national attention. But there are other significant effects as well.

Increased Pro-life Activities

One theologian maintains that as a result of rescuing, "Not surprisingly, peaceful, legal action is being neglected."[18]

I believe this assessment is completely inaccurate. I have never seen more legal efforts to stop abortion than in recent years, and rescuing has been a major catalyst to this in many lives. Rescuing has not generated less prayer, personal intervention and political action, but far more. When it comes to legal pro-life action, most of the rescuers I know are on the front lines.

More pro-life people now than ever before call and write legislators, speak out at public forums, support pro-life candidates, run for political office, and picket abortion clinics and hospitals. They give money to pro-life groups, and donate office space, materials, goods and services. They write letters to the editor, put advertisements in the paper, call in and speak up on talk shows, and talk to their friends about alternatives to abortion.

More and more Christians are refusing any indirect or business support of abortion mills, and are boycotting pro-abortion companies. More than ever before wear pro-life symbols and use pro-life bumper stickers. (There is a case where a baby's life was saved because the abortion-bound mom saw a bumper sticker.) More are volunteering at Crisis Pregnancy Centers and are sidewalk counseling outside abortion clinics. More open their homes to pregnant girls, and to an "unwanted" child through adoption or foster care. Six years ago, however, the picture was not so encouraging. It was evident to many of us that the pro-life movement, while very much alive, was growing weary and discouraged. Annual pro-life marches and abortion protests in our area were smaller than in the past, and pro-life efforts were increasingly being seen as token expressions. Of course, many faithful people remained diligent over the years, but numbers and energy were waning.

When rescuing gained public attention in 1987 and 1988, through the large

Operation Rescue interventions, this served to rejuvenate a sagging pro-life movement. Even those pro-life organizations that are not supportive of rescuing have benefited from the renewed interest in saving the unborn children.

For instance, one church concludes its statement of strong opposition to rescuing by saying, "We do, however, with new energy and vigor commit ourselves to use every measure that we believe to be consistent with Scripture to end the holocaust of abortion in America."[19] This "new energy and vigor" was inspired by rescuing, even though those inspired actually oppose it. This significant "coattail effect" has been obvious in our area. Many who would not picket or sidewalk counsel even a year ago have been stretched into doing such things. These activities used to be viewed as extreme and fanatical. Now, compared to rescuing, they seem reasonable and almost conservative. The largest gatherings of pro-lifers in Portland have been organized around the unjust treatment of rescuers and the concentrated media coverage of rescues. One nonrescuing pro-life leader told me, "Rescuing has been the beachhead of pro-life activity in Portland. It has been the catalyst we need to finally wake up and mobilize the churches."

Increased Evangelism

I have shared the gospel at rescues with people I never would have met otherwise. I saw one girl come to Christ at a rescue, and know of others who have. When people see you standing up for what you believe, those with hard hearts resent you. But those whose hearts are being softened by God's Spirit are interested and will genuinely listen. They will often be open not just when you talk about the unborn, but when you talk about Christ.

One of the most fertile fields in rescuing has been the "jail ministry." Many rescuers have found that jail ministry is more effective when you're in jail with the people you're ministering to! One pastor in Atlanta spent twenty-one days in jail for rescuing, and while there led twelve inmates to Christ. I've personally been able to share the gospel with inmates and police officers in jail. In a recent jail term for Portland rescuers, fifteen people came to Christ, and others recommitted their lives. Seeds of Christian witness were planted in literally hundreds of lives. As Paul and Silas led the Philippian jailer to Christ, many men and women have come to the Lord through the testimonies of those arrested in rescues.

Impact on Police, Judges and Other Authorities

Many of those in authority become irritated and angry with those who rescue. However, many others are genuinely touched. While few judges have ruled in favor of rescuers, many have given light sentences, understanding not only the sincerity but the moral rightness of the rescuers. I stood before a judge who said, "I want you to know I defend your right to do what you did. No one knows what I think on this issue. For all I know some day I may join you down there at the clinic. Today I'm a judge and I have to mete out the consequences, but I still believe you were within your rights."

One district attorney in New York said that neither he nor anyone on his staff would prosecute rescuers because, in his words, abortion is "a grievous wrong," and the rescuers' actions were "justified."[20]

When rescuing I have seen police officers angry and sometimes, frankly, mean. But I have also seen them kind, gentle and sympathetic. I have seen police officers search their hearts and examine their consciences about the issues of rescuing. I watched one cry as we sang "Great Is Thy Faithfulness." I have heard them say they are in favor of what we are doing.

At one rescue, the abortionist "doctor" had swung a baseball bat at some rescuers near a back door to the clinic, hitting one of them in the knee. Every once in a while a police officer would come back and ask me, with genuine concern, "Are you OK back here?" It was encouraging to have an officer protecting us from the crazed abortionist rather than dragging us away from protecting the babies from this same man!

Once after I defended myself in court, I was approached by a police officer who had arrested me at the rescue. He shook my hand and told me he wanted me to know that he respected my beliefs and my willingness to act on them. While in jail, one police officer told me he thought what I was doing was right. He had heard that I was an insulin-dependent diabetic, and he sought me out and asked if he could do anything to help me.

Officer Chet Gallagher took a courageous stand by not only refusing to arrest rescuers at a Las Vegas abortion clinic, but *actually joining them in blocking access to the clinic.* It was not a spur-of-the-moment action, but carefully thought through in advance. "I had determined, after much investigation, that real babies were dying," Gallagher stated. "I didn't go there as part of my religious or political beliefs. Even an officer with no real religious convictions should not arrest rescuers—should even stand with them—because it is their sworn responsibility to protect human life."[21]

Family Growth

Ironically, many Christians criticize rescuing because it is hard on the family of the rescuer. Of course, in one sense this is true—rescuing and its consequences are stressful. This must be weighed by anyone deciding to rescue. But nothing is so good for children than to see their parents acting on their biblical convictions at personal cost. What were sterile Sunday-school stories become living realities. Dad and Mom are showing they really believe these things they've taught the children about justice and mercy and the value of the unborn children. My secretary's husband has been in jail three months for rescuing. She and her children are fully supportive of their husband and father. They speak often of God's grace and the positive effects on their family.

My wife has become involved in sidewalk counseling at abortion clinics. My daughters regularly pray for her. They have stood and listened and prayed as she has shared the gospel outside an abortion clinic. Once I joined hands with our daughters to pray for their mom as she talked with a pregnant woman during a rescue.

The day before I was going to jail, our family had our own little service at home. We looked at several passages. My youngest daughter, then eight, shared that she had been reading Psalm 7:1-2 and thought it was a good reminder of why "we" should be rescuing the children. Though I am the only family member who currently violates the law, rescuing is a family ministry in which each of us has a vital role.

Personal Spiritual Growth

Every person I know who has become involved in rescuing has grown spiritually. The decision to rescue is difficult and by our standards the personal costs are great. The one who makes such a choice steps out in faith, and is thrown unto Christ to depend on him for strength and encouragement. Every rescuer finds deeper meaning than ever in the Scriptures that speak of God as rock and fortress and rescuer. Passages that seemed distant or irrelevant before now come alive (e.g., Heb. 10:32-36). There is an acute awareness of the reality of spiritual warfare and the power of prayer.

The rescuer is reminded that this world is not the real home. This is not the true country. We are ambassadors representing another King (2 Cor 5:20). We are aliens and strangers in this world (1 Pet 2:11). Our citizenship is in heaven, from which we await our Savior (Phil 3:20). Faced with the possible loss of money and possessions, and in some cases jobs, material things take on another perspective.

Rescuers often learn courage and boldness while rescuing. This affects the way they share their faith. It strengthens their ability to stand up for what is right in other areas of life. They learn, perhaps for the first time, the cost and the rewards of discipleship. They also begin to feel a sense of solidarity and oneness with Christians who, in standing for their faith, faced difficult circumstances. Rescuers stand not only for today's unborn, but for their own children and grandchildren. They have not forgotten the price paid for their own welfare by godly people of the past.

Rescuing forces Christians to come to terms with whom they are trying to please in this life. They come to understand the words of Paul, "If I were still trying to please men, I would not be a servant of Christ" (Gal 1:10). As we stand in the courts of earth before human judges, we are reminded that we will some day stand in the court of heaven before a higher Judge. We are reminded that in that day it will be *his* verdict on our lives, and no other, that will matter.

12
Concerns about the Rescue Movement

It is a great poverty that a child must die
that I may live as I wish.
Mother Theresa

*I*n this chapter I will respond to criticisms of the rescue movement, some of which I believe to be valid, some not. I will also express some concerns of my own. While I believe in the legitimacy of civil disobedience to save the unborn, this by no means justifies all methods or attitudes that may go into rescuing at a particular place and time. The rescue movement needs continuous healthy self-examination and constructive criticism to become an increasingly effective instrument of intervention on Christ's behalf.

This chapter focuses on concerns regarding the rescue movement itself. The following two chapters respond to theological, social and personal arguments against rescuing.

Rescuing and Randall Terry
Rescuing was practiced on a small scale in the 1970s.[1] But it came to prom-

inence with the national organization Operation Rescue, founded by Randall Terry in October 1986.[2]

The first large Operation Rescue was November 28, 1987, where nearly three hundred people blocked access to an abortion clinic in Cherry Hill, New Jersey, near Philadelphia. The May 1988 New York City rescue was another milestone, but the rescues that captured the most attention were those in Atlanta in August 1988. For a better understanding of the history, philosophy and goals of Operation Rescue I recommend Randall Terry's book, *Operation Rescue*.[3]

Since he was the catalyst behind the spread of the rescue movement, it isn't surprising that some rescuing critics have objected to Randall Terry and his leadership style.[4] Prior to 1990, the secular media and sometimes the Christian media tended to inaccurately portray rescuers as the cult of Randall Terry. Dynamic and controversial, Terry was the major human catalyst to the rescue movement, but it is not *his* movement, as he himself has been quick to say.

Randall Terry has been criticized for being too young, too dogmatic, too blunt, too cocky, and too reactionary.[5] He is seen by some as too antagonistic, not only to people who are pro-choice and to the media, but to anti-rescuing church leaders. Some of these criticisms are unfair, some may be partially accurate, but all must be put in perspective.

Randall Terry is not a diplomat. He is a prophet. Prophets are imperfect people, just like everyone else, but their imperfections become more obvious due to their bold uncompromising leadership style. Elijah, John the Baptist and Martin Luther were all prophets, not diplomats. Prophets are often admired after they die, but very few of a prophet's contemporaries are ever comfortable with him at the time.

At times I have deeply appreciated Randall Terry's words and actions. At other times his approach has not set well with me. Nonetheless, I believe there is a critical need for his bold, prophetic approach, to awaken church and society to the reality of child-killing. The pro-life movement and the evangelical church as a whole has plenty of diplomatic spokesmen. We may not like what our prophets say to us, but we need their hot blood and piercing words to move us to biblical response.

Rightness must be determined on its own merit. No one should favor rescuing because they like Randall Terry; no one should oppose it because they don't. Randall Terry is not, and never has been, the issue in rescuing. Neither is any other rescue leader.

Nevertheless, for the sake of Christ and the children, leaders in the rescue movement need to take seriously the criticisms of their attitudes and methodology (Prov 15:22, 31-33). It is a reasonable expectation for rescuers and rescue leaders to be listened to by evangelical leaders. Therefore, they should set the example by listening themselves.

Behavior at Rescues

In our area the loud and angry behavior of one woman (not a rescuer, but an outspoken pro-life activist) has resulted in many pro-lifers fearing to join any gathering where she is or may be present. Though this woman is genuinely concerned for the lives of the unborn, she is keeping others from intervening for them. She is thereby indirectly contributing to their destruction.

If rescuing saves lives, and having more rescuers will mean more lives saved, then actions that turn others away from rescuing will result in fewer saved lives. Some people congratulate themselves that they have stood boldly and without compromise, when a little moderation and common sense would have solicited participation that would save the lives of more children.

It only takes one person shouting, pushing, name-calling or struggling with a police officer to put a cloud over a rescue. We would never say evangelism is wrong because someone shouted or pushed someone to whom he was witnessing. But people will naturally judge the rightness of rescuing by how well the people doing it behave.

I have determined that I will not stop rescuing simply because some rescuer occasionally responds with human emotions. This *is* an emotional issue. Sometimes the intensity of the situation will result in words or actions I am uncomfortable with. However, this must not be made into an excuse. Rescuers must diligently seek to be self-controlled and Spirit controlled. If they are not, then they are responsible for the bad impressions of rescuing left with others.

For this reason, most rescue groups have given careful attention to developing standards of behavior. The group I rescue with has printed guidelines which are reviewed carefully before a rescue and enforced during it. Among them are these:

Please don't talk with or shout at the police, passers-by, abortion-mill personnel or anyone else. *Violators will be asked to leave if it becomes a problem.*

Always walk, do not run. Ignore hecklers.

Do not lock arms or hold on to each other if police are arresting. Never block access to police.

We are not at war with the police, abortionists, escorts or hecklers. All our actions go back to the primary goal of saving babies' lives and mothers from being exploited. We must keep focused on our goal of serving the Lord. *This is not the place to enact any "personal agenda" one may have.*[6]

In addition, before participating in a rescue with this group, every person must sign the following pledge:

I pledge to be Christlike in my behavior and to cooperate with the leaders, spirit and goals set forth by Advocates for Life. I will remain peaceful and nonviolent in word and deed during all the activities associated with the rescue.

Having prayerfully considered this pledge, I sign it with the determination to fulfill it as an obligation before God.

Single-Issue Christians?

One pastor maintains, "In Operation Rescue I see a lot of single-issue Christians . . ."[7] A church position paper says, "This [abortion] is only one issue. There will be others equally as offensive to our Christian convictions."[8]

It is certainly true that baby-killing is not the only issue. In addition to the primary fact that people need to know Christ as their Savior, there is world hunger, poverty, war, the ghettos, economic and social injustice, drugs, alcoholism, and a myriad of other moral, spiritual and social issues. There are innumerable problems we must face, and many other ministries in which we must be involved. In a letter to my own church I said,

Pro-life issues are not the only issues in the Christian life! Many Christians are called to other ministries that are just as legitimate and essential as trying to save the lives of babies.

Furthermore, rescuing is only one part of the pro-life movement. Certain ones of our church body will focus on certain pro-life ministries, others on ministries unrelated to pro-life, but the overall balance of ministries requires that not everyone tries to do everything. God has gifted and called people to *differing* ministries. Recognizing this unites the body rather than dividing it. (1 Cor 12:14-31)

Though not the only important issue, it is possible for one issue to raise itself above others at a particular place and time in history. In South Africa that issue is apartheid, and the church there must be excused for focusing on this issue. If they did not rise to the occasion, they would not be the salt and light Christ called them to be. In the middle of the last century, slavery was not the only issue facing the American church and society, but certainly it was a central one. In occupied Europe there were many problems, but the Jews' right to live was obviously a paramount concern. Most churches, tragically, failed to address this issue because they had "other pressing concerns."

The dying unborn are one such central issue of our time. Is it not appropriate that some of us in Christ's body, even many of us, devote extra time and energy to intervening for the unborn, in all the traditional and legal ways, as well as in rescuing?

Though the rhetoric of the rescue movement may sometimes leave that impression, are most rescuers really "single-issue Christians"? In my experience, the answer is no. Though doing so is risky, let me use my family as an example. Above and beyond our regular giving to our local church, we give a significant portion of our monthly income to foreign missions. Another portion goes to feeding the hungry in the name of Christ. In fact, much more goes for both of these purposes than for "pro-life" causes.

To be honest, the greatest burden of myself and my family is not rescuing but foreign missions, and relief work in particular. Our concern for the unborn is real, but it is no greater than our concern for the unsaved and the unfed. Our pro-life interests are neither exclusive nor myopic. When I examine my schedule, I find that only five to eight hours of my week are devoted to pro-life concerns. To those who question the legitimacy of this, of course, it will seem like much more. Those who label us "single-issue Christians" usually do so on the basis of our more visible and controversial actions for the unborn. But they do not see the other dimensions of our lives and ministry that are far more quiet *and* more time-consuming.

Furthermore, a person can devote a great deal of effort to one part of the whole without losing sight of the whole. I have been impressed with the fact that many missionaries home on furlough become vitally involved in the cause of the unborn children. Chuck Colson devotes most of his time to prison ministry. But anyone who has read his books could never accuse him of being a single-issue Christian. One can see many legitimate needs and ministry opportunities, then choose to focus on one of them while still maintaining a vital concern for others. Even full time pro-life workers should not be, and often aren't, single-issue people. Pro-lifers and rescuers can focus their efforts on intervening for the preborn without losing sight of the fact that there are many other legitimate and critical ministries besides their own.

The Need for Patience

One pastor says rescuers "are impatient with people who want to examine the Bible to see if it indeed does justify that kind of activity."[9] This is sometimes true. Rescuers must remember that there is natural resistance to civil disobedience. I was once skeptical of rescuing. Why should I not expect others to be? Where, five years ago, were all the people who are now impatient with those who don't support rescuing?

In some parts of the country a number of pastors are involved in rescuing. In my part of the country, as I write, very few are. I am concerned at the impatience some rescuers have displayed in regard to pastors. "Why don't more pastors get involved in rescuing?" The question is easy for me to answer. Most of us pastors are constantly bombarded by people and ministries who want us to take on their agendas as our own. Pastors can't be involved in everything, no matter how worthy. Rescuers need to be patient with their pastors, pray for them, and request to meet with them to humbly share their thinking and sincerely ask their advice.

Above all, pastors should not be put in the binary trap of thinking they either have to rescue or come up with some reason to oppose rescuing. They *can* genuinely support rescuing and encourage their people who rescue without necessarily rescuing themselves. They can also be supportive of missions and encourage others to go to the mission field without doing it themselves. In my experience, most pastors will not be pushed into rescuing or even into being supportive of rescuing. They must be pulled, not pushed, by the positive and sensitive examples of people they respect.

A common problem in the rescue movement has been the fact that the heated rhetoric and forceful drawing of lines has pushed Christian leaders into hasty evaluations. These evaluations are often not well thought through, but once made, they subsequently feel obligated to defend them. Many criticisms of rescuing, including some of those cited in this book, are defensive and reactionary in nature. They show clear signs of being hastily formulated, with unclear and contradictory sentences. At times they appear to be the proverbial straws grasped at by those who are offended by certain people pushing a certain position on them. If taken to mean what they say, the position papers of some churches would require that churches no longer support missionaries in China, the Middle East and other parts of the world where civil disobedience is a daily necessity.

Some of the greatest resistance to rescuing is found in the very cities targeted for large rescues by Operation Rescue. Pastors in these cities have had to take a public position on rescuing in a short time. They have felt pressured to take a stand, then feel obligated to defend their position. They may end up mustering every argument they can, including unbiblical and illogical ones. Once the initial position is taken, there is the matter of face-saving. The more one has argued for a certain position, the more embarrassed he would be to back down from it. Even if it is incorrect or unbalanced. This is as true of rescuers as anti-rescuers. One's vested interests in his initial position become greater and greater with time.

Whenever possible, rescue groups should work closely, positively and humbly with local church leaders to avoid lines being drawn and defensive positions being taken.

Harsh Criticisms of Those against Rescuing

One Operation Rescue publication, excellent in many respects, accuses the church of being willing to purchase its tax-deductible status at the expense of permitting murderous doctors to kill babies.[10] It also speaks of the church "paying homage to a new deity, the state." While this may indeed be true of some, it is an unfair caricature of many who honestly don't know whether rescuing is right, or honestly believe it is wrong. Is everyone who does not rescue a coward or a state-worshipper? I'm sure that's not the intention of this literature, but that's the impression it could easily leave.

When one Atlanta church issued a statement criticizing civil disobedience in general and Operation Rescue in particular, some rescue leaders publicly accused it of "siding with the baby-killers." I agree that the church's statement was flawed, and the consequences of the statement were unfortunate, but the intention was not to defend abortion or those who commit it. Though I strongly disagree with their conclusion, I believe it is important not to impugn the motives of fellow Christians who are sincerely trying to deal with an issue.

A popular seminar speaker who argues against rescuing is similarly said to have "sided with the murderers." I understand the point, and no one disagrees with the seminar speaker's conclusions more than I do. However, he is committed to Christ and the Scriptures, and is genuinely pro-life.

It is not the rescue leaders' criticism per se, but only the inflammatory language to which I object. This seminar speaker, who has an unusual degree of influence, has spoken to pastors at seminars across the nation, and has probably talked hundreds, perhaps thousands of pastors into a position against rescuing, based on his unbalanced and inaccurate presentation. This may mean that these pastors in turn have discouraged hundreds of thousands of Christians who otherwise might have intervened at the clinics for the unborn. It is therefore understandable that rescue leaders will feel he has done great damage to the cause of the unborn. Still, we have to choose our words carefully when we criticize our brothers, especially in public.

On the one hand, we have to allow people the right to become emotional over the slaughter of the unborn. Something is wrong with us if we can discuss this matter with a total calm and coolness that forgets the dying babies. On the other hand, we need to graciously encourage and challenge each other to reexamine our positions in light of God's Word.

I have heard unwholesome, unhelpful and unedifying talk leveled by anti-rescuers against rescuers, and rescuers against anti-rescuers. I have also seen bitterness, anger, slander and malice in Christians on both sides of the issue.

This is in direct violation of Ephesians 4:29-32. According to this passage, such behavior grieves the Holy Spirit of God. The appropriate attitude is not arrogance and aloofness, but repentance.

Noncooperation and Deception

One of the criticisms of rescuing which must be taken seriously is the occasional practice of refusing to give names to police. I have never participated in a rescue where this was done. I understand the motives behind this practice, primarily the symbolic identification of the rescuer with the anonymous "Baby Doe" unborn being killed. But I believe rescuers must ask if this practice directly or essentially relates to intervention for the unborn. Is the antagonism and misunderstanding this practice generates worth the statement being made, or has the real purpose already been accomplished in the rescuing itself? Despite his support for rescuing, Charles Colson objects to the practice of withholding names, and I must concur.[11]

On the other hand, I cannot say that I believe Joan Andrews, for instance, has been wrong in her courageous identification with the unborn, even though it has involved a policy of passive noncooperation in the courtroom and in prison. It has cost her years of imprisonment, much of it in solitary confinement, and I believe God has greatly used her integrity and commitment. I do think, however, that for most of us in the rescue movement, the best course is full cooperation with the authorities once we are removed from the rescue site and can no longer help the dying babies that day.

A reasonable exception to this principle of cooperation following arrest is the matter of paying fines. If all rescuers paid all fines, the fines would simply be increased to the point of bankrupting people out of life savings. In some cities rescuers have been threatened with $25,000 fines for a single rescue. If everyone pays fines, it only encourages larger fines, motivating the legal system to make bigger and bigger profits from inflicting greater punishments on rescuers. This, in turn, means more babies dying.

Furthermore, many judges recognize the legitimacy of choosing jail time rather than paying a fine. Hence, one is still accepting the ultimate legal consequences, even if he does not choose to pay a fine. In some cases fines have been awarded directly to abortion clinics, creating a very serious question of conscience. Is it right to voluntarily turn over money to a child-killing center?

Another issue that rescue leaders must carefully think through is the matter of making false appointments at abortion clinics and using similar means to accomplish the ends of rescuing. I am not saying this is always wrong. After all, the midwives and Rahab and others deceived the enemies of the innocent, and were still approved by God. The Christians of the Underground Railroad, the Warsaw Ghetto, and others necessarily used deception to save precious lives. Secrecy and deception, such as in Bible smuggling and illegal church meetings, are common and necessary practices for Christians in China, the Middle East and other parts of the world.

I realize that we are involved in a type of warfare and that "intelligence gathering" is commonly part of such warfare. Still, we must seek to determine when deception is absolutely necessary and when it is not. We must not get caught up in a game of covert activities that undermines the simplicity of faithful intervention for the unborn.

At the same time, if we are to rescue, then surely we should try to do so wisely. Does it make sense to show up and rescue at a clinic that might not be open that day anyway, when on the other side of town there is a clinic killing thirty babies? This can be determined by trying to make an appointment at several clinics, or using other means to get inside information. Obviously the abortion clinics will not knowingly volunteer this information to rescuers. But in any case, we must examine our hearts and seek to be as wise as serpents, without losing the innocence of doves.

Pressuring Rescuers

I believe rescue leaders should make sure rescuers are not pressured into conforming to certain practices that may violate their consciences. Some rescuers, understanding the "buy time for the babies" logic, nevertheless feel that going limp unnecessarily antagonizes police officers. Some do not feel right about crawling under police barricades to place themselves back in front of the clinics after they have been removed but not arrested. Some believe they should pay all fines. Others are concerned that they will lose their jobs or that their family needs them at home right now, and feel that on certain occasions they must pay their fines to avoid jail.

It is my conviction that every Christian who chooses to rescue must make these decisions for himself. Though seeking advice is appropriate, he should not be pressured into doing anything he thinks may be wrong.

One of the main reasons some rescuers are lost to the movement is not because they are unwilling to rescue, but because they don't feel good about a certain element of rescuing. Personally, I would encourage all people to do whatever they believe they can do in good conscience on behalf of the unborn. If this means sidewalk counseling but not picketing, or picketing but not rescuing, or rescuing but not going limp, or if it means paying fines or whatever it means, God bless anyone who is willing on any terms to peacefully intervene for the unborn children.

Distracted by Peripheral Issues

Most rescue literature and oratory emphasizes that obeying God and trying to save lives is the central purpose of rescuing. Unfortunately, however, I have noticed that some rescuers subtly move away from this to other things. They start to focus on the jails, the fines, the courts, the lawsuits, police brutality, the media coverage, and any number of secondary issues. Some may even use rescuing as an avenue to promote their particular convictions about minor doctrinal matters or other issues. If rescuing is to maintain its focus and integrity, rescuers must resolutely keep their focus on Christ and the children.

I get concerned when I hear too much talk about clogging up the courts, creating social tension, and using the media to draw attention to rescuing. Though these things can in their own way result in the long-term saving of lives, they can also become ends in themselves. God doesn't command us to clog the system or to create social tension. He *does* command us to glorify him by defending the cause of the weak and fatherless, and delivering them from the hand of the wicked. We must never forget that this is what rescuing is all about.

Rescuers must also avoid focusing on their past experiences in rescuing. Though the camaraderie naturally runs deep, there is a soberness, a sense of tragedy, attached to rescuing. The tragedy is not only the babies, but that we have had to resort to civil disobedience to rescue them. We must not take this lightly or give the impression that we are taking it lightly, and neither must we ever focus on our personal achievements. We are the Master's lowliest servants, God's errand boys, no less and no more. I appreciate Randall Terry's reminder in this regard. He said, "There are no heroes in the rescue movement—we're all fifteen years too late."

Facing Off with Abortionists
One of the most uncomfortable and controversial aspects of the rescue movement is the direct confrontation with abortionists that takes place at the clinics. Most pro-life activities are done at a distance from the place the children are being killed. Rescuing's "face off" with the abortionist is objected to by some evangelicals. For instance, a well-known Christian leader states, "Abortion clinics are being singled out as the primary offenders by those who are advocating civil disobedience. Great animosity is being generated toward these 'Murder Mills' and toward the doctors who are performing the murders."[12]

I have heard several people say: "We must never forget that the abortionist is not our enemy." If by this we mean the *ultimate* enemy, then of course this is true. Only Satan qualifies for that title (1 Pet 5:8). But in any normal sense of the term *enemy*, is the abortionist *an* enemy? I believe the answer is yes. He is certainly the enemy of the child. He may feel no malice toward the child, but anyone who is about to destroy someone else is surely functioning as his enemy. He is not the child's only enemy, but right now he is the one who has the authority, knowledge, license and intention to kill him or her.

Furthermore, there are enemies of God, and abortionists are certainly among them (Phil 3:18; Heb 10:27; Ps 5:6). They are specifically cursed by God, for Scripture places a curse on anyone who profits through slaying an innocent person (Deut 27:25). One of the seven things God says he hates is "hands that shed innocent blood" (Prov 6:17-18). Christ died for everyone, including the abortionist, but this should not mislead us into thinking God does not feel animosity toward the abortionist.

In the evangelical church today there is a serious misunderstanding about whether Christians have enemies. The Bible does *not* tell us we don't have enemies. It specifically says we *will* have enemies. We must have them if we are faithful to Christ (Mt 10:36; Lk 1:71, 74; Rom 12:20). But the Bible says we are to *love* our enemies and we are to *pray* for them (Mt 5:44; Lk 6:27, 35). We cannot love and pray for enemies unless we have enemies.

Over eighty times in the Psalms alone we are told about the enemies of the righteous. These are human beings who oppose God's people, curse them, mock them, resist their righteous efforts, and who even seek to take their lives. The abortionist is functioning as the enemy of the child and the enemy of God. If we are on the side of the child and the side of God, then the abortionist must also be *our* enemy. We are to love him and pray for him and seek to win him to Christ. But we should not forget that battle lines have been drawn, not by us, but by God on the one hand and by the abortionist on the other.

Our hesitancy to regard the abortionist as our enemy was not at all shared by the American Medical Society a century ago. The AMA publicly compared abortionists to Herod, the child-killer, and Judas, who betrayed God's son for thirty pieces of silver. They called abortionists "monsters" and men of "corrupt souls," a "blight" on society and a "shame" to the medical profession. What follows is a portion of the AMA's official position on abortionists, issued in 1871. It reminds us how desensitized to this "profession" we have become:

... There we shall discover an enemy in the camp; there we shall witness as hideous a view of moral deformity as the evil spirit could present. There we shall find a class of men ... who seek not to save, but to destroy; men known not only to the profession, but to the public, as abortionists. ... Yes, it is false brethren we have most to fear; men who are false to their profession, false to principle, false to honor, false to humanity, false to God.

"Thou shalt not kill." This commandment is given to all, and applies to all without exception. ... notwithstanding all this, we see in our midst a class of men, regardless of all principle, regardless of all honor, who daily destroy that fair fabric of God's creation; who daily pull down what he has built up; who act in antagonism to that profession of which they claim to be members. ...

... it matters not at what state of development his victim may have arrived—it matters not how small or how apparently insignificant it may be—it is a murder, a foul, unprovoked murder; and its blood, like the blood of Abel, will cry from earth to Heaven for vengeance.

We have no foreign enemy to contend with, but we have a domestic enemy, and that enemy is in our midst . . . an enemy to the human family, as dark and as malignant as the spirit that sent it.[13]

I recently heard a former abortion clinic owner, now a follower of Christ, speak about Christians standing outside her clinic. At the time she hated it. But she said that God used it to change her thinking. A pro-choice newspaper reports, "Under siege from protestors and largely isolated from medical colleagues, doctors who perform abortions say they are being heavily stigmatized, and fewer and fewer doctors are willing to enter the field."[14] The article states that in some areas "abortion services" are no longer offered because being an abortionist is no longer as lucrative or socially acceptable due to "protesting" at the clinics.

Rescuers should love abortionists, pray for them, and reach out to them. We should never view them as beyond the reach of God's grace. I recently had the joy of rescuing alongside a former abortionist, who told me, "One day I looked at one of the babies I had killed and I suddenly came to my senses." I know four former abortionists who are now pro-life Christians. Three of them actually owned abortion clinics, and three have now participated in rescues.

In this chapter I have agreed with some criticisms of the rescue movement. However, I do not believe anyone should apologize for going directly to the abortion clinics to save the babies. Nor should we apologize for any side-effect of drawing attention to the evil the abortionist is doing. It is an evil against God, against society and against our most vulnerable children.

Imperfect Efforts Are Better than None

D. L. Moody was frequently criticized for his evangelistic techniques. Pointing out that at least people were coming to Christ rather than dying in their sins, Moody stated, *"I like the way I do it better than the way you don't do it."* Some who criticize rescuing are active in saving the lives of the unborn. Many, however, are not. To those latter critics I would say this: "I like the way rescuers do it better than the way you don't do it."

I often hear critics of rescuing question the motives of rescuers. I will grant that maybe 10 per cent of those involved in the rescue movement are rescuing with wrong motives. But even if it were 50 per cent—and I'm sure it's not—this would still not invalidate rescuing. People often have wrong motives for doing the right things. This includes prayer, evangelism, Bible study and helping the poor. The question is not whether rescuing is ever done with wrong motives, but whether rescuing is ever a right thing to do.

Even in the worst case scenario, we should consider rescuing from the victim's point of view. If I was drowning, I for one would rather be rescued by a guilt-ridden fanatic than be watched drown by a group of well-motivated and emotionally healthy bystanders.

There are few things in life that I have weighed more heavily and prayerfully than my decision to rescue. I have determined to not just make the decision once for all, but to reevaluate it each time to make sure I am convinced God is in it. I know many others who take it equally seriously and continually reevaluate their motives.

For those who know better ways than rescuing, I can only say, "Do them, and show us the better way. Show us how the children dying today can be saved more effectively than through our methods." If I can be shown this, I will gladly quit rescuing today and devote my energies to the better way. Until then, I will continue to rescue, not out of stubbornness, but out of loving desperation for the dying little ones.

Conclusion

I believe that rescuing is a viable, legitimate and biblically justifiable Christian activity. But this does not mean that every rescue is done well, every method is right, or that every rescuer is in submission to the Holy Spirit. Rescuing needs to be continually reexamined and "fine tuned." Rescuers must check their attitudes, reexamine their methodology, and prayerfully ask Christ's wisdom and direction. We must always look for the better way to save these innocent lives today. If we find such a way we should gratefully embrace it, and abandon "rescuing" in favor of the better way to rescue the unborn.

Regardless of our position on rescuing, we need more understanding, more openness, more prayer, more Scripture-searching and more soul-searching. We also need less caricature, less accusation, and less name-calling of our brothers and sisters in Christ who love him, respect his Word, and desire to help his unborn children.

When Peter asked the Lord his plans for the apostle John, Jesus said, ". . . what is that to you? *You* must follow me" (Jn 21:21-22). All of us, whether or not we choose to rescue, must focus on God's calling in our own lives, and trust God and our brothers to work in theirs. "Who are you to judge someone else's servant? To his own master he stands or falls. And he will stand, for the Lord is able to make him stand" (Rom 14:4).

We must pray for each other, talk to each other, lovingly try to persuade each other of what we believe is biblically right. But in the final analysis, we must leave God to call our brothers where it pleases him. No matter what others believe or don't believe, no matter what others choose to do or don't do, the Lord says to each of us, *"You* must follow me."

13
Biblical & Theological Arguments against Rescuing

My conscience I have from God
and cannot give to Caesar.
John Milton

Many arguments against civil disobedience in general and rescuing in particular have surfaced in the last few years. If, as I believe, there is a place for civil disobedience to rescue the unborn, then these arguments demand an adequate response. Some of them have been dealt with already in the course of this book. I will try to address the others in this and the following chapter.

I want to emphasize that I have great respect for most of those pastors, Bible teachers and others whose arguments I will address. Though I disagree with them, I do not want to be perceived as criticizing them as persons or impugning their motives. They have stepped boldly into the public forum to state their objections to rescuing. My desire is simply to respond to those objections in what I believe is a biblical and sensible way.

"Third Parties Aren't Responsible"

We dealt earlier with the question of whether the government is mandating believers to sin by commanding them not to interfere with child-killing. Beneath this question is the issue of responsibility for situations in which someone is not directly involved. A Bible teacher argues, "No one is being commanded to have an abortion that would require them to break the law by refusing. The trespassers are all third parties to the situation and not directly involved in any dictate."[1]

Another rescuing critic says,

> We are considering what should be our response to how others (the doctor and the pregnant woman) respond to that legal permission, not how we would respond to that same permission. It is our indirect response, as third parties, that we are looking into here.... How a person responds by noncompliance to a direct legal edict that directly affects him as the primary participant is a different issue from how a person should react to another person or persons opting to take advantage of a legal permission.[2]

Notice that this argument recognizes the existence of a first and second party, the abortionist and the mother, and the third party, the Christian wondering what to do about abortion. Significantly, it completely ignores the *fourth* party, who is really the primary party, the one who has everything at stake—the innocent victim about to die. Though the author prefaces his critique with the statement, "I do believe absolutely that abortion is the murder of an unborn person," the fact is that in his entire treatment of the issue he never once takes that unborn person's welfare into consideration.

This "third party" mentality suggests to us that child-killing is none of our business. Many Europeans believed that Jew-killing was none of their business, and many Americans of the last century believed that slave-holding was none of their business.

Furthermore, no mention is made of Obadiah, Jehosheba, the men of Israel, Esther, and others who were third parties and not directly commanded to do evil. They stepped into situations which were legally none of their business, to intervene to save lives. Though they were merely "third parties," these people felt morally obligated to intervene.

The reasoning reflected in the third-party argument misses an entire dimension of biblical and moral responsibility. Do I fulfill my responsibility to the poor just by not stealing their food? Do I fulfill my responsibility to love my wife simply by not beating her up? Do I fulfill my responsibility to the innocent unborn children just by not killing them myself? Have we forgotten that omitting right actions can be just as sinful as committing wrong ones? (Jas 4:17).

God says to "third parties" not directly involved in hurting others: "rescue from the hand of his oppressor the one who has been robbed, or my wrath will break out and burn like fire because of the evil you have done—burn with no one to quench it" (Jer 21:12). Notice that the "evil you have done" is the fact that they did not rescue the innocent. It is not good enough that we do not oppress someone in need. We must rescue him from the oppression of others.

"We're Not Accountable for Pagan Children"

Speaking against rescuing, one seminar leader argues that God holds us accountable for how we treat our own children, not how others treat theirs. "God did not tell the parents of Moses to start a crusade against the slaughter of innocent children. He held them accountable only for the lives of the children He had given them."[3]

If we see our next-door neighbor beating his children to death, are we forbidden to intervene, or are we *compelled* to intervene? Will God really hold us accountable only for how we treat our own children, and not for the child whose cries we turn our backs on? And is there something bad about "a crusade against the slaughter of innocent children"? God also did not tell Moses' parents to start a crusade to oppose child abuse or feed hungry children or help the handicapped, but can we thereby conclude that these things are not worth doing?

One pastor questions our "responsibility to pagan women who sacrifice their children" and wonders about "our responsibility to the unborn children of pagan women." He asks, "Should *our* wives and children be sacrificed (when we go to jail or worse) to save *their* children? I think not." After saying it is our business to preach and teach against abortion, he adds, "But as far as putting my wife and children at risk to keep a pagan woman from sacrificing her child, I believe that's going too far."[4]

An extension of this argument is made by still another pastor who questions whether we are to "indiscriminately" rescue babies, in light of such acts of divine judgment as "Noah's flood, which drowned unborn babies, and Sodom and Gomorrah, in which unborn babies were burned up by God." "What," he asks, "are the implication of these facts for our *indiscriminate* attempts to save babies?"[5]

I frankly find the we/they distinctions of these arguments to be frightening in their implications. Is the sanctity of human life limited to the sanctity of *Christian* lives? Shall we punish the children of "pagan women" for their parents' unbelief by failing to intervene for them? And if this is really their argument, would these pastors allow rescuing in the case of saving a child of Christians? If we led a woman to Christ outside an abortion clinic, would we suddenly have an obligation to intervene for her child's life that we did not have a few moments earlier?

The pastor's comparison is invalid when we look at the risks to the rescuer's family in contrast to the absolute certainty of the child's horrible death apart from intervention at the clinic. Yes, one's family will suffer inconvenience, anxiety, perhaps even some financial burden from rescuing. But this is hardly comparable to the certain slaughter facing the child if no one stands between his mother and the clinic door.

I suppose the good Samaritan had a family, and the delay in his journey may have caused them great anxiety. Perhaps he had promised to buy a badly needed table or oil lamp, but now he couldn't because the money was indiscriminately spent to rescue some stranger. What effect did this have on the family when they found out what he had done? Hopefully, it had the effect of modeling for them what it means to love your neighbor, even at personal cost.

"God Allows Children to Die—Why Shouldn't We?"

"God condemned child sacrifice in the Old Testament. God's prophets boldly condemned it. But he didn't ask the Israelites to do rescues in the pagan temples of the surrounding nations."[6] Mark Belz addresses this argument:

This objection also assumes facts not in evidence. There is no biblical data informing us of the Israelites' failure to intervene on behalf of Canaanite babies being sacrificed in the fires of Molech; there is no record of God's affirmation of their failure to intervene; there is no mention of the proximity of the infant human sacrifices to the homes of the Israelites. We do not know if there were twenty-three or twenty-three million babies killed in this way. A theology of nonintervention should not be constructed on such sparse evidence. By contrast . . . there is an abundance of Scriptural evidence concerning the duty of Christians to preserve and protect the lives of others—"others" being all those made in the image of God.[7]

An argument against "indiscriminate" rescuing I quoted earlier cited examples of children dying in judgment along with adults. The Old Testament does indeed give examples when God in his sovereignty judged people, and certain children died in the process. But nowhere are we told to draw our own conclusions about when this is happening and to decide not to intervene because of it. One layman asks,

> Can any reasonable person argue that we should do nothing when our neighbor sheds the blood of his child because, in the past, God has shed blood, too? This, to my mind, would be ludicrous. There is a vast difference between my sinful, selfish, depraved neighbor and the holy, righteous omniscient God who is the only one who has the authority to say who will die and when they will die. I would say that until we receive direct revelation from God to the contrary we should identify with God's heart by caring for and protecting little ones as precious, fragile beings made in the image of God.[8]

One pastor told me, "When you read your Bible you see that God is not always pro-life." He could prove his point from some of these passages where God takes human life. But what is the bottom line of such reasoning? What is its proper application to the unborn children? Are we saying that God is killing these children and we are not to intervene? Is such a posture trusting in his sovereignty or is it avoiding our responsibility?

One theologian's assessment of rescuing boils down to this: "If we place saving babies above obedience to God, we wind up doing neither the born nor the unborn any good, and we separate ourselves from God."[9] Isn't it revealing that saving the lives of innocent babies is set in contrast to "obedience to God." When I read the Scriptures it appears to me that saving innocent lives created by God is thoroughly compatible with obedience to God! It is also hard to argue that "saving babies" does no good for the unborn, since they are the ones saved.

When someone pointed out to a rescuer that "saving a life is not God's highest priority" and "God is more concerned with the quality of life than just life and breath being preserved," this was his response:

> I agree. The saving of physical life is not God's highest priority. But it *is* important to Him. I dare say if someone were murdering my child the last thing that would come to my mind would be the fact that God has higher priorities than my child's physical life. Although God does have higher priorities, this is no argument against our involvement in things of less priority but still very important to Him.
>
> In answer to God being more concerned with the quality of life ... there is *absolutely no quality of life* at all if the life is killed. I agree that God is concerned with more than just existence in this world, and we should be more concerned with a person than just that he is alive. However, can't we be concerned with *both*? God is.[10]

Some argue against rescuing on the basis that abortion has been directly sent by God as a form of judgment. "Abortion is a curse—God's curse—on our ungodly society. Most people fear God's judgment in the future as a result of the widespread practice of abortion in our land. This is a mistake. Abortion *is* the judgment."[11]

What are the intended implications of saying that abortion is God's judgment? That we should not be trying to stop it lest we oppose God? That we should not try to save lives, legally or illegally, because God may have appointed them for death?

While God obviously has allowed abortion, I believe it originates with Satan, the murderer, from the beginning. It is his attempt to retaliate against God and man. Because little children are particularly precious to God and are stamped with his image, abortion is Satan's attempt to kill God in effigy. It is the Devil's desperate and malevolent effort to reach from the very heart of hell, to strike out at God. It was Satan, not God, who was behind the horrors of child sacrifice in the Old Testament. It is Satan, not God, who is behind the horrors of child-killing today. And it is God, not Satan, who calls upon his people to intervene and save these precious lives.

"God Has a Sovereign Plan in Abortion"

Speaking against civil disobedience to save lives, one seminar teacher uses this example: "Joseph was unjustly held captive. How different the account would have been if some well-meaning abolitionist had convinced him to run away and return home!"[12] This also has some frightening implications. Of course God used Joseph's situation—he always does. He uses cancer for his purposes—but does this mean we would not give someone a cure for cancer if we had one? God uses pain—but would we withhold a pain reliever from someone in agony?

What does this teacher mean by "some well-meaning abolitionist"? Is he suggesting that the slaves weren't really so bad off, and the abolitionists just should have minded their own business? Is he saying God's real desire for the slaves was to continue to live in slavery, to continue to be beaten and have their wives and children beaten and raped at the whim of their masters? The obvious implication is that the abolitionist was "well-meaning" but *misguided.* Shall we conclude the same of the well meaning (but misguided) Rahab and the well-meaning (but misguided) Obadiah?

Whether God can use a bad thing for his purposes has no bearing on whether we should try to prevent the bad thing if he's told us to do so. Were abolitionists really not to intervene for the slaves? Are we not to intervene for the unborn? If everything, good or bad, is going according to God's plan, why intervene for anyone at all, legally or otherwise?

It is certainly convenient to appeal to God's sovereignty when the cost of intervention is great. But is it biblical and right to do so?

"Babies Will Go to Heaven Anyway"

One church's statement against rescuing reassures us that " . . . the death of the children will not alter the sovereign plan of God. The testimony of David was that he would see his dead infant son (2 Sam 12:16-23) and Jesus spoke of children taking part in His Kingdom (Mt 19:13-14)."[13]

Ah, now we can feel relieved. Abortion really isn't so bad for the babies.

I have actually been told, "Don't you believe babies go to heaven when they die? That means they're better off anyway. In fact, if you 'rescue' them, they may grow up to be non-Christians who go to hell. Dying now is probably the best thing for them."

What are the implications of this approach? If it is sound logic for opposing rescuing, it also must apply to legal attempts at life-saving. Why write letters, vote, or counsel pregnant women not to have abortions? Indeed, why not actively *encourage* abortions if they are really in the best interests of the children?

Shall we kill our own children in their sleep so that they will go to heaven? Otherwise they will grow up, pass "the age of accountability" (a term not used in Scripture) and possibly go to hell. If a believer is about to be killed in cold blood shall we passively let him die? If we see a Christian friend about to fall off a one-hundred-foot cliff to a certain death, shall we let him fall so he can be better off in heaven?

If one's eternal destination is all that matters, why should we feed the hungry, clothe the naked and meet the material needs of people? Perhaps we could justify keeping pagans alive just long enough to see them come to Christ, but that's it. Then we could just let them die so they could leave their miserable existence here on earth. Why keep believers alive when they'd be better off if we let them die and go to heaven? Apparently Jesus doesn't follow the "let them die and go to heaven" logic. In fact, he puts even greater stress on meeting the material needs of fellow believers, those going to heaven, than he does on those whose current eternal destiny is hell (Mt 25:34-40; Gal 6:10).

Where is our compassion to save the child from the agonizing pain of abortion? I emphatically agree that life in this world is not our ultimate focus, but it *is* a life that God values, that he gives, and that he alone has the right to take. And it is a life for which God has told us to actively intervene, not to passively stand by while it is brutally taken away.

"Rescuing Is Impulsive and Impatient"

"There is an increasing and unhealthy thirst for immediate results among pro-life activists. . . . this is a symptom of the modern mentality of immediate gratification, rather than God's ideal of patient faith. We may have to wait generations."[14]

I agree we must be patient. At the same time, we must be sure it is a patience accompanied by diligent and prayerful action. The church in Germany might have said, "We must be patient with this Jewish problem. We may have to wait generations." They waited less than a generation. But meanwhile six million Jews and perhaps five million others had paid the price for their waiting. One does not stand on the shore and say of drowning children, "If we are just patient, they won't be drowning much longer."

Is every act of civil disobedience an act of impatience, stemming from a "mentality of immediate gratification"? Were Rahab and Obadiah guilty of impatience when they intervened *at the moment* to save the lives of God's people?

As long as we are intervening for the children in every peaceful way we know how, then we must indeed wait patiently on God. But we must not mistake indifference for trust, or inaction for patience. There is a sense in which the church has been notoriously "patient" with the killing of children.

Since our government receives its just powers from the consent of the governed, we must ask, "What are we willing to consent to?" Are we willing to consent to the killing of four thousand innocent human beings each day? Are we willing to consent to being told we cannot and must not intervene to try to save innocent preborn children from slaughter? Mark Belz says this:

> It is to be expected that good citizens will be putting up some kind of fuss where an atrocity is being carried out. When part of a healthy body is infected, antibodies rush to the scene. There will be soreness and swelling. There will be, that is, if the body's immune systems are working. We should not be surprised if there is a showdown in front of the abortion clinic. Rather, we should be very concerned about the health of the country if in such a situation good people remain perfectly quiet and well-ordered. But in America, thank God, it is becoming evident that you cannot kill babies without someone trying to stop you.[15]

"If Rescuing Is Urgent, Then Why Not Rescue Every Day?"
I have been asked, "If you believe rescuing is right, why aren't you down there

doing it every day?" This is a fair question.

I believe the ideal is that every abortion clinic in America would have Christians standing in front of it each day. This is not an impossible task. If 200,000 people nationwide, less than 1 per cent of those who profess to be believers—and only a tiny portion of those who believe abortion is murder—were each rescuing once a week, this could be done. There are more than a hundred Christian churches in the greater Portland area where I live. There are only four abortion clinics, which account for the great majority of abortions in our entire state. If only eight people from each church rescued once a week (or thirty from each church rescued once a month), there would be about forty people in front of *each* of the four clinics *every* "working day," more than enough to prevent the killings. Because of the increased numbers the adverse consequences would be reduced, being spread out and dissipated among the many, rather than focused so heavily on the few.

I realize some people would still get abortions, in private doctor's offices and other places. But the fact is that huge numbers of lives would be saved, perhaps thousands each day, and society would have to, for the first time, take seriously the scientific facts and moral implications of the humanity of the unborn.

"If these are dying babies, shouldn't you be out there every day?" Yes, I believe *someone* should be, but not always the same people. The problem is that while rescuing is important, it is not the only thing God calls me to do, nor is it the only important thing. I must also work for a living. I must pray, share my faith, preach, teach, counsel, study, write, spend quality time with my family, develop relationships with my neighbors, minister to the poor, do chores and sometimes even relax. I am not making excuses. I am simply acknowledging the fact that God does not call me to do just one thing, no matter how vital that thing may be. If I rescued every day, how could I justify my neglect of my other God-given responsibilities?

Isn't it more consistent to try to save some lives, even if you can't save them all, than not to try to save any?

Perhaps we can understand this better by comparing it to evangelism, something which *all* of us are commanded to do. People are dying without Christ every moment. So why aren't all of us out there witnessing every moment of the day? Of course, some of us aren't witnessing at all, simply because we are disobedient to God and lack compassion for the unsaved. But let's talk about obedient Christians. Why aren't *they* witnessing every hour of every day? Because while God calls us to witness he also calls us to do other things, including eat, sleep, work, read the Bible, intervene for the poor, and raise a family. None of this changes the urgency of the fact that people are dying without Christ and desperately need to hear the gospel.

Fortunately, however, there are good life-saving alternatives to rescuing every day. Even where numbers are so limited that rescues can only be done once a month at a single clinic, throughout the week sidewalk counselors can be at each clinic each day. They can interact with women getting pregnancy tests and give one last chance—often the first chance—for those coming for an abortion. Except where court injunctions have created no-access zones in front of clinics, sidewalk counseling is perfectly legal. In fact, counselors can stand on the perimeter of the forbidden zones and still talk to most of the abortion-bound mothers. Because they are not arrested, prosecuted, jailed or sued, they can spend their ministry time right at the clinics. Others can join them, holding signs that offer help and support.

If only one hundred Christians in the greater Portland area of one million people, an average of one from each church, devoted just one half day a week to sidewalk counseling, every clinic in the entire area would have two people legally intervening for the babies and the women all day every day. Sidewalk counseling is not enough, because most women will move on by to kill their children. Still, it is a lot—some babies are saved from death, women are saved from abortions, and the gospel is shared with the lost.

"Preaching and Prayer Are All We Need"

"Preaching the gospel is sufficient to change all things. It does no good to look for physical solutions, such things as demonstrations or planned civil rebellion. Preaching is sufficient."[16]

Preaching the gospel certainly is necessary, but it is *not* sufficient. Our words ring hollow when they are unaccompanied by loving actions. Faith without deeds is dead (Jas 2:26). Words without action are hypocrisy. What we do—and what we *don't* do—for the unborn speaks so loudly no one hears a word we are saying.

Teaching the truth about the unborn children is important and can be effective. Just yesterday, as I write, a woman came up to me with her beautiful newborn baby and said, "I thought you'd like to see a result of your message last January." Seven months earlier I had preached about the unborn, and the mother had decided not to have an abortion.

I am absolutely committed to the preaching of the gospel, which I believe includes teaching people to obey *all* that Jesus commands us (Mt 28:20). But what kind of a gospel are we preaching? Does it or does it not involve loving God and loving your neighbor as yourself? Is it a gospel that focuses exclusively on inner spiritual experience? Or is it a gospel that also intervenes for others, bringing them compassion and justice in the name of Christ?

"Instead [of rescuing], God instructs Christians to pray for those who are in authority, that they might be saved."[17] I fully agree with the statement that God instructs us to pray. But the Bible does not say to pray "instead" of intervening for the helpless. Why are action and prayer presented as two conflicting alternatives? Are they not both important, both appropriate, both essential, both specifically commanded in Scripture? If I knew my child was about to be killed in a certain place, would I start preaching? Would I get down on my knees to pray? No, I would pray fervently *as I took action* to intervene for my child. Prayer *and* action, not prayer *instead* of action.

Arguing against rescuing one pastor asks, "Why not do some really radical stuff like forty days of fasting? . . . Why not prayer?"[18] Once again we see a lack of awareness of what goes into rescuing. Prayer is not inhibited by rescuing. On the contrary, in the fourteen years I have been a pastor *I have never seen as much prayer go into any Christian event or ministry as goes into a rescue.* It is literally bathed in prayer weeks in advance, the night before, and throughout the day of the rescue. This is followed by more prayer for those who were met and spoken with at the rescue. Not only do rescuers pray throughout the day, but there are special teams of people who come to the rescue and do nothing but pray, not to mention the many people praying at home. Prayer is the very lifeblood of rescuing. Many rescuers practice fasting as well (though I admit this pastor's suggestion of forty days exceeds most of our averages). Can we not pray, fast *and* love our littlest neighbor by intervening directly to save him from death?

One rescuing critic says, "The abortion epidemic is not a purely political problem and the real solution is not to be found in political action, nor in the action of the high court. The real problem is moral and spiritual and the solution is repentance."[19]

I could not agree more with the fact that the real problem is moral and spiritual and the solution is repentance. But I see absolutely no incompatibility between such a belief and a commitment to personal intervention on behalf of the needy and victimized. We should certainly pray for rapists to repent. But is it really spiritual to wait for rapists to repent as an alternative to intervening to save victims from rape? As for our repenting, can't we repent down at the abortion clinic while trying to save innocent lives? Or can repentance only take place in the sterile safety of our homes and churches?

"Rescuing Distracts from the Main Thing"

A Christian friend told me, "Abortion is politics. All this stuff about rescuing gets us off on rabbit-trails and puts the focus on secondary issues."

Is it politics to save a drowning child? Was it politics for the Samaritan to save the half-dead man, or for the men of Israel to save Jonathan, or Esther to save the Jews? Just because abortion has become the center of political controversy and political action we must not lose sight of the bottom line— *the victim.* The slaves and the Jews were not just political issues, they were people. The lives of innocent babies must be viewed as more than a political rabbit-trail.

I was talking with a full-time Christian worker who expressed the concern that rescuing was distracting Christians from "the main thing." I asked her what she thought "the main thing" was. "Evangelism," she replied. Interestingly, in an earlier conversation the same day she had confided in me that she rarely shared her faith with anyone. I couldn't resist pointing out to her that she was in no danger of being distracted from the main thing by rescuing, since by her own admission she was not doing the main thing in the first place.

Rescuing has opened up tremendous evangelistic opportunities, far more than I would have by staying home from rescuing. Rather than distracting me from evangelism, it has been a catalyst to it. This is true of many others as well. I know of a recent rescue where three pro-abortionists were led to Christ.

The day after the largest abortion clinic in Oregon filed suit against me and twenty-two others, my wife was there at the clinic as a sidewalk counselor. She had been praying specifically for the manager of the clinic. That day she talked with him for about an hour, sharing the gospel in detail. He seemed genuinely attentive, asked questions and opened up about his personal spiritual struggles. Opportunities to share the gospel with pregnant women, bystanders and others are common in pro-life activities.

Furthermore, there is often a faulty assumption in our definition of "the main thing." Certainly speaking the gospel is central, but we must also *live* the gospel. In Matthew 25 Christ makes a distinction that puts eternal destinies in the balance. The distinction is based on what one has actually done for the weak and needy. One cannot read this sobering passage and conclude that intervening for the needy is a *peripheral* issue! It is not some fringe or secondary concern that distracts us from our "real business." On the contrary, it is at the heart of a truly Christian faith.

Jesus said the main thing was loving God and loving our neighbor. *Rescuing is not a diversion from the main thing, but an extension of it.* "Vigorous and systematic social involvement requires not that Christians weaken the structure of their piety but rather that they carry it through to its natural social consequences."[20]

Many of the most evangelistically oriented Christians of all time were also on the cutting edge of social action. John Wesley encouraged mine workers to unite in order to resist the inhuman treatment their employers gave them. Wesley was also active in opposing slavery. Evangelist Charles Finney had a major role in the illegal Underground Railroad. D. L. Moody opened homes for underprivileged girls, rescuing them from hopelessness and exploitation. Charles Spurgeon built seventeen homes to help care for elderly women, and a large school to provide education for hundreds of children. Spurgeon and his church built homes for orphans in London, rescuing them from starvation and vice on the streets. Amy Carmichael intervened for the sexually exploited girls of India, rescuing them from prostitution in the temples. She built for them homes, a school and a hospital.[21]

Wesley, Finney, Moody, Spurgeon and Carmichael are all known for their focus on "the main thing" of winning souls to Christ. Yet all five of them were *deeply* involved in intervening for the needy, weak and socially oppressed. They saw no contradiction, but an essential connection between evangelism and need-meeting love. Perhaps the effectiveness of their evangelism was due to the fact that they lived out the gospel that they preached.

"We Can't Prevent Every Sin"

In a personal note to me a godly brother and good friend states that, logically, if we are to disobey the state in intervening to stop abortions, "we must also recognize that legalized divorce, pornography, homosexuality, fornication, atheism, polytheism, astrology, New Age Humanism, ad infinitum, must also invoke an explicit response by Christians to disobey the state."

One pastor told me that abortion is no worse than other destructive sins, including alcoholism and sexual immorality. So why don't we break the law to keep people from committing those sins too? Another pastor and Bible teacher stated on his radio program,

So what you're doing is disobeying governmental law in an effort to stop an individual from committing a sin. Now how far are you going to carry that? . . . *are you going to stop all the other sinners from sinning?* Are you going to go lie down in front of the bars—going to lie down in front of the X-rated movies? Are you going to go to any place where sin might occur and lie all over the building?[22]

The elders of this pastor's church have issued a statement that says,

If we are going to prevent sinners from sinning, we have a lot of work to do. We need to prevent people from going into bars and gay bathhouses. We need to prevent parents who are abusing their children. We even need to prevent some people from watching television! . . . We cannot be selective in our prevention of any of God's laws being broken.[23]

But these arguments simply don't hold up under analysis. Who among us would feel we have to prevent people from watching the television programs of their choice? Or that we would enter private homes and try to prevent partners who are choosing to commit sexual immorality? No one, I trust. But would we feel we should prevent a man from raping the woman of his choice?

Would we try to stop someone from beating and robbing the elderly man of his choice? Or from killing the person of his choice? Things like rape and assault and murder are entirely different matters, because *the issue is not someone's private sinful behavior but whether an innocent person is victimized, and even whether he lives or dies.*

The men in the gay bar consent to their act of immorality. The woman being raped, the elderly gentleman being beaten and robbed, and the baby being killed by abortion are *victims!* Can't we see the difference between stopping all sin and trying to save innocent victims?

If my child was about to be abducted, my purpose in intervening would not be to prevent the sin of kidnapping, but simply to protect the life of my child. If saving a life results in "stopping sin" then this is a byproduct, not the purpose.

One pastor told me, "Drunk driving is a sin that kills people too. Should we 'directly intervene' to keep drunk drivers off the road?" My answer is yes, to the degree that we know someone is drunk and is putting lives in jeopardy by choosing to drive. If necessary, we might even take the car keys away from someone who is liable to kill people once he gets on the highway. That's probably illegal, since it's a free country. But if it was your wife and children he hit head on, you'd wish someone had taken his keys. So would he. There's another important difference, though. Drunk driving *sometimes* results in death, but often it doesn't. Abortion *always* results in death—no exceptions. Furthermore, I don't know where all the drunk drivers are, or when and where their victims will be killed. But I do know exactly where and when the unborn children will be killed.

Comparing abortion to private sinful habits and preferences is comparing apples and oranges. Watching bad television programs is not an equivalent to abortion. Using a proper equivalent, let's repeat the question asked by the radio preacher: "Where is it going to stop—are we going to try to stop men from raping women?" When we make an accurate comparison, then the answer is obvious—*yes, of course we are.* Why? Because rape does direct, immediate and severe harm to an innocent person. The same is true of abortion. Someone may say, "But that's different, rape is illegal." So? If it were legalized, would that change the issue? Legal rape is rape. Legal murder is murder. It is not the legality or illegality of rape or murder that makes it what it is, but the nature of the crime itself.

No one recovers from murder. There are no therapy groups for people who have been murdered. Murder is not an "ordinary sin" that inflicts harm on self, or even that inflicts "recoverable" harm on others. It is final and irreversible. It cannot be undone. After abortion a woman can be healed, but a baby cannot be. Yes, abortion *is* different from most sins—it is the innocent baby who makes it different and justifies unusual efforts.

"Rescuing Is Post-Millennial"

A Bible teacher concludes his verbal critique of rescuing by saying this on his radio program:

This [rescuing] is a bigger issue than just that. This is the issue—the church of Jesus Christ has lost its vision of the Second Coming. The new thing is not we're waiting for the coming of Christ. The new thing is we're going to make America Christian. This is our utopia. And we have traded in our historical pre-millennialism for a post-millennialism.... Listen, that is the dominating new doctrine—post-millennialism. The world is going to get better and better. We're going to get Christian senators, Christian presidents, Christian judges, Christian everything and we're going to get Christian laws.

... We're going to get a Christian nation. This is what's called dominion theology, kingdom theology, reconstruction theology, liberation theology—it's coming in a lot of forms. But that's what this [rescuing] is all about. It's all about forcing the government of the United States to bow the knee to Christianity so that we can have Christian laws and Christian leaders and Christian this and Christian that.

It's the new wave, I think, that is born out of a comfortable indulgent lifestyle that really isn't that interested in heaven. So if we're going to have our kingdom now, let's force it to come. I don't think all the people involved in it understand all that but that's what's behind it.[24]

I find this critique remarkable for many reasons. For one, I am thoroughly pre-millennial in my theology. I have graduated from and taught at two staunchly pre-millennial schools. Yet I see no discrepancy whatsoever between being pre-millennial and saving the lives of innocent children! For me, the timing of Christ's return has no relationship at all to the issue of rescuing.

Most of the rescuers I know are also pre-millennial. But what is even more ironic is that the strongest criticisms of rescuing I have heard come from post-millennial "dominion theology" reconstructionists. I respect them as brothers in Christ, even though our theologies differ considerably at certain points. However, these are the exact people that this Bible teacher claims are really behind the rescue movement! In fact, many of the criticisms of rescuing quoted from in this book come straight from reconstructionists.

Certainly there are reconstructionists who rescue, just as there are those who evangelize, go to the mission field, and work in prison ministries. Dominion theology has no doubt influenced some rescue leaders. Yet in my research I have come across only one leading reconstructionist who has written in favor of rescuing, as opposed to many who speak out against it.[25]

Certainly many reconstructionists would object to being told it is their distinctive theology that is at the heart of this rescue movement that they so vigorously oppose! I and most of those I rescue with would likewise object to being told that our convictions are rooted in post-millennialism.

Furthermore, the radio teacher unfairly impugns the motives and character of rescuers when he suggests they are uninterested in heaven, and are wrapped up in comfortable and indulgent lifestyles. I am keenly interested in heaven, as are many of those with whom I rescue. In fact, my perspective on heaven, the eternal state, and the reality of eternal rewards has had a profound impact not only on my life in general, but my decision to rescue in particular.

Finally, if I wanted "a comfortable indulgent lifestyle," the last thing I would do is rescue, because it is the furthest thing from either comfortable or indulgent that I have ever experienced.[26]

The issue is not eschatology. The issue is biblical morality, justice and mercy.

14

Social & Personal Arguments against Rescuing

We may preach with all the fervor of a reformer,
and yet succeed only in winning a struggle here and there,
if we permit the whole collective thought of the nation
to be controlled by ideas which, by the resistless force of logic,
prevent Christianity from being regarded as anything more
than a harmless delusion.
J. Gresham Machen

I n the previous chapter we considered biblical and theological arguments against rescuing. In this chapter we will turn to social and personal arguments against rescuing. First, several social arguments.

"We Can't Impose Our Morality on Nonbelievers"

According to one pastor who opposes rescuing, ". . . we will never be able to convince the pagans of America to stop sacrificing their children until they convert to Christianity."[1]

It is obvious that the hearts of men must change for there to be a thoroughly Christian morality. Conversion to Christ, not mere social reform, is the answer to the deepest needs of men. Yet the fact is that *prior to 1973 most of the "pagans of America" did not believe in child-killing.* Indeed, there is hardly a nation in the world where abortion was legal prior to World War 2. *One does not have to be a Christian to believe the unborn are children, or that it is wrong to kill children.* Is it really impossible to call our society back to an ethical principle that was so deeply embedded in it only a short time ago?

If we can do nothing significant to influence our society apart from directly leading everyone to Christ, then why do we try to influence our schools and communities? Why vote? The pastor who stated people won't change their minds about abortion unless they're converted says that he pickets against abortion. Why? How many people have been won to Christ by picketing? Apparently he feels it really *is* possible to affect the moral persuasions of others even if they aren't converted.

Jonah, Nahum, Obadiah, Ezekiel, Isaiah and Jeremiah all addressed some or all of their prophetic instruction to heathen nations such as Nineveh, Ammon, Moab, Tyre and Sidon. We *can* influence people, including nonbelievers, on matters of justice, compassion and human decency. And in the process we can not only tell them about Christ, but show them the full implications of Christian truth and compassion.

"Operation Rescue is trying to force, to compel, to coerce (even though they are not using the sword) a non-Christian, pagan culture to conform to the Word and will of God."[2]

If rape were legal, as child-killing is, by making organized efforts to save women from rape would Christians be attempting to coerce society to conform to God's Word? Or would they simply be trying to save women from rape, with the hope that society would eventually come to its senses? Would this be coercion? If so, would it be wrong?

John Jefferson Davis states,

The charge of "imposing morality" reflects confusion about the relationship of law and morality. . . . The real issue is not *whether* laws will reflect a moral point of view, but rather, what *type* of morality they should reflect. There is simply no compelling reason why moral insights drawn from the Judaeo-Christian tradition should be disqualified from legal and public policy debates.[3]

Furthermore, many Christians have greatly overestimated how many people really favor abortion on demand. In 1989 the *Boston Globe,* a vocally pro-abortion newspaper, reported the results of its own survey: "Most Americans would ban the vast majority of abortions performed in this country."[4]

The *Globe* reported that "while 78 per cent of the nation would keep abortion legal in limited circumstances, those circumstances account for only a tiny percentage of the reasons cited by women having abortions."[5] The "limited circumstances" were rape, incest, the life of the mother, and deformity. But in cases when pregnancy poses financial or emotional strain, or when the woman is alone or a teenager—in other words, in 97 per cent of actual situations—an overwhelming majority of Americans believe abortion should be illegal.

Similarly, a *Los Angeles Times* poll indicated that 61 per cent of people believe that abortion is immoral, and 57 per cent actually believe it is murder. In response to this, Chuck Colson states,

We must appeal to the sensibilities of people. . . . The pro-life movement has been very successful in convincing 57 per cent of the people that abortion is murder.

So we must constantly talk about the murder of the unborn children until it sinks down into the public consciousness. People must be brought to deal with the incredible schizophrenia of recognizing it as murder on the one hand, and favoring it on the other. Eventually you will get some consistency.[6]

According to the two pro-choice newspapers quoted above, to achieve the milestone of eliminating abortion on demand would not be "imposing our morality" on the majority, but in fact would reflect what the majority already believe! It was the Supreme Court that in 1973 imposed its minority morality on our nation. We must not be so quick to give up, either in intervening for the children dying today or in working to change the law to protect the children of tomorrow.

"We Can't Violate the Right to Choose"
One of three major points in the argument against rescuing made by one large pro-life church is, "The women who choose to have an abortion are free moral agents responsible before Almighty God for their actions, including the exercise of the rights of their innocent, unborn child."[7] Of course these

women are responsible for their actions. But how does this relate to the rescuing issue? Is it not also true that "men who choose to rape women are free moral agents responsible before Almighty God for their actions"? Does the fact that someone will be judged for his act of violence upon an innocent person take away my responsibility to intervene to try to save that person from the violence? What consolation is it to the victims that their killers were free moral agents?

Which is more sacred, human life or the human choice to take someone else's life? In some of the arguments against rescuing, even by pro-lifers, there emerges a "choice is sacred" mentality that demonstrates how effectively the pro-choice advocates have done their job in affecting even the church's attitudes. We must realize that "choice" comes down to a person's wants. But wants and rights are very different things. *Any civilized society is based on the restriction of the individual's choice.* What are laws, but the setting of limitations on personal choice? When we talk about being "free to choose" we must always ask, "Free to choose what?" Who is pro-choice when it comes to theft, rape, kidnapping, and murder? No civilized society is "pro-choice" regardless of the harm inflicted on others by that choice.

A Bible teacher objecting to rescuing states, "Performing an abortion is legal and though we recognize that it is immoral, that viewpoint is not shared by the women seeking it."[8] If wife-killing were legal, would we decide not to rescue women about to be killed because our "viewpoint" that wife-killing is immoral is "not shared" by the men seeking to kill them?

Not only the woman's, but the abortionist's right to choose to kill a child is defended by a Christian judge, who criticizes rescuing on this basis:

Society says, I am entitled to the peaceful (and legal) use of my property for income or pleasure without interference from civil government and certainly not from my neighbor. To take that from me constitutes, in my opinion, a violation of the Eighth Commandment, "Thou shalt not steal." The demonstrators [rescuers] have stolen the physician's right to earn a living by a legal enterprise (albeit a sinful enterprise).[9]

Does the "physician" (baby-killer) really have a right to "earn a living" by killing the innocent? The judge says abortion is a sin, but he still believes that the doctor has the "right" to do that sin simply because it is legal. If it is the

Creator who grants rights, however, then the doctor has no right whatsoever to earn a living killing babies. (In any case, the rescuers' goal is not to punish the man for choosing a sinful enterprise, but to save the innocent baby from death.)

The theology of choice is so deeply ingrained in us that a Christian judge actually believes that attempts to keep innocent people from becoming the victims of the violation of the sixth commandment (do not murder) are in fact a violation of the eighth commandment (do not steal). It is amazing the extent to which the tables are turned to make those trying to peacefully prevent innocent children from being killed appear to be worse than those who are killing them!

An evangelical theologian says that rescuers "have sinned and they have 'judged' their neighbor. . . . the demonstrators trespass violates the scripture which says 'Love does no wrong to a neighbor, love therefore is the fulfillment of the law' (Rom 13:10)."[10]

It is astounding that the principle "Love does no wrong to a neighbor" is used to condemn a peaceful, nonviolent, life-saving action, rather than to justify it. Even apart from our duty to love the innocent child, there is the faulty perception that the "loving" thing to do for an abortionist is not to interfere with his plan to kill babies all day!

Rescuers maintain that the right to privacy should extend to everyone, including the child. How easily we forget that it is the "doctor," by request or permission of the mother, who is trespassing into the child's private living space. It is the doctor who is breaking and entering the womb and violently killing its resident. The person whose residence it is did *not* grant anyone permission to enter, much less to cut him to pieces. The one trespass may save a life and result in the doctor/hired killer losing a few hundred dollars. The other trespass takes a life, and prevents that life from ever growing up and making any of his or her own choices.

If rape were legal, would interfering with rape also be violating the command to do no wrong to one's neighbor? If people were raped on private property and we interfered, this would be trespassing. But hopefully we would remember the victim of rape, and be prompted to intervene despite the law.

"Rescuing Encourages Disrespect for the Law"

"By breaking the law the rescuers frustrate the justice system which was designed to put fear into the evil doer who will now have less fear of breaking the law."[11] The point is that rescuers are demonstrating disrespect for the law and are encouraging that disrespect in others.

Even apart from the question, "Whose law are we breaking and whose are we keeping?" we must ask, "Who do we know that has gone out to break good laws because rescuers are breaking a bad one?" Did the people in Israel start violating good laws because Obadiah broke the law to save the prophets? Were the citizens of America led into situational ethics by the activities of the Underground Railroad?

Given the punishments inflicted upon those who rescue, I can't imagine any person being encouraged to do anything illegal unless he was absolutely convinced it was morally right to do so and was willing to pay a high price for it. This does not appear to be a serious danger in our self-centered society.

But even if this imaginary problem becomes real on some occasion, can this dissuade us from obeying higher law? Can you imagine Peter and John saying to the Sanhedrin, "We thought about obeying God rather than men, but some people might have misunderstood and started breaking good laws, so on further consideration we won't obey God after all."

Would it be so bad if a small minority of normally law-abiding Americans were willing to endure sacrifices by violating those few civil laws that clearly violate natural law? Rather than resulting in chaos, would it not more likely result in positive social and legal reform? Would it not bring civil law more into line with natural law, and thereby procure God's blessing rather than God's curse upon the nation?

I think the truly bad examples of Christians breaking the law come in those many areas where we do so for our personal convenience or profit. I know Christians, for instance, who feel it is wrong to disobey trespassing laws to save lives, yet who deliberately disobey seat-belt laws, even though these laws save lives. Why would we think it acceptable to disobey a good law that saves lives, then say it is wrong to disobey an evil law that prevents life-saving?

I know believers, even fellow pastors, who think nothing of violating copyright laws by making illegal copies of cassette tapes, sheet music, booklets and computer programs. Yet the same men oppose rescuing on the grounds that it is illegal. In my opinion, Romans 13 and other basic principles of biblical ethics clearly forbid us from violating copyright laws, even for what we may consider "a good cause." Why, then, are we quick to apply Romans 13 when God doesn't want us to—when higher law is at stake—but slow to apply it to those situations for which it was actually written?

When it comes right down to it, many of us are willing to violate good laws when it is beneficial for us but costly to others. But we are unwilling to violate evil laws when it is costly for us, but beneficial to others.

"The Law Being Broken Is Not the Law Objected To"

"The law being broken (in this case, the ordinance designed to insure free access to business) has nothing whatsoever to do with abortion. Those arrested are not being arrested because they are protesting abortion."[12] This is the first of three reasons given by one group of church leaders as to why rescuing is wrong.

Suppose this argument is true. Now apply it to a born child. A trespassing law has nothing to do with a child being beaten to death either, but would I not still break the law to save him? The point in rescuing is not to object to trespassing laws but to give one last chance for a life to be saved. This just happens to require that someone trespass. *The focus of rescuing is not the law being broken but the life being taken.*

Everyone involved in rescuing, including police and judges, knows that rescuers are not protesting the trespass laws. Police and judges will freely admit that they would not arrest or put someone in jail for trespassing to save a born child's life. Indeed, such a person would be praised as a hero. Those of us who have been taken to court know that the real issue being discussed in the courtroom is whether a woman or a doctor has the right to kill a baby, or whether that baby has a right to live. It is *not* the trespassing law that is at issue, but the law that requires that no one interfere with a woman killing her preborn child. Everyone, including the abortionists, the prosecutor and the judge, knows this to be true.

In anti-Christian countries religion is usually legal, but is controlled through the use of minor violations. No one is told, "You can't meet here because we forbid you to worship," but instead "meeting here violates zoning ordinances." Church buildings are often torn down because they "don't meet building codes" or "the permit wasn't valid." Believers in such countries are constantly violating rules and regulations in order to obey God in evangelism and worship. Similarly, Chuck Colson states,

Many Jews and Christians during World War 2 refused to obey Nazi laws requiring registration of aliens. On the surface those might have seemed just laws, no different than alien registration laws on the books of most Western countries today. But the citizens disobeyed because they knew those laws were being used to identify individuals for extermination.[13]

Even if the law objected to isn't the one being violated, what does this prove? Would we deprive the unborn of one last chance to live, simply on the basis of a technicality? We would pull an ox out of the ditch on the sabbath. Would we fail to intervene to save a human life just because it breaks a rule, or the wrong rule?

"Once You Disobey the Law, Why Not Use Violence?"

One of the most common arguments against rescuing involves the question of where the line is drawn once we move to civil disobedience.

Those participating in Operation Rescue also need to explain why they should limit their direct action options to trespassing and the passive, non-violent blocking of abortion center entrances. They could let the air out of the abortionist's tires. . . . They could splatter the building with chicken blood. If legality is no longer an issue, then the possibilities are endless. If trespassing is legitimate, then why not these others?[14]

Another pastor takes the question a step further to show the supposed absurdity of rescuing, saying:

If we really want to rescue, if we really want to "physically intervene" to save the children, surely the most efficient ways would be to poison all the abortionists [sic] doctors in the country, to bomb the clinics, or to kidnap the girls who attempt to go in the clinics.[15]

But there are perfectly logical and consistent reasons why we draw lines and do not use violence in rescuing. Violence puts human life at risk, and we are there to save lives not endanger them. We want to rescue victims, not create victims. Violence is punitive—we are intervening for the innocent, not doling out punishment on the guilty.

The same objections apply equally to Rahab. If she was willing to violate the law to save the spies, why not poison the king or kill the soldiers? Obadiah was a trusted officer with weapons and soldiers at his disposal—he could have assassinated Ahab and Jezebel and solved the problem that way, rather than going to all the trouble of hiding the spies. The Magi could have gone back to kill Herod rather than simply disobey him by leaving the other way. Participants in the Underground Railroad could have burned the homes of slave owners to the ground, or even "splattered them with chicken blood." Do we believe their actions were illegitimate simply because they could have taken them to violent extremes, but didn't?

Though I believe our nonviolence is both biblical and logical, I do not pretend to take everything to its absolute possible extreme. But I do believe it is *more* consistent, that it is *more* logical, that it treats the unborn *more* like human beings to rescue than to passively stand by while helpless human beings are slaughtered. Surely the legitimacy of an act cannot be disproven because it is not taken further and further and further until it becomes illegitimate. Otherwise the only consistent position is total inaction.

Is there a danger that disobeying one law could escalate into breaking other laws? I have not found it to be true for myself or those I know who rescue. But suppose there is the danger of such a thing.

It is not fair or even logical to say that a thing is inappropriate simply because it might evolve into another totally different inappropriate thing. For example, sharing one's faith is not invalidated by the possibility that one might then become so consumed with evangelism that he might begin to scream at everyone that they are going to hell if they don't turn to Christ and he might neglect his own marriage and the parenting of his children in his distractions of proclaiming the gospel. In the case of rescuing, as in all other aspects of life, the word of God through the work of the Holy Spirit gives us the balance to live in action that glorifies the Father.[16]

"Innocent Citizens Are Going Unprotected"

Some have argued that certain homicides would have been prevented if the police would not have been at a rescue. However, even if it is true, this statement by a pro-life Christian is revealing. As one writer put it, while rescuers are merely trying to keep the unborn from abortion, elsewhere "innocent people are being killed." Here is a clear indication of what we *really* believe. Why try to save the unborn when *real* people are being killed?

Rescues have saved hundreds if not thousands of babies' lives. What if it were demonstrated that the presence of police trying to stop rescues has resulted in twenty deaths of other citizens that could otherwise been prevented? Shall we blame the deaths of the twenty on the people who were saving the hundreds? The rescuers neither asked nor wanted the police to leave other citizens unprotected. They merely said, "Since the state refuses to protect these babies from a brutal death, we will try to protect them." Society and the state, not the rescuers, must accept responsibility for this situation.

"Abortions Should Be Prevented before Women Reach the Clinic"

One pastor says, "To confront an already distraught woman at the door of an abortion clinic and attempt to correct her for what she is about to do is not the solution. Nor is the solution concerned citizens allowing themselves to be arrested. The solution to her problem should have begun in her home and in her church long before that day arrived."[17]

Of course, the point of rescuing is not to correct the woman for killing her child, but to give her a chance to decide *not* to kill her child. After a woman has had an abortion and has come outside the clinic, rescuers have a strict policy of saying nothing to condemn her, but offering only love and friendship. It is too late now to avoid the death. But it is not to late to express love and concern.

I completely agree that "the solution to her problem should have begun in her home and in her church long before that day arrived." Unfortunately, the facts are *it did not,* or in the few cases where it did, she did not respond. Furthermore, the assumption that she *has* a church is a faulty one. In my part of the country, for instance, only one in twenty people go to church regularly. Even those that do may go to one of many churches that are "pro-choice."

Legal pro-life actions, including education, can prevent many women from coming to the abortion clinic in the first place. But once the woman is there, rescuing gives one last opportunity for her to come to grips with the fact that this is a valuable human being inside of her.

If we saw a man beating his wife to death, it might indeed be accurate to say that "the solution to his problem should have begun in his home and church long before." True as this is, it would hopefully not prevent us from intervening to save the woman's life.

The pastor's phrase "the solution to *her* problem" is revealing, for it leaves someone out of the equation. The woman does indeed have a problem, an unwanted pregnancy, but the major problem at the abortion clinic is that of the child. His or her problem is imminent destruction. Who will solve *that* problem?

In fact, the woman's greatest problem is not really the unwanted pregnancy, but the fact that she is about to become guilty of taking an innocent life. Her problem will be facing the moral, mental and emotional consequences of so doing. Her home and church apparently did not solve this problem, just as they did not solve the baby's problem. Shall we then punish both mother and child by withholding one last opportunity for her to change her mind?

"Rescuing Will Turn Society against the Church"

"What is to prevent pro-abortion people from blocking access to churches, or even entering them to disrupt services? If we allow lawless protest to one side, we justify it for all."[18] One person uses the example of an "atheist sit-in" in churches, asking how we would like people to do to us what we are doing to the abortion clinics.

I have heard Christians argue that it is inconsistent to expect to exercise our religious freedoms if we don't give others the freedom to do as they wish within the framework of the law. Certainly this is true in any number of discretionary areas. But when the freedom at issue is the freedom to brutally kill an innocent human being, can't we see the fundamental difference between this and "normal" freedoms?

Is it really inconsistent to maintain that the "atheist sit-in" violates the law of God, while the attempt to rescue innocent children is in keeping with the law of God? Trying to prevent worship and trying to save a baby's life are not the same thing. One is wrong and the other is right. "But many people don't believe that"—perhaps not, but it is still true! Shall we buy our religious liberties at the cost of allowing the lives of the innocent to be taken? If we do so in this area, won't we do so again in others? How valuable is a religious liberty bought at such a cost?

One Bible teacher argues against rescuing on the grounds that unbelievers may react negatively toward it: ". . . we are called to have our behavior honest among the Gentiles. We are called to live in such a way that by our good behavior and conduct they glorify God, and I don't think that that's what that [rescuing] causes. I think it causes the very opposite. It causes bitterness, animosity, hostility toward Christianity."[19]

One man responds to the above statement this way:

Here the argument is that things that cause bitterness, animosity and hostility toward Christianity are the opposite of things that glorify God. I would ask those who hold this view to consider 1 Peter 3 & 4. These Christians were often the object of the above negative emotions. For doing what? For doing *good.* "Who is going to harm you if you are eager to do good? But even if you do suffer for what is right, you are blessed" (1 Peter 3:13-14). Peter goes on to tell the believers how to act when they are recipients of direct insults. He said not to be surprised at these responses to their good deeds. So, we cannot say that because some things bring about bitterness, animosity and hostility, they therefore do not glorify God.[20]

Scripture is full of reminders that the world will actively oppose us (Mt 5:11-12), hate us on account of Christ's name (Lk 21:17), will not understand our behavior (1 Pet 4:4) and will persecute us for our deeds of righteousness (1 Tim 3:12). Jesus said, "In this world you shall have trouble . . ." (Jn 16:33). His apostle said, "Do not be surprised, my brothers, if the world hates you" (1 Jn 3:13).

Why will the world hate us? For the same reason it hated Jesus. "The world . . . hates me because I testify that what it does is evil" (Jn 7:7). Is our goal to stand against evil, or to avoid the world's hatred? Ordinarily we will not be able to do both at the same time.

Haman argued to the king concerning the Jews. Their "customs are different from those of all other people, and [they] do not obey the king's laws;

it is not in the king's best interest to tolerate them" (Esther 3:8). The people of God, no matter how peaceful and humble, have a way of irritating the enemies of God, by challenging their assumptions and shaking their foundations.

The German laws depriving the Jews of rights were obeyed by the German Christians out of fear of hostility and persecution. The result was the death of many people who could have been saved with illegal but moral intervention. We must not make the same mistake.

Having now reviewed typical social arguments against rescuing, let us now turn to personal arguments.

"Rescuing Damages Our Witness"

I have heard people say, "Getting arrested and going to jail is a bad witness to others. It undermines our credibility as Christians."

The issue is not *whether* a person is in jail but *why* a person is in jail. Jeremiah went to jail. So did John the Baptist. Jesus got arrested, went to jail, stood before civil judges and even received capital punishment. So did Paul and Peter, the same ones who wrote Romans 13 and 1 Peter 2. John Bunyan and Dietrich Bonhoeffer went to jail. Pastors in the Soviet Union and Eastern Europe used to go to jail routinely. They still do in China, the Middle East and many other places.

Were all these people having "a bad testimony"? We in the Western church have largely forgotten all the good reasons for which the people of God have always gone to jail!

Jesus said his disciples would be hauled before civil authority. He said, "On account of me you will stand before governors and kings as witnesses to them" (Mk 13:9-11; Lk 21:12-19). Arrests, trials, imprisonment and punishment were common for the disciples. It was also common to be subjected to public insult and to have one's property confiscated (Heb 10:32-34).

Paul told Timothy, "Do not be ashamed to testify about our Lord, or ashamed of me his prisoner. But join with me in suffering for the gospel" (2 Tim 1:8). He commended Onesiphorus because "he often refreshed me and was not ashamed of my chains" (2 Tim 1:16). We should be willing to be arrested for what is right, and we should not be ashamed of our brothers who are willing to be arrested for what is right.

We say going to jail is a bad witness. Jesus says there are times when we will go to jail precisely *because* we are good witnesses. And once in jail, we become witnesses to those who otherwise would not hear the gospel.

The terms *good* and *bad* witness are not as helpful as the terms *accurate* and *inaccurate* witness. If the Bible teaches that the unborn are human beings, it is an accurate witness to act consistently with that truth.

William Booth, founder of the Salvation Army, said that two kinds of people go to jail—those who behave worse than their neighbors and those who behave better than them. In a statement directly relevant to rescuing and other forms of civil disobedience he said, "The repeal of an unjust law is seldom carried until a certain number of those who are laboring for the reform have experienced in their own persons the hardships of fine and imprisonment."[21]

"Rescuing Makes People Look Like Fanatics and Fools"

It has always fascinated me that Christians can go to Portland's Memorial Colosseum and jump up and down and cheer at a slam dunk or a three-point shot and be respectable "fans." But if they go out to the abortion clinic and try calmly to save the lives of babies about to be killed they are derisively called "fanatics." As to the label "fool," Paul bore it well (1 Cor 4:10). We must sometimes choose between being called a fool *for* Christ now and being judged a fool *by* Christ later.

Our commitment to looking acceptable is so strong that radical actions for Christ are generally discouraged in the Christian community. This is a tragedy. Of course, we should not seek to look foolish. But the danger is that we would gain respectability at the cost of fear or apathy. As to being afraid of people becoming too zealous for righteousness, a missionary once told me, "It's easier to cool down a fanatic than to warm up a corpse."

William Wilberforce, a devout Christian, was the British parliamentarian whose single-minded efforts finally brought an end to the slave trade in England. For many years his colleagues would not pay attention to his words about the realities of slavery. Wilberforce would periodically reach under his chair and pull out chains, draping them over himself to symbolize the inhumanity of slavery. His fellow parliamentarians would roll their eyes, snicker, mock him, and call him a fool. But it is Wilberforce, not they, who is remembered—by God and men—as the one who stood for justice and mercy.

"Rescuing Isn't Christlike"

Some have seriously argued that rescuing is disrespectful of police authority and have said they cannot imagine Jesus acting in such a way.

Why is it unimaginable that Jesus would rescue? Because it is not status quo? Because it would have been disapproved by the religious leaders? Because it requires boldness? Jesus was not status quo, cared nothing for approval by the religious leaders, and was very bold in his actions.

If we cannot imagine Jesus rescuing, can we imagine him creating a public scene by overturning (illegally) the tables of the moneychangers, throwing their coins to the floor, and making a whip out of cords and driving men and beasts out of the temple? (Jn 2:14-16). Can we imagine him standing before the mighty tetrarch Herod and refusing to speak when spoken to? (Lk 23:9). Can we imagine him deliberately and repeatedly violating Jewish law by putting human life above law and healing on the sabbath, knowing it would infuriate the religious leaders? There is much that Jesus did that most of us cannot imagine him doing. Our lack of imagination, however, did not stop him from doing it!

"But Jesus never broke the law to save infants from destruction." This is an argument from silence. Scripture doesn't record most of the things Jesus said and did (Jn 21:25). Jesus lived with Jews, among whom abortion was virtually unheard of. In other places Roman women used abortion-inducing drugs privately. Jesus probably never came near the equivalent of an abortion clinic the entire time he was on earth.

What do we suppose Jesus would have done if he had come across one of the infants abandoned outside the gates? Turn his back and look the other way? Leave him to suffer and die because the law forbade intervention? Now on this point I would say, "One cannot imagine Jesus acting that way." If we cannot imagine Jesus rescuing the preborn at an abortion clinic, perhaps the problem is not with Jesus, but with who we imagine him to be.

"Some Christian Leaders Oppose Rescuing"

Most of the men I have quoted who oppose rescuing are sincere and godly. However, we must realize that there has never been a movement of God—whether the Protestant Reformation, the Underground Railroad, the Christian resistance in Germany or any other—that has not been strongly opposed by respected Christian leaders.

Many men who are themselves in positions of authority find the thought of disobedience to authority repulsive or frightening. Some will forever relate civil disobedience to long-haired students of the sixties, burning the flag, burning draft-cards, yelling obscenities, and refusing to fight for their country. These leaders will always tend to see civil disobedience as cowardly, not courageous. They will find it difficult to discern the difference between civil disobedience for one reason as opposed to another.

We in America, Canada, Great Britain and other Western nations have seen our countries stand for freedom and human rights. It is a great temptation to take the position, "my country right or wrong." For many American Christians, especially, it is easy to mistake the flag for the cross, and to substitute loyalty to the flag for loyalty to the Savior.

As I look at some of those people most resistant to civil disobedience in any form, I see men who find it inconceivable to disobey a law of the country for which they and others have fought. This is the land we love, a land that was founded on Christian principles, and for which blood has been bravely shed. Of course, none of this takes away the agony of the unborn children, and none of it takes away our responsibility to intervene. But all of it makes it more difficult for some people to see the legitimacy of any form of civil disobedience.

Other leaders, without realizing it, may be protectors of the status quo. They may say, "Things are going fine, our church is enjoying popularity in the community, let's not spoil it by doing something crazy." Some pastors are afraid of lawsuits from abortion clinics to the point that they even oppose legal picketing or any activity near the killing places. Some react defensively to rescuing, some out of a sense of guilt.

In many cases, I think, Christian leaders are afraid if they leave a door open to rescuing they might be expected to do it themselves. They do not feel drawn to rescuing, and are already involved in so many other good ministries that they don't want to even think about it, much less do it. Some pastors are also afraid, and understandably so, that their people will run off half-cocked and follow someone else's leadership, especially leadership with which they are uncomfortable.

At any rate, I do not question the integrity of these men who oppose rescuing. I do, however, believe that they have reached a faulty conclusion that needs to be carefully reexamined in light of Scripture, history and basic Christian morality.

We must also remember that there are many fine Christian leaders who have spoken out in favor of rescuing. James Dobson has said,

> The crux of the entire issue is, do we believe our own rhetoric? Do we really believe we're killing babies? . . . If 1.5 million children were being slaughtered per year, who are *here* . . . what would we do about it? Would we stand behind our pulpits and say, "We don't believe in civil disobedience. If the law says these children must die, then they must die." No! We wouldn't do that. We'd be in there trying to rescue them any way we could. And if that meant going to jail, we'd go to jail. We don't believe our rhetoric. That's the problem. There are children at stake . . .[22]

In an open letter to Christians, D. James Kennedy states,

> Thankfully in many cities Christians are putting feet to their faith . . . in obedience to Proverbs 24:11 which tells us to rescue the innocent being dragged to the slaughter. . . . I encourage the body of Christ to join in this action as salt and light to our communities. . . .
>
> We need Corrie ten Booms of the 1980s who will stand up to man's repudiation of God's law and follow Jesus' command to love our neighbors as ourselves.[23]

Chuck Colson says of rescuers, "In terms of blocking abortion clinics and violating no-trespassing laws and getting arrested, I think what they are doing is appropriate."[24]

Bill Bright was asked to respond to contributors who cut off support to a Campus Crusade for Christ couple arrested for rescuing. He concluded by saying, "I'd rather stand before the Lord with a prison record and a pure heart than to stand before men with a clean record and blood on my hands."[25]

Though he died before the rescue movement was established, Francis

Schaeffer advocated protesting abortion through illegal sit-ins not just at abortion clinics, but in legislatures and courts, including the Supreme Court.[26]

But creating a "board of reference for rescuing" would no more prove rescuing is right than citing other well-known names proves it is wrong. We must draw our conclusions on something other than a majority vote. Even if we determined how many leaders favor rescuing and how many are against it, it would mean little. The majority is seldom the repository of the truth.

Pastors need to be encouraged by rescuers and nonrescuers alike to take a balanced position in this matter. They need to give their people biblical instruction, guidelines and advice, but leave the final decision to the individual and family involved. It is my opinion that any Christian leader who leaves the impression either that rescuing should be done by everyone or that rescuing should be done by no one, has gone beyond the boundaries of Scripture. He has therefore gone beyond the boundaries of proper leadership. He has failed to leave room for the conviction and illumination and guidance of God's Spirit in the lives of believer-priests and their families, who must prayerfully search the Scriptures and discern God's leading in their own lives. Christian leaders should seek to promote the personal study of Scripture and the illuminating ministry of the Holy Spirit, not replace it.

"Rescuing Creates Disunity in the Church"

One Christian leader, questioning the validity of rescuing, stated, "We must not allow our personal opinions, passions, or rhetoric to desecrate the much larger and more significant issue of the body's oneness."

I agree that unity is very important. But is it not equally important that we not allow our concern for unity to desecrate the welfare of the innocent children? We must ask if certain things—or people—are worth being divided about. Our country was divided by the human rights issues related to the slaves, which brought on the Civil War. This was unfortunate, but Abraham Lincoln and others felt the lives and freedom of human beings were worth it. Is the cost of differing opinions on rescuing really greater than the cost of innocent human lives who will be killed if rescuing is not done?

Christians who are pro-life will be divided against those who defend abortion, whether in church or society. Sometimes divisions among believers are necessary (1 Cor 11:18-19). What is called "unity" in churches too often is nothing more than a "let's not rock the boat" policy of avoiding conflict at all costs. We must encourage open Bible-centered dialog, rather than sweeping the rescue issue under the church rug and hoping it just goes away.

In some churches rescuing has indeed created disunity. But this is not necessary. If rescuers and nonrescuers and even anti-rescuers can talk, search the Scriptures, pray together and control their tongues, the unity of the body can be maintained. If people begin to resent the fact that others are rescuing, or that others are not rescuing, this is when the body is divided.

The day I shared with my own church my decision to rescue, I went through thirty-five ways in which we could intervene for the unborn. The final and only illegal one of these was rescuing. I explained why I had made that decision, and emphasized again that it was only one of many available avenues to try to save lives. Seven months later, at my seventh rescue, I was shown being arrested on all the local television news programs. When a lawsuit came to trial a few days later, there I was in the news again, with my family and twenty other rescuers, including a few others from our church.

Realizing this could cause misunderstanding, I drafted a letter to the church, to remind them of what I had said earlier:

At our church we have always given each other the freedom to prayerfully study the Scriptures and follow God's leading according to our consciences. Hence, someone is not considered spiritual or unspiritual for either rescuing or not rescuing—any more than he would be considered spiritual or unspiritual for being involved (or not involved) in a jail ministry, Hispanic ministry, lay counseling ministry, teaching Sunday School or working in the nursery.

Furthermore, I can fully believe in the rightness of a ministry, for example, foreign missions, without believing God has called me personally to that particular ministry. I say all this because I feel deeply about the unity of the church body. I never want to be perceived as thinking others should do exactly as I do. The fact that I choose to be involved in rescuing is a difficult matter of conscience that my family and I have come to after considerable Bible study, soul-searching and prayer. My involvement in rescuing in no way implies that I think it is the most important ministry, or that other ministry choices are less legitimate or significant. I do not, never have and never will think this.

The important thing is not exactly *how* we serve Him but *that* we serve Him—in no matter what capacity He calls us to.

Of course, rescuing will inevitably produce some discomfort in the church. It has in mine. I believe there is a place for rescuers to compromise and bend to give others time to work through their objections to rescuing. In fact, I have chosen not to attend several rescues, and to avoid arrest at several others, during times when this issue was particularly sensitive for some of my coleaders.

But being challenged and stretched and brought to our knees to seek God's wisdom isn't bad and unhealthy. True biblical unity is achieved through the honest recognition of different convictions, not through the silencing of those convictions. "Unity" based on a refusal to deal with issues, or unity resulting from indifference to human suffering, is not a unity worth having.

The long-term solution, then, is not for all Christians to stop rescuing simply because some people oppose it and because stopping would create a superficial appearance of unity. We must always seek peace, yet weigh the price of peace. When we "bury the hatchet," let's be sure we don't bury it in the unborn children.

Conclusion: Reality, Not Fantasy

A Bible teacher says, rescuing is appealing because it "sounds romantically exciting."[27] Unlike this professor, I have actually rescued, and I find the word "romantic" amusing. He sums up his position by saying, "We cannot just mount our gallant steeds, ride into the abortion clinic, and rescue the innocent babies. We live in reality, not fantasy." He adds, "Whether we like it or not, many millions of babies will die before change comes to the abortion laws, and the laws may never change."[28]

Yes, we live in reality, not fantasy. Yes, millions more children will probably die despite our efforts. But shall we resign ourselves to the wide-scale killing by appointment in our communities? Shall we write off the children to be killed today and tomorrow? Shall we abandon the painful but peaceful efforts of rescuing that sometimes result—and this is *reality*, not fantasy—in the saved lives of innocent children?

15
Rescuing, the Church & the Future

All that is necessary for the triumph of evil is that good men do nothing.
Edmund Burke

*T*he bodies of aborted children, sometimes while they are still alive, are being cut apart, and their organs and tissues sold for commercial and research purposes. Fresh organs and tissue from babies are being bought from abortion clinics at $50 per tissue sample to be used in research to treat Parkinson's disease and insulin-dependent diabetes.[1]

In his novel *Weeping in Ramah*, J. R. Lucas envisions a future where unborn babies are kept in medical labs to produce spare parts for other people.[2] This is not far-fetched. Doctors have already transplanted cells from the pancreas of unborn children to that of diabetics, to reduce their insulin requirements. A man who suffered from Parkinson's disease has two daughters who have volunteered to get pregnant and abort their babies to provide brain cells for a transplant. The attitude of researchers is "there is no reason to waste such a potentially beneficial biological resource obtained from a perfectly legal procedure."[3]

The estimates are that the potential market in using fetal tissue from induced abortions exceeds six billion dollars. The probable result will be delayed abortions in which women will sell their unborn children to the highest commercial bidders, who will use baby flesh for their own purposes.[4]

A survey of a dozen villages in India, near the Pakistan border, uncovered a frightening statistic—out of a total population of 10,000 people, including thousands of children, only fifty were girls.[5] The other girls, thousands of them, had been killed.

The reason is that girls are regarded as an economic liability. Those who shudder at this should realize it is happening right now across America. Amniocentesis is being used to detect the gender of a baby early in his or her development. That way, if you want a boy, you don't have to go through all those months of inconvenience till you can get a reliable ultrasound. You can tell within a month or two, then kill your little girl by abortion and start over again. Increasing numbers of married couples are in fact killing their girls because they want boys.

Medical World News reported a study in which, by means of amniocentesis, ninety-nine mothers were informed of the sex of their children. Fifty-three of these preborn children were boys, and forty-six girls. Of this number, only one mother elected to kill her boy, while *twenty-nine* elected to kill their girls.[6] Since many more girls than boys are being killed this way, some outraged feminists have labeled this practice "femicide."[7] The term betrays what those who use it deny, but which even they know deep inside—that the unborn are people, and to kill an unborn female is to kill a human female.

Amniocentesis is opening the door to a society of designer babies. People will keep having abortions till they get just the right one. You want a boy? Throw out the girls. You want an athlete? Throw out the physically handicapped. You want a doctor, lawyer or teacher? Throw out the mentally handicapped. This practice is quiet, but already common, and it won't stop with gender or physique. You want a blonde one? Throw out the black-haired ones. You want blue eyes? Get rid of the brown-eyed.

Once you say strong human beings can take the life of weak human beings—which is exactly what legalized abortion has said—then where do you stop? The current euthanasia movement is simply applying to people before life's end the identical rationale that justifies abortion after life's beginning. Why should a person be forced to undertake the personal and financial hardship of bringing a dependent child into the world? Why should a family be forced to undertake the personal and financial hardship of keeping a dependent elderly parent in the world? The former Surgeon General of the United States publicly stated, "One day for every Baby Doe there will be 10,000 Grandma Does."

While society is shocked at the dramatic rise in child abuse that began in the seventies, it should come as no surprise to thinking people. If it's all right to kill your child up to the day of birth, why isn't it all right to "just" beat up the same child a few months or years later?

Why is all this happening? What has caused this fundamental shift in morality, and what will it take to reverse it? Francis Schaeffer skillfully diagnosed the condition of the Western church, and how it has led to the loss of the sanctity of human life in society:

Accommodation, accommodation. How the mindset of accommodation grows and expands. The last sixty years have given birth to a moral disaster, and what have we done? Sadly we must say that the evangelical world has been part of the disaster. More than this, the evangelical response itself has been a disaster. Where is the clear voice speaking to the crucial issues of the day with distinctively biblical, Christian answers? With tears we must say that largely it is not there and that a large segment of the evangelical world has become seduced by the world spirit of this present age. And more than this, we can expect the future to be a further disaster if the evangelical world does not take a stand for biblical truth and morality in the full spectrum of life. *For the evangelical accommodation to the world of our age represents the removal of the last barrier against the breakdown of our culture.*[8]

We must not see the lives of unborn children as an isolated issue. How we respond to the issues related to the unborn's desperate struggle for survival will have sweeping implications not just for the future of millions of babies, but the future of both church and society.

The Dynamics of Denial

Abortion was conceived in the very pit of hell by the Lord of Abortion, who is both a murderer and a liar, and who lies to cover his murders. Our tendency will be to go on with business as usual, to occasionally say a word or write a letter on behalf of the unborn, to look at a colorful bulletin insert and listen to an anti-abortion sermon once a year on the Sanctity of Human Life Sunday. Somehow we will believe this is enough. But day after day the innocent blood keeps spilling and the precious children keep dying. As long as our own rights aren't threatened, as long as our own lifestyles aren't interfered with, as long as no one is killing our *own* children, we will let them kill God's. Or will we?

In a documentary on the holocaust, one German who lived near a death camp was asked whether it bothered people to hear the screams. He responded, "At first it was unbearable; then you get used to it."[9] As Scott Peck puts it, "It is a simple sort of thing. The horrible becomes normal, and we simply tune it out." The unspeakably horrible practice of child-killing has become normal in our country. Though the church may decry the practice, it has accommodated and adjusted to it.

How do people with consciences allow themselves to go on day after day indifferent to, or even directly involved in, the slaughter? One of the most compelling books I have ever read is Robert Jay Lifton's *The Nazi Doctors: Medical Killing and the Psychology of Genocide*.[10] Lifton states that "psychologically speaking, nothing is darker or more menacing, or harder to accept, than the participation of physicians in mass murder."[11]

Interviewing both the doctors and their victims over a period of years, Lifton was struck most with what he called the "ordinariness" of the Nazi doctors. He says they were "by no means the demonic figures—sadistic, fanatic, lusting to kill—people have often thought them to be."[12] His simple conclusion is that "ordinary people can commit demonic acts." The final section of his book deals with the phenomenon of "doubling," the formation of a second, autonomous self, which enables a "decent person" to participate in evil.

What struck me most in reading this book is not the obvious application to abortionists, but that everything Lifton says of the psychological mechanisms that allow people to *participate* in evil applies even more readily to those who simply *tolerate* evil. What is it that allows good men to do nothing in the face of evil? What is it that allows most evangelical Christians to go on day after day believing abortion is killing an innocent child, but not taking substantial efforts to save these precious lives? The key to nonintervention to save lives is the same for us as it was the decent normal Christian citizens who permitted it in Germany. The key is denial. Denial is the simple refusal to recognize reality, or the deliberate choice to not think about what one concedes to be reality.

Our coping mechanism of denying the reality of the horrible is demonstrated every time we turn away from the picture of a mother and child starving in Mozambique, or a picture of a child who has been killed by abortion. In the early 1940s, when the pictures of the death camps were circulated to the Western world, many people refused to believe what they saw. They turned from the pictures in disgust. They said it was a Russian propaganda trick, an attempt to incriminate the Nazis. People said it wasn't real, or if they suspected it was real, they turned away in revulsion and went back to their normal lives.

When I was on a live television program with a number of pro-life and pro-choice guests, one of the pro-life participants held up a picture of an aborted child. There was an immediate panic, cameras turned away, and one of the pro-choice leaders gasped, "God, don't let them show that." *But why not?* Does anyone really believe this is trick photography? If we are going to honestly discuss abortion, what could possibly be wrong with showing an actual picture of it? If a fetus is merely a blob of tissue, why not show the mere blob of tissue? Is a blob of tissue really so offensive? Why is any other piece of evidence admissable except the one that actually shows what we are talking about?

Pastor and rescuer Dr. John Piper states, "If all America could be made to watch the shredding of a three month old pre-born baby, the debate would shift dramatically."[13] It is for this reason that I urge Christians to not turn away from the pictures of the preborn. Much as we hate to, we *need* to watch *The Eclipse of Reason, The Silent Scream, Baby Choice* and similar films and videos. They will likely cause us to weep and may literally cause us to vomit. But we need to watch them anyway. Why? For the same reason that the world needed to see the horrible pictures coming out of Auschwitz and Buchenwald. These things compel us to believe this was really happening and to be forced to deal with it. Even if we don't look at the aborted babies, we can look with wonder at the magnificent intrauterine photographs that show live unborn children. Can we really gaze at these creations of God and then go right on without trying to save their precious lives?

Holocausts happen. Stalin killed at least four times more than Hitler, Mao Tse-tung more than Stalin. Wide-scale holocausts have been perpetrated in Cambodia and Uganda and dozens of other countries. What happened under Nazi Germany fifty years ago was not *the* holocaust, but *a* holocaust, one in a long and ongoing tradition of holocausts. The holocaust of the *unborn* is happening today. And what makes holocausts work is simply that the larger group of citizens does little or nothing to stop them.

After the command to rescue those being led away to slaughter, Proverbs 24 anticipates our excuse for not doing so: "If you say, 'but we knew nothing about this,' does not he who weighs the heart perceive it? Does not he who guards your life know it? Will he not repay each person according to what he has done?" (Prov 24:12)

God tells us we cannot plead ignorance. We know who the unborn are, and we know (or could if we chose to) how and where they are being killed. God also reminds us that we will one day be held accountable for whether or not we tried to rescue those being led away to death. In that day, the judge will repay each person according to what he has done for innocent victims about to die.

Alternatives to Denial

Do you want to see how society's values have come to the place that something like child-killing could be legalized and accepted? Read Robert Bellah's *Habits of the Heart.* How a small group of people could in one decision sweep away the constitutional rights of an entire class of people? Read *The Brethren.* How ordinary people could stand passively by and watch others suffer, and even make them suffer, all in the name of obeying authority? Read *Obedience to Authority.* How a church and community could stand together and illegally save the lives of 2,500 Jews? Read *Lest Innocent Blood Be Shed.* How one family could save the lives of the innocent? Read *The Hiding Place.* How the early Christians obeyed God, even when it meant disobeying the state, and the price they paid for it? Read *Foxe's Book of Martyrs.* The proper relationship of

Christians and civil law? Read Francis Schaeffer's *A Christian Manifesto* and
Charles Colson's *Kingdoms in Conflict*.

Above all, read the Bible itself. Then become a student of church history
and the church around the world. Become mentally connected with the people of God throughout history and the people of God scattered across the
globe today.

But please do one more thing. My request to any Christian reading this
book, in fact my earnest plea, is to *go spend time outside an abortion clinic*. You
may need to watch the *Eclipse of Reason* just before you go, or bring along a
picture of a preborn or an aborted baby to visualize what is actually going
on in there. But go. You don't feel you can violate a civil law? Fine. Just go
stand on the public sidewalk. Picket or pass out literature if you wish. But even
if you don't do that, go anyway.

Go and pray. Go and watch the women go in with a live baby inside them
and walk out with no baby at all. Look at the clinic dumpsters that have been
the graveyards for millions of innocent children. Look at the fancy cars the
abortionists drive. Ask yourself where the money came from. Think and pray.
And weep. And if you cannot weep, ask yourself why. If you cannot act, ask
yourself why.

If you choose not to rescue, that's fine. If you still feel rescuing is wrong,
OK. But until you go to Auschwitz, do not criticize the Christians of the
Warsaw Ghetto for breaking the law to save Jews. Until you go to the plan-
tations and see men whipped and women raped, don't criticize the Christians
of the Underground Railroad for breaking the law to save slaves. Until you've
put yourself in their place, don't blame the midwives for rescuing the children, Rahab for rescuing the spies, Obadiah for rescuing the prophets, Jehosheba for rescuing baby Joash, or Esther for trespassing to rescue the Jews.
And until you go to where innocent children are being torn to pieces, don't
criticize those who trespass to save babies.

Don't draw any final judgments until you've spent at least a day where the
children are *really* being slaughtered.

The Burden of Proof

Imagine fifty years ago some Christians coming across a group of Jews being herded toward ditches where they will be legally shot. One Christian says, "Let's try to save their lives." Can you imagine his companions asking, "Why? Prove to us that this is ethical." *Why* is not the appropriate question. Why is obvious. These are innocent human beings. One does not have to come up with five good reasons to justify breaking the law to save their lives.

We need not search for some clever or compelling argument to justify saving an innocent life. But to *not* intervene to save the innocent demands a clever and compelling argument! The eternal law of God is that innocent people should not be killed, and that righteous people should not stand back and let them be killed. The current law of society is that innocent people can be killed by another person's choice, and that citizens must not step onto private property to attempt to save their lives. Which of these laws commands our obedience?

In the "rescuing debate," the burden of proof lies not on the arguments *for* saving lives today, but on the arguments *against* doing so.

Examining Our Vested Interests

To be human is to be subjective. Whenever we make a difficult decision or moral judgment, we should always asked ourselves, "What are my vested interests?" I must be sure that whether I favor or oppose rescuing, it is not because I will benefit from doing so.

I must ask myself, What do I really *want* to believe? What is most comfortable for me? What will require the least amount of challenge and risk and change in my life? Most of us resist change—the status quo is always more comfortable. We tend to avoid risk and embrace comfort. Most of us are strongly motivated to believe anything that justifies our past behavior and allows us to live in the present without significant change.

We all bring a lot of freight to this issue, and that freight will often tip the balance for us, whether or not we realize it. The greater our vested interests in coming to a particular conclusion, the more suspicious we should be when that is the conclusion we come to. We should search the Scriptures to *determine* what we believe, not merely to *defend* it. Too often our position is determined in advance. We approach Scripture deductively rather than inductively, changing it to fit our preconceived position, rather than changing our position to fit it.

I too have vested interests. But part of my belief that I have reached the right conclusion concerning rescuing comes from the fact that from the beginning I have had strong vested interests against it. I have never wanted to do it, and still don't. I have a strong respect for the law and law enforcers. I am patriotic. I have a definite aversion to looking foolish. I am supposed to be careful with my health. Furthermore, I am sufficiently busy that I desperately don't want to do anything new that takes my time and energy, much less that means going to jail and possibly losing my money and possessions. (As I write, two abortion clinics have filed lawsuits and are attempting to take whatever they can from me.)

My theological training was at schools that are as conservative in actions as they are in doctrine. My church is not a "civil disobedience type of church." I deeply respect my fellow church leaders. They are not prone to this sort of position or action. By rescuing I have lost respect in the eyes of some in the evangelical community. In short, neither I myself, nor the context out of which I have come, nor the context in which I now am, are conducive to rescuing. I had and still have strong vested interests *against* rescuing.

It has been interesting to find others just like myself, who rescue or believe in rescuing because they have come to that conclusion after an agonizing process of studying the Scriptures and praying. I have often prayed, and still do, that God would show me if I am wrong. In fact I have specifically prayed *that* he would show me I *am* wrong! Whenever I read some new criticism against rescuing, I ask that God would teach me, correct me, show me something I have overlooked. I would rather swallow my pride and say "I was wrong when I favored rescuing" than continue to bring on my life the adverse consequences of rescuing. But for the present my family and I find our consciences compelling us to remain involved in rescuing.

Fear or Cowardice?

Nearly four hundred times Scripture tells us not to fear. Our natural tendency is to be afraid to stand up for Christ and for innocent victims. Courage is not the absence of fear, but the determination to obey God despite our fears. Cowardice is when we give in to our fears and place our own temporal comfort and security over obedience to the will of God. Fear is understandable. Cowardice is a sin (Rev 21:8).

I do not for a moment believe that someone is cowardly because he chooses not to rescue. However, like any difficult activity—including evangelism—there is a tendency to build one's opinions and actions about rescuing upon a base of cowardice. If we look full face into Scripture and history and prayerfully and honestly conclude civil disobedience to save the lives of preborn children is wrong, then that is one thing. If our conclusion secretly stems from the fear that God would call us to it, and of what that would cost us, then that is another.

If—apart from the idea of breaking civil law—there were no negative consequences of violating trespassing laws to save innocent children, would we really oppose it? Isn't it the conflict, the ridicule, the suffering, the jail time, the possible loss of money and possessions that we are really resisting?

Standing By Rescuers

Mark Belz says of rescuing, "This crossing of a line that is done with such fear and trepidation, and which is criticized and condemned outright by so many Christians, is an act which lends credibility to everything else which we are saying and doing in the pro-life movement."[14] He adds, "Just as it is essential for each of us to demonstrate solidarity with the unborn, so it is essential for us to demonstrate solidarity with each other."

Rescuers need support, and from a much broader base than just fellow rescuers. One man in our church told me he was still searching the Scriptures on the issue of rescuing, and felt that he himself should not participate. Yet when some of us from church were arrested for rescuing, this same man wrote a letter to the newspaper defending us. He regularly prays for us and has offered financial support to rescuers. In contrast, one woman had served the Lord and her church faithfully for many years, only to see her church leaders draw back from her when she started rescuing. She admitted to a friend, "When I've needed most the support of my spiritual leaders, I've had it the least."

In one area a group of Christian leaders concerned with social issues called a press conference and publicly stated their opposition to rescuing. This group did not even ask to meet with their brothers and sisters who were rescuing to try to understand their actions. Instead, they publicly criticized and disassociated themselves from them. This not only won the group a public commendation by the National Abortion Rights Action League (which it no doubt found embarrassing), but it naturally put a damper on rescuing for the entire Christian community.

Was a public forum the best way to deal with fellow Christians, rather than private discussion? I do not for a moment question the motives of these men, but I do question their approach. Couldn't they have gone to, learned from and better understood the convictions of their brethren before going into the public eye to disassociate themselves? Perhaps through dialog they could have come to unity, even if not agreement, and a public statement would not have been necessary.

Many rescuers come and go. They don't keep rescuing long. Often this is not because their convictions change, but because they feel they cannot go on without emotional support. It is difficult enough to do something so costly, but when your brothers and sisters in Christ question your motives—and some even publicly rebuke you—it becomes almost unbearable. I asked a seminary professor how his colleagues felt about his rescuing. With a pained expression on his face, he said, "Well, they tolerate me." Tolerance is better than aggressive opposition, but it still leaves you feeling alone and misunderstood.

A church in Georgia issued a policy statement opposed to rescuing. They said that while they would allow their people to rescue, they would *not* give them or their families financial help related to fines, lawsuits, loss of income due to jail sentences, or other rescue-related matters. I neither ask nor expect such help from my church. Yet I cannot help but think how sad it would be to be part of a church that will give financial help to cancer victims, alcoholics, the unemployed, the divorced and any number of others, but as a matter of policy will not help the families of those who rescue! In contrast, in 1989 the Baptist General Conference, by an eighty per cent affirmative vote, passed a resolution to encourage their churches to give financial and legal help to their members who rescue.

Matthew 25:36 and Hebrews 10:34 tell us what our response should be to our brothers and sisters in Christ who violate the law for the cause of right-eousness. We are to visit them in jail, sympathize with them, and stand up for them.

When a pastor shared with his board that he had prayerfully and carefully come to the conclusion that he needed to rescue, the response of one board member was, "We can't have a pastor who's in and out of jail." Why not? Paul was in and out of jail. John Bunyan was in and out of jail. Martin Niemöller was in and out of jail. Instead of being irritated or ashamed of our brothers and sisters who are willing to pay a price to stand for righteousness, shouldn't we offer them our support?

Don't Forget the Children

I have listened to and studied many arguments against rescuing. In a number of cases, as I have read page after page of argumentation, I've had a haunting feeling. The feeling is that with all the talk about mothers and doctors and judges and policemen and Christians and churches and pro-choice and pro-life, something is desperately wrong. Some *one* is being overlooked. If we talk long enough, we seem to always forget about the baby.

How do you argue against rescuing without arguing against the babies that are here because of it? Hold in your arms one of the many rescue babies around the country, and then picture yourself explaining to him your oppo-sition to rescuing. If those who oppose rescuing had persuaded certain Chris-tians not to rescue, it is a simple fact that these babies would have been cut to pieces. If you adopted a child and when he was five years old you discov-ered that child had been saved in a rescue, how would it affect your view of rescuing? Are we getting too personal here? Don't we need to make this issue personal, if these babies are indeed persons?

As long as the children remain unseen and nameless, it is easy to forget them and focus on an endless array of arguments. But if we would disobey the law to save five-year-old children from death, then our real problem is not with civil disobedience but with the value of unborn children. If we would break the law to save *older* children, if we would break the law to save *our* children no matter what their age, why would we treat these children differ-ently? Is it because the womb has no window? Is it because we do not see them? This does not change the fact they are there. The anonymity of those four thousand children a day allows us to treat them as a mere factor in a theological discussion rather than as what they are—precious human beings created in the image of God. We may not know them, but God does.

Suppose you heard that I drove a car eighty miles an hour down a freeway. Was I right or wrong? I was wrong, of course. After all, I broke the law. If you heard that a policeman had pulled me over you'd say, "Fine, he deserved it."

But suppose you found out later that lying in the back of the car was my little daughter, who had a ruptured appendix. She could have died any minute, and I broke the law in an attempt to get her to the doctor to save her life. Would this additional factor affect your opinion about whether my action was right or wrong? Of course it would. As long as you focus on the law, on the speed limit, on why Christians must always obey such laws, you will condemn my action. But when you remember the little child in the back seat, it changes everything. The child about to die makes all the difference.

Whenever I look at a child, it seems strange to think that taking peaceful nonviolent action to save him from being slaughtered is such a controversial issue in the Christian community. When he is old enough to understand, either in this world or the next, I'm sure he will also wonder why honest attempts to save his life were met with such opposition by some Christians.

Take all the arguments against rescuing you can think of. Now, prepare to present them as persuasively as you can to an audience of four thousand people, gathered in an auditorium. The audience in this case does not consist of pastors, theologians, teachers or scholars. The audience consists entirely of four thousand preborn children, who were killed today by abortion. How persuasive will your arguments against rescuing sound to this audience? How persuasive will they sound to you?

The Judgment Seat of Christ

How will history judge today's church? How will it judge our treatment of the preborn? Will we be condemned by others as we have condemned the church that spoke against breaking the law to save the lives of slaves, and the church that refused to break the law to save the lives of Jews? Will our grandchildren be ashamed of us for what we have failed to do to save the lives of unborn children?

These are good and legitimate questions, and we must ponder them. But they pale in comparison to another question. The ultimate question is, How will the Lord of the Church judge us? How will *Christ* evaluate our actions on behalf of the unborn children when we stand before him at the judgment seat (Rom 14:10, 12; 1 Cor 3:12-15; 2 Cor 5:10)?

The following is Charles Beecher's question in the introduction to his 1851 sermon that resulted in his expulsion from the ministerial association.

> My object tonight will be to take such a view of the late Fugitive Slave Law, passed by the Congress of these United States, and approved by the President. I wish to inquire how that law will look when examined before the bar of God. I wish to ask how the men that made it, the men that execute, the citizens that obey, and the nation that tolerates that law, will look when they stand before the judgment seat.[15]

We must weigh each other's counsel, search the Scriptures, and seek the face of God in prayer. But we cannot be each other's consciences. Ultimately we must play out our lives before an audience of one. In the final analysis it is God's applause, and his alone, for which we should live.

A Stubborn Refusal to Be Silent

In our battle for the unborn we need to take our cues from the likes of William Wilberforce, the British Parliamentarian mentioned in the previous chapter. Shortly after his conversion to Christ in 1784 Wilberforce began his battle for the Black man's freedom. Relentlessly, year after year—in the face of apathy, scorn and all the opposition the bloody slave industry could offer—this man reintroduced to Parliament the motion for abolition. Rejected again and again, Wilberforce was encouraged by only a few, among them John Newton and John Wesley.

"We are all guilty" for tolerating the evil of slavery, Wilberforce said, "Never, never will we desist till we . . . extinguish every trace of this bloody traffic, of which our posterity, looking back to the history of these enlightened times will scarce believe that it has been suffered to exist so long a disgrace and dishonor to this country."[16]

Year after year, while both non-Christians and Christians denied or ignored reality, Wilberforce suffered sleepless nights, plagued by dreams of the suffering Black man. Finally, in 1807, against incredible odds, Wilberforce saw the slave trade outlawed. But even then, he was to fight eighteen more years for the emancipation of existing slaves. Wilberforce died in 1833—three days after the Bill for the Abolition of Slavery passed its second reading in the House of Commons, bringing slavery in England to its final end.

I use Wilberforce as an example partly because, as far as I know, he did *not* practice civil disobedience in his fight against slavery. I emphasize this because, whether one chooses the path of civil disobedience or not, it is the diligence and persistence of Wilberforce that we need among Christians today.

While I have tried to persuade the reader that there is indeed a place for civil disobedience in saving the lives of unborn children, my primary concern is that we would all do whatever we can to intervene for them in whatever way we believe is right.

"The LORD looked and was displeased that there was no justice. He saw that there was no one, he was appalled that there was no one to intervene" (Is 59:15-16). Wilberforce intervened for the innocent victims in the cause of justice. He stubbornly refused to be silent or inactive. The unborn children need our help, and they need it *now*. Who else will take care of them if we don't?

Conclusion

Martin Luther said that in any time certain issues become the focus of attention and must be addressed by Christians:

> If I profess with the loudest voice and clearest exposition every portion of the truth of God except precisely that little point which the world and the devil are at that moment attacking, I am not confessing Christ. Where the battle rages, there the loyalty of the soldier is proved, and to be steady on all the battle front besides is mere flight and disgrace if he flinches at that point.

Despite our many words to the contrary, is the evangelical church flinching on the point of the value of the lives of unborn children and the worthiness of extraordinary action and significant sacrifice to give them a chance to live?

Beliefs have no credibility when unaccompanied by sacrifice. We must stubbornly refuse to remain silent in the face of the holocaust of God's unborn children. Not all of us in the church will be called upon by our Lord to do the same thing in the same way. All of us can, however, be supportive of sacrificial intervention that gives credibility to our words. This must involve much more than peaceful civil disobedience at abortion clinics to save the lives of unborn children. But surely it can include it.

Afterword

While I was writing this book, my daughter and I were rescued.

My family and I were spending two weeks in Alaska. I had spoken to two hundred missionaries at their annual conference near Palmer, outside of Anchorage. Afterward, we were to fly to Galena, three hours north by small plane. There we would stay with our friends and observe their ministry in Indian villages on the Yukon. My ten-year-old daughter and I were flying with our missionary friend and his daughter. My wife and youngest daughter were leaving with the rest of our friend's family an hour later in another plane, going a different route.

An hour after take-off we were flying over a beautiful waterfall at 3,000 feet elevation, when, without warning, the engine lost power. Oil and smoke poured out. Seeing there was no oil pressure, my friend had to shut off the engine, which wasn't working anyway and looked like it might blow up. Suddenly we were descending rapidly in a rough mountain pass where there was almost no place to land. It looked like we might not make it. By God's grace and my friend's skill, he spotted a possible landing site. Had we been only a few miles farther, there would have been nowhere to land. We would have crashed into the side of the mountain.

After making a beautiful emergency landing at 4:30 P.M., we set off the emergency locator transmission, tried to reach help with the radio, built an SOS, set up shelter, ate C-rations, and prayed for our families who would know we were down but wouldn't know our condition. Then we waited, hoping and praying that we would be rescued before the black cold night came upon us. At 10:30 P.M. a Search and Rescue plane saw one of our flares. After seven hours on the ground we were picked up at 11:30 PM by a Search and Rescue helicopter. When the pilot got out and flashed his broad grin, he was one of the most welcome sights we'd ever seen. He said, "We expected wreckage. We didn't think you'd be alive."

Three planes had flown over us earlier. Two were flying high. They apparently weren't listening to the emergency frequency, didn't see our SOS or fire, and didn't notice us waving our white flags down below. They went right on as if we didn't exist. The third airplane could have easily seen us but the pilot simply wasn't looking. He no doubt had other things on his mind besides finding people to rescue!

It was a strange feeling to see and hear these planes go over, flying along so casually with no knowledge of or interest in our dilemma. I thought about the preborn child in the womb. The world goes by as if he or she isn't there. Even as they are physically taken inside the abortion clinic, no one seems to care. They cry when they are cut to pieces, but no one hears them cry. No one is listening. No one is looking for them. It seems that no one believes they're really there.

At least when we were stranded in that mountain pass, we could do something to take care of ourselves. The little child is helpless. At least we had flares to try to get someone's attention. The little child has nothing. We found out later there were four Search and Rescue airplanes and two helicopters combing the mountains looking for us. The little child has no one.

I'll never forget the girls' squeals of delight as that huge Rescue helicopter with its powerful searchlight and deafening roar landed only forty feet away from us. When they put the four of us on board, gave us food, and flew us to spend the night in a hunting lodge, it was an indescribable feeling.

I know what it means to be rescued. And I think I can ask with a little more empathy a question on behalf of the precious preborn child about to die:

"Is there somebody out there who will try to rescue me?"

Notes

Chapter 1: Purpose & Foundation

[1]The number was set at "more than 26,000" by Tom Hess in "Three Tough Questions for Randall Terry," *Focus on the Family Citizen,* June 19, 1989, p. 4. An Operation Rescue pamphlet *(Repentance and Rescue,* December 1989) stated that 55,000 had risked arrest that year. The rescue movement has continued to grow since that time, and by now the numbers are undoubtedly considerably higher.

[2]I recommend John Jefferson Davis, *Abortion and the Christian* (Phillipsburg, N.J.: Presbyterian & Reformed, 1984); Landrum Shettles and David Rorvik, *Rites of Life: The Scientific Evidence of Life Before Birth* (Grand Rapids, Mich.: Zondervan, 1983); Paul Fowler, *Abortion: Toward an Evangelical Consensus* (Portland: Multnomah Press, 1987); J. C. Willke, *Abortion Questions and Answers* (Cincinnati: Hayes Publishing Co., 1988); Curt Young, *The Least of These* (Chicago: Moody Press, 1983); and R. C. Sproul, *Abortion: A Rational Look at an Emotional Issue* (Colorado Springs: NavPress, 1990).

[3]For example, a Harvard Medical School text states flatly that "the development of a human being begins with fertilization." See Alan K. Ota, "Senate Panel Opens Hearing on Pro-Choice Legislation," *The Oregonian,* March 28, 1990.

[4]Shettles and Rorvik, *Rites,* p. 113.

[5]Shettles and Rorvik, *Rites,* pp. 112-13.

[6]The terms *zygote, embryo* and *fetus* are to some no different than *infant, child* or *teen-*

ager—all legitimate terms describing a human being at a certain stage of development. But the widespread use of the terms *zygote, embryo* and *fetus* has in fact greatly depersonalized our references to, and consequently our thoughts about, the unborn children. This is why I choose to avoid these terms. It is better to call them what they are—unborn babies. Personally, I also prefer the term *preborn* over *unborn,* because it emphasizes the fact that unless someone interferes, these children will in fact be born. However, *preborn* is still a strange term to many people, and I don't want them to miss the focus of the book through being distracted by unfamiliar terminology.

[7]Shettles and Rorvik, *Rites,* pp. 112-13.

[8]See Willke, *Abortion Questions,* pp. 44-55, and Shettles and Rorvik, *Rites,* pp. 41-65.

[9]Willke, *Abortion Questions,* p. 46.

[10]See, for example, Dr. Rainer Jonas's breathtaking photograph of a fifty-six-day-developed unborn child (available from Right to Life of Michigan Educational Fund, 920 Cherry, S.E., Grand Rapids, MI 49506). Eyes, ears, nose, mouth and fingers are all unmistakable.

[11]Willke, *Abortion Questions,* p. 45.

[12]A classic example of imposing personal opinions on the scientific facts is Carl Sagan's and Ann Druyan's "Is it Possible to be Both Pro-Life and Pro-Choice?" *Parade Magazine,* April 22, 1990, pp. 4-8. The authors' evolutionary presuppositions lead them to compare the unborn child to a worm, amphibian, reptile and lower mammal. This distracts the reader from the scientific fact that the unborn is actually none of these, but is indisputably a human being.

[13]Lawrence O. Richards, *Expository Dictionary of Bible Words* (Grand Rapids, Mich.: Zondervan, 1985), pp. 156-57.

[14]See Michael J. Gorman, *Abortion and the Early Church* (Downers Grove, Ill.: InterVarsity Press, 1982).

[15]Many prefer not to use the term *murder* for abortion, even if it is acknowledged that a baby is a person. Murder is by definition the deliberate, unjustified taking of a human life. In my experience, due to the pro-choice indoctrination of society, most women don't fully understand that they're killing a baby. So while the abortion is deliberate, the killing of a person isn't. To say to a woman who has had an abortion, "You murdered your baby," implies a knowledge and understanding that in many cases she did not have.

On the other hand, I am hesitant to abandon the use of the term *murder* in this book. Why? Because every semantic advantage has been taken from the unborn children. *Murder* may not be the best term to ascribe to those doing the killing, but it is one of the few remaining words that tells us the truth about who the unborn are.

A dog or a cat or even a plant can be killed, but not murdered. Though the life-taker may not always understand the full implications of the humanity of his victim, do we not still use the term *murder* if the victim is indeed a person? If a Nazi sincerely believed a Jew was sub-human, does this mean killing him would no longer be murder? If a slave owner honestly believed a slave was sub-human, would whipping him to death no longer be murder?

Abortion is an intentional action that results in the death of a human being, even if the person taking the action doesn't think it's really a human being he's killing. We must not use words that communicate the perceptions of the victimizer, but the reality of the victim. For this reason, though I generally use the word *killing* in this book, I sometimes retain the word *murder.*

The rescue movement has taken the semantic question a step further and refused to use any terms which lend a sound of respectability to child-killing. Chief among these is the term *abortion clinic*—instead rescuers usually use terms such as *abortion mill, abortuary,* or *killing place.* Those who perform the abortions are called "abortionists" or "baby-killers," rather than doctors or physicians.

Personally, I agree with this "call it what it really is" type of word usage. However, I have refrained from using these terms in most of this book, because I know they sound unfamiliar, dramatic and combative to many readers. People in the rescue movement will be disappointed by this, but I do not wish to lose the bulk of the readers of this book, who are not rescuers and are unaccustomed to such terminology.

Chapter 3: Test Cases of Civil Disobedience

[1]Gary North, *Trespassing for Dear Life* (Fort Worth, Tex.: Dominion Press, 1989), p. 1.

[2]By "civil disobedience" I simply mean disobeying any civil law on the basis of Scriptural command, conscience or a sense of moral obligation.

[3]John Whitehead, *The End of Man* (Westchester, Ill.: Crossway Books, 1986), p. 195.

[4]Bruce W. Nelan, "Slaughter in the Streets," *Time,* January 1, 1990, p. 36.

[5]John Greenwald, "A Revolution's Unlikely Spark," *Time,* January 1, 1990, p. 37.

Chapter 4: Civil Disobedience in the Bible

[1]Bill Gothard, "Five Ways in Which Civil Disobedience Violates Scripture" (Oak Brook, Ill.: Institute in Basic Youth Conflicts, 1989), p. 2.

[2]In his arguments against civil disobedience, Charle Ryrie admits, "The Sanhedrin . . . had not only religious power but also wide political power at the time." See *You Mean the Bible Teaches That . . .* (Chicago: Moody Press, 1974), p. 19.

[3]John Stott, "When to Obey God and Disobey State," *Cross Times,* December 1988, p. 46.

Chapter 5: The Laws of Man & the Laws of God

[1]Francis Schaeffer, *A Christian Manifesto* (Westchester, Ill.: Crossway Books, 1981), p. 91.

[2]Ibid., p. 124.

[3]Ibid., p. 132.

[4]R. C. Sproul, *Table Talk*, October 1988.

[5]John MacArthur, "Grace to You" radio program, May 26, 1989.

[6]Charles Ryrie, *You Mean the Bible Teaches That* . . . (Chicago: Moody Press, 1974), p. 17.

[7]Ibid., p. 17.

[8]Ibid., p. 22.

[9]Stephen Charles Mott, *Biblical Ethics and Social Change* (New York: Oxford University Press, 1982), p. 148.

[10]Suetonius, *Claudius* 25.4.

[11]Dietrich Bonhoeffer, *Ethics* (New York: Macmillan, 1955), p. 344.

[12]Ibid., p. 7.

[13]Charles Colson, *Kingdoms in Conflict* (Grand Rapids, Mich.: Zondervan Publishing House, 1987), p. 155.

[14]John Stott, "When to Obey God and Disobey State," *Cross Times*, December 1988, p. 46.

[15]Pastoral Staff and Deacons, First Baptist Church of Atlanta, "A Biblical Perspective on Civil Disobedience," August 28, 1988.

[16]MacArthur, "Grace to You."

[17]Jim Feeney, "Abortion 'Rescue Missions': Are They Biblical?", *Abbot Loop Christian Center and Operation Rescue* (Anchorage, Alaska: 1988), p. 7.

[18]Thomas Aquinas, *Summa Theologica*, 1.2 qu. 96, art. 4; qu. 95, art. 2.

[19]Schaeffer, *Manifesto*, p. 100.

[20]These quotes are from a paper presented by one elder to his fellow elders in a local church context, on March 3, 1989. (Anonymity has been requested.)

[21]For a sampling of this, see Ex 19:5; Lev 18:4; Deut 6:25; 13:8; 28:1; Josh 1:7; 23:6; 1 Kings 6:12; 2 Chron 14:4; Neh 1:7; Ps 119:4, 44; Is 42:24; Mt 28:20; Lk 11:28; Jn 14:15; Rom 2:13; 1 Jn 2:3; 5:3; Rev 12:17.

[22]Charles Colson, "A Time to Disobey?" *Focus on the Family Citizen*, June 1989, pp. 14-15.

Chapter 6: Which Authority Do We Obey?

[1]Stanley Milgram, *Obedience to Authority* (New York: Harper & Row, 1974).

[2]Ibid., p. 4.

[3]Ibid., pp. xi, 5.

[4]Ibid., pp. xii, 8.

[5]Ibid., p. 2.

[6]Ibid., p. 6.

[7]Ibid., p. 10.

[8]Ibid., p. 9.

[9]Ibid., p. 38.

[10]Bernard Nathanson, *Aborting America* (Garden City, N.Y.: Doubleday, 1980), p. 69.

[11]Bob Woodward and Scott Armstrong, *The Brethren: Inside the Supreme Court* (New York: Avon Books, 1979), pp. 265-67.

[12]Ibid., p. 272.

[13]Ibid., p. 215.

[14]Ibid., p. 276.

[15]Judge Randall Hekman, "Letter to the Editor," *Grand Rapids Press,* November 19, 1982.

[16]Robert McAfee Brown, *Saying Yes and Saying No: On Rendering to God and Caesar* (Philadelphia: Westminster, 1986), p. 39.

Chapter 7: The Law of Love

[1]Grover E. Gunn, "Operation Rescue: An Ethical Evaluation," *The Counsel of Chalcedon,* December 1988, p. 22.

[2]Bill Gothard, "Five Ways in Which Civil Disobedience Violates Scripture" (Oak Brook, Ill.: Institute in Basic Youth Conflicts, 1989), p. 7.

[3]B. D. Colen, "The Anti-Abortion High Ground," *New York Newsday,* November 8, 1988.

[4]A. W. Tozer, *The Root of the Righteous* (Camp Hill, Penn.: Christian Publications, 1955), pp. 51-53.

Chapter 8: Civil Disobedience in Church History

[1]Roland H. Bainton, *Early Christianity* (Princeton, N.J.: D. Van Nostrand Company, Inc., 1960), p. 23.

[2]Francis A. Schaeffer, *A Christian Manifesto* (Westchester, Ill.: Crossway Books, 1981), p. 92.

[3]Bainton, *Early Christianity,* pp. 29, 49.

[4]John Foxe, *Foxe's Book of Martyrs,* ed. Marie Gentert King (Westwood, N.J.: Fleming H. Revell, 1968).

[5]Ludwig Hertling and Englebert Kirshbaum, *The Roman Catacombs and Their Martyrs,* trans. M. Joseph Costelloe (Milwaukee, Wis.: The Bruce Publishing Co., 1956), pp. 88-89.

[6]Ibid., p. 97.

[7]Tertullian, cited by Lynn Buzzard and Paula Campbell, *Holy Disobedience: When Christians Must Disobey the State* (Ann Arbor, Mich.: Servant Books, 1984), p. 120.

[8]Hertling and Kirshbaum, *The Roman Catacombs,* p. 115.

[9]Buzzard and Campbell, *Holy Disobedience,* p. 120.

[10]Gary North, *Trespassing for Dear Life* (Fort Worth, Tex.: Dominion Press, 1989), p. 1.

[11]Hertling and Kirshbaum, *The Roman Catacombs,* p. 102.

[12]Buzzard and Campbell, *Holy Disobedience,* p. 123.

[13]James Childress, *The Westminster Dictionary of Christian Ethics,* eds. James F. Childress

and John Macquarrie (Philadelphia: Westminster Press, 1986), p. 95.

[14]Thomas Aquinas, *Summa Theologica*, 1.2 qu. 96, art. 4.

[15]Schaeffer, *Manifesto*, p. 19.

[16]Roland Bainton, *Here I Stand: A Life of Martin Luther* (Nashville: Abingdon Press, 1950), p. 185.

[17]Peter Meinhold, *Caesar's or God's?* (Minneapolis: Augsburg Publishing House, 1962), pp. 108-9.

[18]John Calvin, *Institutes of the Christian Religion*, Book IV, Chapter 20, Section 32.

[19]John Knox, *The Works of John Knox*, vol. six (New York: AMS Press, 1968), pp. 236-38.

[20]Schaeffer, *Manifesto*, p. 99.

[21]Foxe, *Martyrs*, p. 369.

[22]William Perkins, *A Discourse of Conscience*, p. 31, cited by Stephen P. Beck, "Protesting Abortion: A Puritan View of How to Do Lawfully What Is Unlawful," *World Magazine*, July 15, 1989, p. 5.

[23] William G. McLaughlin, "Civil Disobedience and Evangelism among the Missionaries to the Cherokees, 1829-1839," *Journal of Presbyterian History* 51 (1973): 116-39; cited by Stephen Charles Mott, *Biblical Ethics and Social Change* (New York: Oxford University Press, 1982), p. 153.

[24]Slavery among the Hebrews, regulated by Old Testament laws, was by no means ideal, but it did lack the racism, cruelty and exploitation that characterized American slavery. This is an important distinction for those who would justify the latter on the basis of the former.

[25]Abraham Lincoln, cited by Mark Belz, *Suffer the Little Children* (Westchester, Ill.: Crossway Books, 1989), pp. 89-90.

[26]Randall A. Terry, *Operation Rescue* (Springdale, Penn.: Whitaker House, 1989), p. 105.

[27]W. H. Siebert, *The Underground Railroad* (Columbus, Ohio: Ohio State University Press, 1898), p. 111.

[28]Belz, *Suffer*, p. 166.

[29]Levi Coffin, *Reminiscences of Levi Coffin*, third edition (Cincinnati, 1898), republished by Arno Press and the *New York Times* (New York, 1968), pp. 192-193; cited by Belz, *Suffer*, p. 90.

[30]Schaeffer, *Manifesto*, p. 66.

[31]Charles Beecher, *The Duty of Disobedience to Wicked Laws* (Newark, N.J.: 1851); cited by Belz, *Suffer*, pp. 161, 163.

[32]I am heavily indebted in the section on Niemöller to Charles Colson's excellent work *Kingdoms in Conflict* (Grand Rapids: Zondervan Publishing House, co-published with William Morrow, 1987).

[33]James and Marti Hefley, *By Their Blood: Christian Martyrs of the Twentieth Century* (Grand Rapids, Mich.: Baker, 1988), p. 204.

[34]Colson, *Kingdoms*, p. 136.

[35]Ibid., p. 140.

[36]Ibid., p. 146.

[37]Ibid., p. 147.

[38]Wladyslaw Bartoszewski, *The Warsaw Ghetto: A Christian's Testimony* (Boston: Beacon Press, 1989).

[39] Corrie ten Boom, with John and Elizabeth Sherrill, *The Hiding Place* (Old Tappan, N.J.: Fleming H. Revell, 1971), p. 99.

[40]Philip Hallie, *Lest Innocent Blood Be Shed* (New York: Harper & Row, 1979).

[41]Ibid., p. 143.

[42]Ibid., p. 129.

[43]Ibid., pp. 110-11.

Chapter 9: Rescuing As a Form of Civil Disobedience

[1]Henry David Thoreau, "On the Duty of Civil Disobedience," *Walden and Civil Disobedience* (New York: New American Library, 1960), pp. 226, 230.

[2]Taylor Branch, *Parting the Waters: America in the King Years, 1954-63* (New York: Simon and Schuster, 1988).

[3]Martin Luther King, cited by Lynn Buzzard and Paula Campbell, *Holy Disobedience: When Christians Must Disobey the State* (Ann Arbor, Mich.: Servant Books, 1984), p. 105.

[4]Stephen Charles Mott, *Biblical Ethics and Social Change* (New York: Oxford University Press, 1982), p. 160.

[5]Ibid., p. 165.

[6]Bill Gothard, "Five Ways in which Civil Disobedience Violates Scripture," (Oak Brook, Ill.: Institute in Basic Youth Conflicts, 1989), p. 4.

[7]Jeffrey Meyers, "An Open Letter to Pro-Lifers About Operation Rescue," *The Counsel of Chalcedon*, December 1988, p. 26.

[8]John Jefferson Davis, *Evangelical Ethics* (Phillipsburg, N.J.: Presbyterian and Reformed, 1985), p. 214.

[9]Cited in "Attention Jurors," *The Advocate*, March 1990, p. 17.

[10]Martin Luther King, Jr., *Strength to Love* (New York: William Collins & World Publishing, 1963), p. 33.

[11]Mott, *Biblical Ethics*, p. 205.

[12]Daniel Callahan, "Abortion: Thinking and Experiencing," *Christianity and Crisis*, January 8, 1973, p. 296.

[13]Rousas John Rushdoony, "Revolution or Regeneration," *Chalcedon Report*, January 1989, p. 14.

[14]Charles Ryrie, *You Mean the Bible Teaches That . . .* (Chicago: Moody Press, 1974), p. 14.

[15]Norman Geisler, quoted by Tom Hess, "Three Tough Questions for Randall Terry," *Focus on the Family Citizen*, June 1989, p. 4.

[16]Ibid.

[17]Jerry Wilkinson, "Sit-ins against Abortion, Again: A Critique of Operation Rescue," *Abbot Loop Christian Center and Operation Rescue* (Anchorage, Alaska: Abbot Loop Christian Center, 1988), pp. 34-37.

[18]"Text of Judgment and Opinion Entered by Judge Gerhard, St. Louis County Circuit Court August 16, 1989," *The Advocate,* October 1989, p. 9.

Chapter 10: What Really Happens at a Rescue?
[1]Margie Boule, "Local Hostages Ignored," *The Oregonian,* November 7, 1989.
[2]"No Choice: Pro-Choice," *Focus on the Family Citizen,* July 1989, p. 7.

Chapter 11: The Purposes & Results of Rescuing
[1]Vicki Kemper, "Closed for the Day," *Sojourners,* July 1988, p. 8.
[2]Paul deParrie, *The Rescuers* (Brentwood, Tenn.: Wolgemuth & Hyatt, 1989).
[3]Rousas John Rushdoony, "Revolution or Regeneration," *Chalcedon Report,* January 1989, p. 14.
[4]D. Jesse May, "An Evaluation of Operation Rescue from a Biblical Perspective," *Abbot Loop Christian Center and "Operation Rescue"* (Anchorage, Alaska: Abbot Loop Christian Center, 1988), p. 20.
[5]Kim Lawton, "Scanning the Pro-life Battlefields," *Christianity Today,* June 16, 1989, p. 54.
[6]"Operation Rescue HQ Closed," *Christianity Today,* March 5, 1990, p. 32.
[7]Ron Norquist, personal letter, May 10, 1989.
[8]Rushdoony, "Revolution," p. 14.
[9]"A Biblical Perspective on Civil Disobedience," First Baptist Church, Atlanta, Georgia, August 28, 1988.
[10]John Lofton, "Operation Rescue's Tactics," *The Counsel of Chalcedon,* December 1988, p. 12.
[11]Jeffrey Meyers, "An Open Letter to Pro-lifers About Rescue Operations," *The Counsel of Chalcedon,* p. 25.
[12]Lawrence O. Richards, *Expository Dictionary of Bible Words* (Grand Rapids: Zondervan, 1985), p. 523.
[13]Joan Andrews, "A Case for Pro-Se Vulnerability in Court," statement from Escambia County Jail, Pensacola, Florida, July 15, 1986.
[14]Charles Colson, *Kingdoms in Conflict* (Grand Rapids: Zondervan Publishing House, co-published with William Morrow, 1987), p. 250.
[15]Mark Belz, *Suffer the Little Children* (Westchester, Ill.: Crossway Books, 1989), pp. 91-92.
[16]J. I. Packer, *Knowing God* (Downers Grove, Ill: InterVarsity Press, 1973), pp. 23-24.
[17]Ibid.

[18]Rushdoony, "Revolution," p. 14.

[19]"The Sanctity of Human Life," *Grace Family Talk,* Grace Community Church, Sun Valley, California, 1989.

[20]Kemper, "Closed for the Day," p. 8.

[21]Chet Gallagher, quoted in *The Advocate,* March 1989, pp. 1-2.

Chapter 12: Concerns about the Rescue Movement

[1]The accounts of four rescuing pioneers are told largely from their courtroom transcripts in Mark Belz, *Suffer the Little Children* (Westchester, Ill.: Crossway Books, 1989), pp. 36-58.

[2]At the time of writing, Operation Rescue has been forced out of existence as an official entity, its bank accounts having been seized after the refusal to voluntarily pay $50,000 due in a lawsuit brought by the National Organization of Women. However, the organization's impact continues. Its influence has shifted from the national level to more local expressions, including more than a hundred rescue groups in the United States. See "Operation Rescue HQ Closed," *Christianity Today,* March 5, 1990, p. 32.

[3]Randall Terry, *Operation Rescue* (Springdale, Penn.: Whitaker House, 1988).

[4]Jeffrey Meyers, "An Open Letter to Pro-Lifers about Rescue Operations," *The Counsel of Chalcedon,* December 1988, p. 26.

[5]For example, see Meyers, "Open Letter," p. 26.

[6]Guidelines for rescuing and other materials available from Advocates for Life, P.O. Box 13656, Portland, OR 97213. Also ask for *The Advocate,* a free monthly magazine centered on rescuing.

[7]Meyers, "Open Letter," p. 26.

[8]"A Biblical Perspective on Civil Disobedience," First Baptist Church, Atlanta, Georgia, August 28, 1988.

[9]Meyers, "Open Letter," p. 26.

[10]Joseph L. Foreman, *Operation Rescue: Good News for the Unborn* (Montreat, N.C.: self-published paper, 1989), p. 6.

[11]Charles Colson, "A Time to Disobey?" *Focus on the Family Citizen,* June 1989, p. 15.

[12]Bill Gothard, "Five Ways in Which Civil Disobedience Violates Scripture" (Oak Brook, Ill.: Institute for Basic Youth Conflicts, 1989), p. 7.

[13]American Medical Association statement on abortion, *Medical Holocausts,* vol. 1 (Houston: Nordland Publishing International), pp. 28-30.

[14]Gina Kolata, "Declining Number of Physicians Willing to Do Abortions," *The Oregonian,* January 13, 1990, p. A2.

Chapter 13: Biblical & Theological Arguments against Rescuing

[1]D. Jesse May, "An Evaluation of Operation Rescue from a Biblical Perspective," *Abbot*

Loop Christian Center and "Operation Rescue" (Anchorage, Alaska: Abbot Loop Christian Center: 1988), p. 19.

[2]Jim Feeney, "Abortion 'Rescue Missions': Are They Biblical?" *Abbot Loop Christian Center and "Operation Rescue"* (Anchorage, Alaska: Abbot Loop 1988), pp. 7, 9.

[3]Bill Gothard, "Five Ways in Which Civil Disobedience Violates Scripture" (Oak Brook, Ill.: Institute in Basic Youth Conflicts, 1989), p. 2.

[4]Jeffrey Meyers, "An Open Letter to Pro-Lifers About Rescue Operations," *The Counsel of Chalcedon,* December 1988, p. 27.

[5]Joe Morecraft, cited in ibid., p. 27.

[6]Ibid., p. 27.

[7]Mark Belz, *Suffer the Little Children* (Westchester, Ill.: Crossway Books, 1989), p. 157.

[8]Ron Norquist, "Answers to Arguments Against Rescues," unpublished paper, August 1989, p. 4.

[9]Rousas John Rushdoony, "Revolution or Regeneration," *The Chalcedon Report,* January 1989, p. 15.

[10]Norquist, "Answers," p. 4.

[11]Meyers, "Open Letter," p. 21.

[12]Gothard, "Five Ways," p. 6.

[13]"The Sanctity of Human Life," *Grace Family Talk* (Sun Valley, Calif.: Grace Community Church, 1989), p. 3.

[14]Meyers, "Open Letter," p. 20.

[15]Belz, *Suffer,* pp. 108-9.

[16]Quoted by Gary North, *Trespassing for Dear Life* (Fort Worth, Tex.: Dominion Press, 1989), p. 34.

[17]Gothard, "Five Ways," p. 2.

[18]Meyers, "Open Letter," p. 27.

[19]Jack Phelps, "A Question of Ancestry," *The Seventh Trumpet,* March-April 1989, p. 1.

[20]Steven Charles Mott, *Biblical Ethics and Social Change* (New York: Oxford University Press, 1982), p. 20.

[21]Randall Terry, *Operation Rescue* (Springdale, Penn.: Whitaker House, 1988), pp. 63-73.

[22]John MacArthur, "Grace to You" radio program, May 26, 1989.

[23]*Family Talk* (Sun Valley, Calif.: Grace Community Church, 1989).

[24]MacArthur, "Grace to You."

[25]Gary North, *When Justice Is Aborted* (Fort Worth, Tex.: Dominion Press, 1989) and *Trespassing for Dear Life* (Fort Worth, Tex.: Dominion Press, 1989).

[26]See Randy Alcorn, *Money, Possessions and Eternity* (Wheaton, Ill.: Tyndale House, 1989).

Chapter 14: Social & Personal Arguments against Rescuing

[1]Jeffrey Meyers, "An Open Letter to Pro-Lifers about Rescue Operations," *The Counsel of Chalcedon,* December 1988, p. 21.

[2]Wayne Rogers, "Operation Rescue," *The Counsel of Chalcedon*, December 1989, p. 19.

[3]John Jefferson Davis, *Abortion and the Christian* (Phillipsburg, N.J.: Presbyterian and Reformed, 1984), pp. 77-78.

[4]*The Boston Globe*, March 31, 1989.

[5]Ibid.

[6]Charles Colson, "A Time to Disobey?" *Focus on the Family Citizen*, June 1989, p. 15.

[7]"A Biblical Perspective on Civil Disobedience," First Baptist Church, Atlanta, Georgia, August 28, 1988.

[8]D. Jesse May, "An Evaluation of Operation Rescue from a Biblical Perspective," *Abbot Loop Christian Center and "Operation Rescue"* (Anchorage, Alaska: Abbot Loop Christian Center, 1988), p. 19.

[9]Robert A. Hamack, "A Magistrate's View," *Chalcedon Report*, January 1979, p. 17.

[10]Rousas John Rushdoony, "Revolution or Regeneration," *Chalcedon Report*, January 1989, p. 17.

[11]Unpublished position paper presented to church leaders, March 7, 1989.

[12]"A Biblical Perspective on Civil Disobedience," First Baptist Church, Atlanta, 1989.

[13]Charles Colson, *Kingdoms in Conflict* (Grand Rapids, Mich.: Zondervan, 1987), pp. 250-51.

[14]Grover E. Gunn, "Operation Rescue: An Ethical Evaluation," *The Counsel of Chalcedon*, December 1988, p. 24.

[15]Meyers, "Open Letter," p. 25.

[16]Ron Norquist, "Answers to Arguments against Rescues," unpublished paper, July 1989, p. 3.

[17]Earl Paulk, "Operation Rescue: Why I Did Not Participate," *Ministries Today*, March-April 1989, p. 63.

[18]Rushdoony, "Revolution," p. 14.

[19]John MacArthur, "Grace to You" radio program, May 26, 1989.

[20]Norquist, "Answers," p. 1.

[21]William Booth, *In Darkest England and the Way Out* (London: Salvation Army International Headquarters, n.d.), p. 174.

[22]James Dobson, "Focus on the Family" radio broadcast, November 25, 1988; *Focus on the Family Citizen*, June 1989, p. 5.

[23]Church letter by D. James Kennedy, Coral Ridge Presbyterian Church, Fort Lauderdale, Florida, no date.

[24]Charles Colson, "A Time to Disobey?" *Focus on the Family Citizen*, June 1989, p. 14.

[25]Bill Bright, "The Atrocity of Abortion," *Bright Side*, May 1989, p. 1.

[26]Francis Schaeffer, *A Christian Manifesto* (Westchester, Ill.: Crossway Books, 1981), p. 120.

[27]Jerry Wilkinson, "Sit-ins against Abortion, Again: A Critique of Operation Rescue," *Abbot Loop Christian Center and "Operation Rescue"* (Anchorage, Alaska: Abbot Loop

Christian Center, 1988), pp. 34-37.

[28]Ibid.

Chapter 15: Rescuing, the Church & the Future

[1]Rick Weiss, "Forbidding Fruits of Fetal-Cell Research," *Science News*, November 5, 1988, p. 296.

[2]J. R. Lucas, *Weeping in Ramah* (Westchester, Ill.: Crossway Books, 1985).

[3]Weiss, "Forbidding Fruits," p. 296.

[4]Ibid., p. 297.

[5]Robert Stone, "Women Endangered Species in India," *The Oregonian*, March 14, 1989.

[6]*Medical World News*, December 1, 1975, p. 45.

[7]John Leo, "Baby Boys, to Order," *U.S. News and World Report*, January 9, 1989, p. 59.

[8]Francis Schaeffer, *The Great Evangelical Disaster* (Westchester, Ill.: Crossway Books, 1984), p. 141.

[9]Mark Belz, *Suffer the Little Children* (Westchester, Ill.: Crossway Books, 1989), p. 32.

[10]Robert Jay Lifton, *The Nazi Doctors: Medical Killing and the Psychology of Genocide* (New York: Basic Books, 1986).

[11]Ibid., p. 3.

[12]Ibid., pp. 4-5.

[13]John Piper, "Civil Disobedience, Abortion and the Bible," *The Berean Statesman*, November 1988, p. 1.

[14]Belz, *Suffer*, p. 130.

[15]Quoted in ibid., p. 161.

[16]Charles Colson, *Kingdoms in Conflict* (Grand Rapids, Mich.: Zondervan Publishing House, 1988), p. 102.